Slavery-Fre

Slavery-Free Communities

Emerging Theologies and Faith Responses to Modern Slavery

Edited by Dan Pratt

scm press

Published in 2021 SCM Press
Editorial office
3rd Floor, Invicta House,
108–114 Golden Lane,
London EC1Y 0TG, UK
www.scmpress.co.uk

SCM Press is an imprint of Hymns Ancient & Modern Ltd
(a registered charity)

Hymns Ancient & Modern® is a registered trademark of
Hymns Ancient & Modern Ltd
13A Hellesdon Park Road, Norwich,
Norfolk NR6 5DR, UK

British Library Cataloguing in Publication data
A catalogue record for this book is available
from the British Library

ISBN 978-0-334-06129-8

Typeset by Regent Typesetting
Printed and bound by
CPI Group (UK) Ltd

Contents

Holy God,
You enabled your people to escape from slavery
and learn to live more fully in your Promised Land.
Inspire your Church to work for freedom
for all who are enslaved in our midst today;
give us grace to bear the light of Christ
to all who are suffering in slavery;
and lead us to reach out with care and compassion,
that your saving love may be made known,
and your healing presence provide blessing and new life.
We make this prayer through Jesus Christ our Lord,
who for our sake took the nature of a slave,
humbled himself and died on the cross,
yet rose again to bring new life
to all who seek freedom and fulfilment. Amen.

The Most Revd Justin Welby

Foreword

BY THE RT HON THERESA MAY MP

The sheer scale of modern slavery is frightening to behold. It is truly a global epidemic; a crime that transcends borders and to which no country is immune. It is estimated that there are over 40 million men, women and children worldwide living in modern slavery today.

It hides in plain sight in our towns and cities, our fields and factories, and it reaches into every corner of our lives – in the clothes we wear, the food we eat and the services we use. Yet for many years it seldom captured the world's attention, allowing those who trade in human misery to quietly continue their work.

When we hear the testimonies of survivors such as Stella, Richard and Amna, who have experienced the indignity and abuse of modern slavery, we are inspired by the strength of the human spirit and reminded of the many millions of voiceless victims who are still suffering.

Tackling modern slavery is a moral imperative. It was a personal priority of mine as Home Secretary to introduce the Modern Slavery Act, which was designed to tackle the scourge of modern slavery in Britain and in the supply chains of British businesses. Its enactment has resulted in a considerable increase in slavery-related offences being processed through the criminal justice system. Six years on, there is more we can do to strengthen our legislation – but laws alone are never enough.

Modern slavery degrades our common humanity – and we must recognize that the responsibility to act is common to all of us. Faith communities are in a powerful position both to offer a unique space for victims to come forward, and to provide support towards healing and recovery. It has been inspiring to see the progress made by churches and charities working in partnership.

This book's exploration of the Church, theologies and modern slavery offers a timely reminder of the complexities involved in the greatest human rights issue of our time. The next generation could be the first in our history to be free from this pernicious form of exploitation, but only if we act collectively now.

Editor's Introduction

DAN PRATT

Modern slavery now ranks as the second most profitable world-wide criminal enterprise after the illegal arms trade. There are an estimated 40.3 million people kept in modern slavery in the world today,[1] including:

- 10 million children
- 24.9 million people in forced labour
- 15.4 million people in forced marriage
- 4.8 million people in forced sexual exploitation
- 1 in 4 victims of modern slavery are children.

Modern slavery is a hidden crime. Estimates of its prevalence in the UK range from 100,000 to 136,000 people being exploited.[2] Consequently, almost every community in the UK is impacted by modern slavery. Modern slavery is one of the greatest injustices of our time and one that the Church and faith communities should develop robust responses to. Theological and practical engagement with these crimes and exploitation can be, however, a complex reality. An understanding of modern slavery is therefore required.

In 2015, the UK Parliament passed the Modern Slavery Act. The Act categorizes offences of slavery, servitude and forced or compulsory labour and human trafficking. These terms are defined below:

- *Slavery* is when someone takes ownership of another person as if they were a piece of property, and often requires them to perform forced or compulsory labour.[3] This usually restricts that person's freedom of movement and exercises power over their choices.

- *Servitude* is similar to slavery, in that a person is under an obligation to provide a service that is imposed on them. An individual might live in someone's premises, work for them, and be unable to leave.[4]
- *Forced or compulsory labour* is 'all work or service which is exacted from any person under the menace of any penalty and for which the person has not offered himself voluntarily'.[5] This can be found in a number of different industries, including manufacturing, food processing, agriculture and hospitality.
- *Human trafficking* is when a person arranges or facilitates the travel of a woman, man or child with a view to that person being exploited.[6] The movement can be international, but can also be within a country, from one city to another, or even just a few streets away.

The intention and structure of the book

Modern slavery is a global crime impacting local communities, and churches and faith communities are increasingly encountering these victims and survivors through their grassroots community engagement. These faith communities can play a vital role in victim identification, safeguarding, slavery-proofing their organizations, developing community resilience, and partnering towards slavery-free communities. Consequently, there is a need to explore and develop more robust theological and practical engagement.

Part 1 (Chapter 1) of the book starts with the UK's first Independent Anti-Slavery Commissioner, Kevin Hyland. Kevin is one of the world's leading and most respected experts on the issues of human trafficking and modern slavery. In this chapter he overviews the present state of modern slavery and responses within the UK; he also highlights the importance and need for churches and faith communities to respond to modern slavery.

Part 2 (Chapters 2 to 4) contains three narratives of survivors of modern slavery. Each experienced a different form of modern slavery, including sexual exploitation, labour exploitation, and domestic exploitation. These survivors bravely share their stories and graciously allow theologians and practitioners to interact with them.

In Part 3 (Chapters 5 to 9), six theologians and practitioners bring their respective fields of expertise to interact with the survivors' narratives. The survivors' narratives will interact with biblical studies, church history and historic slavery, liberation theology, restorative justice and trinitarian theology and suffering. Through the survivors' narratives interacting with these respective disciplines, practical and contextual theologies start to emerge.

A caution in such theological reflection is needed: objectifying the survivors and their narratives results in their treatment being no better than that from their respective exploiters. Self-awareness, as theologians and practitioners, is needed. Sensitivity as well as a constant awareness of each survivor's humanity and dignity is imperative.

As practical and contextual theology is inherently concerned with human experience, these chapters will critically reflect on 'Where is God in the midst of exploitation and suffering?' Likewise, questions concerning the role of churches and faith communities will ensue. The book seeks to explore the complex dynamic of the human experience of modern slavery and to promote best practice and authentic human living.

Part 4 (Chapters 10 to 14) explores wider church and faith community responses. It asks, 'How are churches and faith communities responding to modern slavery within the UK?' Contributions from the Clewer Initiative (Church of England), The Salvation Army and the organization René Cassin (the Jewish voice for human rights) will highlight, from their respective faith communities, responses to modern slavery and exploitation. Wider reflection will then explore missiological responses, as well as the relationship between the exploitation of the earth and exploitation of people.

Part 5 offers prayers in response to the preceding chapters.

Prayers will include: for victims being exploited; for survivors finding freedom; for church and faith communities and, finally, for exploiters and traffickers. Part 6, Resources, concludes the book, citing organizations and information for further engagement, support, advice and safeguarding.

Notes

1 Alliance 8.7, 2017 Global Estimates, available at www.alliance87. org/2017ge/modernslavery.html#!section=0, accessed 29.01.21.

2 Gren-Jardan, T., 2020, *It Still Happens Here: Fighting UK Slavery in the 2020s*, London: Justice and Care, available from www. justiceandcare.org/wp-content/uploads/2020/07/Justice-and-Care-Centre-for-Social-Justice-It-Still-Happens-Here.pdf, accessed 14.10.20; Minderoo Foundation, 2018, 'More than 136,000 people are living in modern slavery in the United Kingdom', *Walk Free Global Slavery Index*, 18 July, available from www.globalslaveryindex.org/news/more-than-136000-people-are-living-in-modern-slavery-in-the-united-kingdom/, accessed 14.10.20.

3 Equality and Human Rights Commission, 2018, *Article 4: Freedom from Slavery and Forced Labour*, available from www.equality humanrights.com/en/human-rights-act/article-4-freedom-slavery-and-forced-labour, accessed 29.10.20.

4 Equality and Human Rights Commission, 2018.

5 United Nations Human Rights, Office of the High Commissioner, *Forced Labour Convention*, 1930 (no. 29), available from www.ohchr. org/en/professionalinterest/pages/forcedlabourconvention.aspx, accessed 29.01.21.

6 Modern Slavery Act, 2015, p. 2, available from www.legislation. gov.uk/ukpga/2015/30/pdfs/ukpga_20150030_en.pdf, accessed 29.01. 21.

About the Contributors

Major Kathy Betteridge is Director of The Salvation Army's Anti-Trafficking and Modern Slavery Unit. As a Salvation Army officer, Kathy has led and worked with many different Salvation Army church communities across the UK. She works with a wide range of stakeholders and the government to deliver specialist support services, as well as move-on support for adult victims of trafficking and modern slavery. Kathy has encouraged and developed partnership working and collaboration within her various roles, which has been important and vital to ensure that the needs of vulnerable and marginalized members of society are met and the appropriate support is available.

The Revd Dr Myra Blyth is Chaplain and Tutorial Fellow in Theology and Ecumenical Studies at Regent's Park College, Oxford. Myra was Director of Programmes for the Churches' Response to Humanitarian Disasters and Refugee Concerns at the World Council of Churches in Geneva (1988–99), and Deputy General Secretary of the Baptist Union of Great Britain (1999–2004). Her PhD thesis is titled 'Local Congregations Responding to Violence'. Myra's publications include *Gathering Disciples* (2017), *Easter People in a Good Friday World* (2006) and *Gathering for Worship* (2005).

The Revd Dr Marion L. S. Carson lives in Glasgow, where she serves as Chaplain to Glasgow City Mission. She is an adjunct supervisor at International Baptist Study Centre in Amsterdam, and an Honorary Fellow of New College, Edinburgh. She is the author of *Human Trafficking, the Bible, and the Church* (2017) and *Setting the Captives Free: The Bible and Human Trafficking* (2015).

Professor Paul S. Fiddes is Professor of Systematic Theology in the University of Oxford, Principal Emeritus of Regent's Park College, Oxford, and Honorary Fellow of St Peter's College, Oxford. He is an ordained Baptist minister and also Ecumenical Prebendary of St Endellion, Cornwall. Among his many books and articles are: *The Creative Suffering of God* (1988), *Participating in God: A Pastoral Doctrine of the Trinity* (2000) and *Seeing the World and Knowing God* (2013).

Joshua Findlay is a PhD candidate in Criminology at the University of Salford, doing research on the UK government's National Referral Mechanism, part of its 'modern slavery' response framework.

Major Heather Grinsted is Deputy Director of The Salvation Army's Anti-Trafficking and Modern Slavery Unit. Heather has been a Salvation Army officer for 27 years, working with UK local congregations and in the Middle East. Her work in the Gulf involved the protection, with responsibility for a residential shelter, and safe repatriation of domestic workers and labourers, many of whom were victims of modern slavery. She has served as a member of The Salvation Army International Human Trafficking Task Force for five years, which was set up to 'support and co-ordinate a response within the Salvation Army around the world'. On her return to the UK in January 2019, she was appointed to her present position.

Mia Hasenson-Gross is the executive director of René Cassin, the Jewish voice for human rights. Mia joined René Cassin in June 2015, bringing with her an in-depth knowledge of international human rights work and experience in human rights education, campaigning and organizational development, acquired over 15 years while working for Amnesty International.

Kevin Hyland OBE is one of the world's leading and most respected experts on the issues of human trafficking and modern slavery. He is the author of the UN's *SDG 8.7*. Kevin has a wealth of experience from over 35 years in senior leaderships roles, such as in the Metropolitan Police Human Trafficking Unit and as the UK's first Independent Anti-Slavery Commissioner (2014–18). He is currently Ireland's representative to the Council of Europe Independent Group of Experts for Trafficking, the Chair of the Responsible Recruitment Group of the Institute of Human Rights and Business, and Chief Advisor to the Santa Marta Group.

Gabriel Kanter-Webber is training to be a rabbi at Leo Baeck College in north London. He was previously a youth worker for LJY-Netzer, the national youth movement of Liberal Judaism, and a freelance journalist.

The Revd Dr Dan Pratt is founder of and anti-slavery co-ordinator for the Together Free Foundation and the Southend Against Modern Slavery Partnership. Dan is associate researcher with the Centre for Baptist Studies at Regent's Park College, Oxford. His doctoral research was in Christian education and contextual theologies of liberation. From 2008 to 2012, Dan taught Practical Theology at the Baptist Convention College in Soweto with BMS World Mission. Upon returning to the UK in 2012, he pioneered a new Baptist church in Southend-on-Sea among the homeless. He is author of *Covenant and Church for Rough Sleepers* (2017).

The Rt Revd Dr Alastair Redfern is Chair of the Clewer Initiative, Chair of the Advisory Panel for the Independent Anti-Slavery Commissioner, Co-Founder of the Global Sustainability Network, and former Bishop of Derby. Publications include *The Clewer Initiative* (2017), *Being Anglican* (2000), *Ministry and Priesthood* (1999) and *Slavery and Salvation* (2020).

The Revd Gale Richards is the pastor of Zion Baptist Church, Cambridge. Gale has encountered those fleeing modern slavery through her role in supporting people newly arriving in the UK, and people experiencing homelessness. Gale is of Caribbean heritage and so is also the descendant of victims of the transatlantic slave trade. In 2012–15, Gale was a member of the steering group of 'The Sam Sharpe Project – for Education, Research and Community Building'. Publications include *Sam Sharpe Project's Text and Story – Prophets for Their Time and Ours Bible Studies* (2014) and *Journeying to Justice: Contributions to the Baptist Tradition across the Black Atlantic* (2017).

Dr Kang-San Tan is General Director of BMS World Mission. He is also official spokesperson for the World Evangelical Alliance on interfaith issues and is a member of the Lausanne Theology Advisory Group. Previously, he has served as Head of Mission Studies at Redcliffe College and Director for Mission Research for OMF. Kang-San completed his doctoral studies in Missiology at Trinity Evangelical Divinity School, USA. He also holds a PhD in Theology of Religions from Aberdeen University. Publications include *Contextualisation and Mission Training* (2013) and *Understanding Asian Mission Movements* (2011).

The Revd Dr John Weaver is a Baptist minister and from 1992 to 2001 he taught Pastoral Theology at Regent's Park College, Oxford, and served as Principal of South Wales Baptist College from 2001 to 2011. He is a former President of the Baptist Union of Great Britain (2008–9), and was the Chair of the International Baptist Theological Study Centre in Amsterdam (2013–19). John is a Vice President of the John Ray Initiative – connecting Environment, Science and Christianity, and is a Trustee of the Industrial Christian Fellowship. He is author of *Christianity and Science* (2010) and *Earthshaping Earthkeeping: A Doctrine of Creation* (1999).

PART I

Setting the Scene

I

Modern Slavery, Churches and People of Faith

KEVIN HYLAND

Policing brings many challenges and opportunities. It involves meeting people at the lowest point in their lives and, conversely, seeing police officers, public servants, charities and the public behave with bravery, integrity and humility, often in the face of adversity, tragedy or disaster. Seeing families lose loved ones to tragedies or at the hands of a murderer, or witnessing the pain of a parent losing a young child, could harden you to become insensitive. But in my own experience I felt the opposite was true, as each time it strengthened my resolve to be of service.

Encounters with vulnerable or abused people is part of the job in policing. In some geographical areas the challenges for the young in communities are heightened simply because of where they are born or live. Societal norms have changed over recent decades, adjusting the way we look at many things. Over the past 25 years, interactions crossing the world have become commonplace for many, and not just because of the growth of the internet. Holidays in exotic locations, globetrotting career breaks, student gap years, cruises crossing oceans, working in foreign stock markets and student exchange programmes, all offer opportunities to explore the world, and for many, until the COVID pandemic, were seen as a rite of passage.

Possibly the greatest change globalization brings is the proliferation of trade and business activity that navigate seamlessly across continents. This is often driven by a rapidly changing market, including factors such as seasonal traditions, planned or unforeseen events, fluctuations in weather and climate, or responding to trends orchestrated by commercial marketing or social media.

Shamefully, another commodity hides in these evolving global markets: human beings changing hands. Our disposable culture now includes disposable people, used and discarded on a whim to meet market demands. The demand for a flexible workforce of temporary status, with so many people across the world desperate for work, has done much to negate many of the universal rights and protections agreed over many years by the UN, Council of Europe, International Labour Organization, the EU and the like.

The trafficking and slavery of people has never been more common throughout history than it currently is. Even when considering population booms of the past century, the numbers pro rata remains greater today. With 40 million people suffering, lost in forced labour, sexual exploitation, domestic servitude, forced criminality, or marriage and organ harvesting, this suffering should shame us all and we should realize, as the current incumbents of this planet, that we are all in some way responsible. And, of course, our fragility on earth has been made abundantly clear through the global pandemic, which tragically has exacerbated exploitation and the vulnerability of the most marginalized in our societies.

Many in the UK and across Europe believe these crimes only occur on far distant shores, but this is not the case. In 2018, the Walk Free Foundation Global Slavery Index estimated 136,000 suffer modern slavery and human trafficking in the UK (Minderoo Foundation, 2018). This estimate was corroborated in 2020 by Justice and Care's report, 'It Still Happens Here' (Gren-Jardan, 2020), which provides regional breakdowns of prevalence across the UK.

Surprisingly, our personal connection to this crime might be much closer than we imagine. For high-street products we buy, the vehicles we drive, and the technology we increasingly use, we need to ask, 'Is there a child working a mine excavating cobalt? Is there a child on a plantation harvesting rubber for tyres? For fashion outlets on London's high streets, is there a woman forced to sew garments in a Bangladeshi factory or in an east Midlands house? Are there men working on North Atlantic fishing vessels who are abused and exploited for catches sold in supermarkets and restaurants across Europe?'

Extortionate recruitment fees are a common feature for migrant workers and can lead to a life of poverty and exploitation. Organizations such as the Institute of Human Rights and Business[1] and the International Labour Organization[2] have advocated the abolition of recruitment fees for some time and for businesses to adopt the UN's Guiding Principles on Business and Human Rights introduced in 2011 with three pillars: 1) the state's duty to protect human rights; 2) corporate responsibility to respect, and 3) access to remedy if rights are not respected.

Global business and trade have grown exponentially in recent years, but so also has the exploitation of workers. Success has been increasingly viewed through the lens of financial prowess and the accumulation of wealth. Prioritization of shareholder dividends, exorbitant bonuses for executives, and the adage 'stack 'em high, sell 'em cheap', have all contributed to a blind spot when it comes to considering the workers in the supply chains. On too many occasions government and business leaders disparage particular races, communities or groups for discriminatory reasons. It is important, however, to remember that in 1954 the UN Secretary General and Nobel Peace Prize winner Dag Hammarskjöld stated, 'The United Nations was set up not to get us to heaven, but only to save us from hell' (United Nations Association). The international community should reflect on these words today given that human trafficking and modern slavery is a living hell on earth for 40 million worldwide – a living hell that requires a coherent global strategy.

The framework for the international response was drafted over 20 years ago at the UN in the Palermo Protocol, to Prevent, Suppress and Punish Trafficking in Persons, Especially Women and Children (United Nations Treaty Collection, 2000).[3] Ratified in 2003, the protocol now has 178 nations as parties, with most introducing their own domestic legislation. To be considered trafficking in persons, the protocol sets three conditions:

1 Act (that is, recruitment, harbouring ...).
2 Means (that is, through the use of force, deception, abuse of authority ...).
3 Purpose (that is, for the purpose of forced labour, servitude, sexual exploitation ...).

The protocol defines trafficking thus:

> Trafficking in persons shall mean the recruitment, transportation, transfer, harbouring or receipt of persons, by means of the threat or use of force or other forms of coercion, of abduction, of fraud, of deception, of the abuse of power or of a position of vulnerability or of the giving or receiving of payments or benefits to achieve the consent of a person having control over another person, for the purpose of exploitation. Exploitation shall include, at a minimum, the exploitation of the prostitution of others or other forms of sexual exploitation, forced labour or services, slavery or practices similar to slavery, servitude or the removal of organs. The consent of a victim of trafficking in persons to the intended exploitation set forth [above] shall be irrelevant where any of the means set forth [above] have been used. (United Nations Treaty Collection, 2000)

In 2005 the Council of Europe Convention on Action against Trafficking in Human Beings[4] was opened for accession and came into force in 2008. The convention established a Group of Experts on Action against Trafficking in Human Beings (GRETA, comprising 15 members), which monitors and reports publicly on the implementation of the convention through reports from various countries. It has been ratified by 46 European states and also adopted by some nations outside of Council of Europe membership.

September 2015 saw great hope when the 193 UN member states unanimously agreed a 15-year plan for a better world in the Sustainable Development Goals (SDGs) launched by Pope Francis in New York. These 17 goals brought unprecedented unity to improve lives across the world, encouraging collaboration between governments, business, civil society, NGOs and multilateral bodies including the UN, EU Organization for Security and Co-operation in Europe (ESCE), Organization for Economic Co-operation and Development (OECD), and the World Bank.

A target I proposed as UK Anti-Slavery Commissioner is dedicated to the eradication of human trafficking and modern slavery, secured with the personal support of Pope Francis:

Take immediate and effective measures to eradicate forced labour, end modern slavery and human trafficking and secure the prohibition and elimination of the worst forms of child labour, including recruitment and use of child soldiers, and by 2025 end child labour in all its forms. (United Nations Department of Economic and Social Affairs)

Without the Pontiff's personal backing, the eradication of modern slavery and human trafficking would have been missing from the targets, and this would have been seriously detrimental to global development. This target has led to greater global emphasis in tackling modern slavery through initiatives like the International Labour Organizations' Alliance 8.7[5] and the Liechtenstein Initiative[6] to deal with the financial assets of modern slavery. Sustainable Development Goal 8.7 created a global priority enabling Official Development Assistance (ODA) funds of OECD countries to be more readily accessible when addressing this issue. However, financial allocations by governments and the private sector to fight modern slavery remain low, falling short of what is needed to counter the $150 billion illicit annual profit this crime generates. The gap between investment to counter this crime and the profits slavery generates will increase further in future years as global aid budgets reduce in 2021, giving the criminals even greater advantage.

With the many international commitments and most countries legislating against this crime, you may think global efforts were having a significant impact in reducing the scale of exploitation. Nothing could be further from the truth. This crime continues to grow with low numbers of victims identified, and perpetrators acting with impunity. The latest annual *Trafficking in Persons Report* published by the US State Department reveals globally only 1 in every 2,150 victims see their trafficker convicted. The bracketed data in Table 1 refers to cases of forced labour included in the totals (US State Department, 2020, p. 43).

Table 1   Cases of forced labour in the USA, 2013–19

Year	Prosecutions	Convictions	Victims identified	New or amended legislations
2013	9,460 (1,199)	5,776 (470)	44,758 (10,603)	58
2014	10,051 (418)	4,443 (216)	44,462 (11,438)	20
2015	19,127 (857)	6,615 (456)	77,823 (14,262)	30
2016	14,939 (1,038)	9,072 (717)	68,453 (17,465)	25
2017	17,741 (869)	7,135 (332)	96,960 (23,906)	5
2018	11,096 (457)	7,481 (259)	85,613 (11,009)	5
2019	11,841 (1,024)	9,548 (498)	118,932 (13,875)	7

The role of faith communities and churches – strategic to grassroots

Among the most active groups fighting human trafficking and modern slavery are churches and people of faith. Vatican leadership comes from Pope Francis himself where he stated: 'It constitutes an unjustifiable violation of the freedom and dignity of the victims, constitutive dimensions of the human being wanted and created by God. This is why it is considered a crime against humanity' (Pope Francis, 2019).

In December 2014, at the Casina Pio IV, Pontifical Academies of Sciences and Social Sciences, Catholic, Anglican, Muslim, Hindu, Buddhist, Jewish and Orthodox religious leaders signed a *Joint Declaration of Religious Leaders Against Modern Slavery* as a public statement of their commitment to work together:

We, the undersigned, are gathered here today for a historical initiative to inspire spiritual and practical action by all global faiths and people of good will everywhere to eradicate modern slavery across the world by 2020 and for all time.

In the eyes of God each human being is a free person, whether girl, boy, woman or man, and is destined to exist for the good of all in equality and fraternity. Modern slavery, in terms of human trafficking, forced labour and prostitution, organ trafficking, and any relationship that fails to respect the fundamental conviction that all people are equal and have the same freedom and dignity, is a crime against humanity.

We pledge ourselves here today to do all in our power, within our faith communities and beyond, to work together for the freedom of all those who are enslaved and trafficked so that their future may be restored. Today we have the opportunity, awareness, wisdom, innovation and technology to achieve this human and moral imperative. (Pontifical Academy of Social Sciences, 2014)

There remains much to be done before eradication is in sight, but aim for it we must as a movement towards abolition. We cannot be complacent with regard to the notion that human trafficking is inevitable in the socio-economic structures of the modern world.

What are faith groups currently doing in the UK and elsewhere?

There are many examples demonstrating the unique reach of churches and faith groups across the UK and elsewhere. However, these represent a fraction of the combined efforts underway across the world. Some examples include:

- *Nigeria*: The Africa Faith and Justice Network-Nigeria (AFJN-N)[7] includes religious sisters working to educate communities in Edo State also playing a vital role in securing state legislation. Project Grow Edo[8] works with communities introducing sustainable livelihoods employment to disempower traffickers from recruiting victims on promises of work in Europe.

- *India*: Caritas India run the All India Network to End Human Trafficking (AINET). Other projects include a school run by the Sisters Adorers in Hyderabad where girls of all ages rescued from exploitation are provided with schooling of a high standard.

- *Australia*: Catholic Anti-Slavery Network (ACAN)[9] brings a range of activities together, including leading transparency in the supply chain throughout Australian Catholic organizations. Domus 8.7 advocates for victims of modern slavery and provides pathways to support them (Sydney Archdiocese). Australian Catholic Religious Against Trafficking Humans (ACRATH)[10] brings together religious orders who provide support and accommodation to those who have suffered in modern slavery.

- *The Orthodox Church*: His All-Holiness Ecumenical Patriarch Bartholomew launched a forum[11] in Istanbul where he said: 'This Forum aims to rectify the direction society is heading in, and to find real and concrete means to fight against this unacceptable expression of abuse and evil in our present day and age' (In Communion, 2019). The Orthodox Christian ministries that were invited to the Forum met for a first-ever inter-Orthodox consultation on modern slavery. Ministry representatives discussed their core activities and key outcomes, identifying opportunities for collaboration and synergy among and between Orthodox institutions and organizations.

- *The Jesuit Refugee Service (JRS)*[12]: The JRS is an international Catholic organization offering legal assistance, social work services, healthcare, psychological support, school outreach and spiritual care to migrants and refugees including many who are victims of modern slavery and human trafficking.

- *Across Europe*: The Salvation Army International Safe Havens project includes a film showing the challenges, which are described in their work as:

  On a daily basis we witness despair, poverty, pain-filled lives, fear, brokenness. To the best of our abilities we side with (potential) victims of trafficking trying to support them in finding a way out, to re-integrate them into their community, re-affirming their God-given human dignity. (Hoogteijling, 2019)

- *Ireland*: Act to Prevent Trafficking (APT)[13], with its headquarters in Dublin, brings together a multitude of religious orders collectively sharing resources, knowledge and expertise from across the world and in Ireland. MECPATHS[14] (Mercy Efforts for Child Protection Against Trafficking with the Hospitality and Services Sectors), founded by the Mercy Sisters, has a national programme of prevention through educating the hospitality sector on risks in their industry. They have also recently developed a human trafficking module at Maynooth University as part of a master's degree in social science.

Within the UK there are many faith-based projects providing advocacy, training, raising awareness and victim support.

The Clewer Initiative is a project founded and chaired by Church of England bishop the Rt Revd Dr Alastair Redfern. As a member of the House of Lords, Dr Redfern was a prominent member of the Parliamentary Scrutiny Committee during the drafting of the UK Modern Slavery Act. As Bishop of Derby, he introduced projects of collaboration between the police, local government and civil society.

The Clewer Initiative is enabling Church of England dioceses and wider Church networks to develop strategies to detect modern slavery in their communities and help provide victim support and care. We are working at varying levels with the majority of the Church of England's 42 dioceses, either on community-based projects or by sharing learning and knowledge through our network (or both!). Through this national network we are able to encourage dioceses to follow similar methodologies. We support and learn from one another and strive towards our common goal: a world without slavery. (Clewer Initiative)

The Jewish organization René Cassin, named after the French jurist known for co-authoring the Universal Declaration of Human Rights and who received the Nobel Peace Prize, launched their initiative in 2017 to raise awareness within their communities. Their project states: 'Slavery is not history. It calls to mind images of the Israelites in Egypt or the trans-Atlantic trade. But it is here and it is now – in the UK today there are as many as 136,000 victims of slavery or trafficking' (René Cassin).

The Medaille Trust[15] is the largest provider of beds in safe houses across the UK. Founded by a religious sister and now working with many church and lay groups from civil society and statutory agencies, the Medaille Trust policy covers the four 'Ps' of Protection, Prevention, Prosecution and Partnership.

London Bakhita House,[16] named after St Josephine Bakhita, provides services in London for women mainly in domestic servitude or forced labour, many of whom are particularly fearful of authorities. In its establishment a great deal of research and communication was conducted with a range of stakeholders, partners and local communities to negate risks and concerns.

The Church of Wales Governing Body unanimously endorsed a motion to combat modern slavery during their 2019 General Meeting. They have since been working on development of a strategy. The motion reads:

The Governing Body: (i) consider that slavery and human trafficking in all their forms are crimes against humanity, and deplore their continuing existence in the modern world; (ii) commend the efforts of the international community, our own governments, law-enforcement authorities and voluntary societies to combat modern slavery and human trafficking; (iii) lament our society's failure to end the plague of modern slavery, acknowledging that ignorance and indifference are forms of tolerance and complicity; (iv) pray for and support cross-sector partnerships, voluntary initiatives, education and business groups, and all efforts to cooperate and harness goodwill to bring an end to modern slavery and trafficking; (v) commit to exploring every opportunity to play our part in working to combat modern slavery, its prevention, detection, and in offering support for its victims. (Church in Wales, 2019, p. 14)

Scotland's successive moderators of the Church of Scotland have given their support to anti-trafficking efforts and have held discussions with the UK Prime Minister.

Christian Action Research and Education (CARE)[17] provides leadership across the UK advising and influencing legislation in Westminster, but also to the devolved administrations of Northern Ireland and Scotland who have separate legal instruments.

Government victim identification – National Referral Mechanism (NRM)

The Council of Europe Convention on Action against Trafficking in Human Beings[18] includes a responsibility of states to introduce a National Referral Mechanism (NRM). The purpose of an NRM is for a state to introduce a system that proactively identifies potential victims, even where such people do not know they are victims. It introduces a reflection period to allow those who have been exploited to deconflict and start their recovery and to better understand their options.

The reflection period recommended in the convention is set at 30 days, but the UK has extended this to 90 days. This period was introduced to allow a victim to consider their course of action and for the 'competent authority' to establish the veracity of the potential crime and come to a conclusive decision. During this period, a potential victim should have unconditional access to healthcare, legal services, financial support and psychological assessment. In the UK, the delivery of the NRM victim care element for adults is contracted by the government to The Salvation Army, while support for children remains the responsibility of local authorities. Currently, The Salvation Army subcontracts services to a range of organizations across the UK. .

Year on year there has been an increase in the number of potential victims referred to the NRM with data published by the Home Office quarterly.[19] In 2019 NRM decision-making transferred to the sole responsibility of the Home Office where on average it now takes over 14 months for a conclusive ground's outcome, with some decisions taking several years. This delay causes distress to potential victims who very often cannot access work or education, receive compensation or plan their future until their case is decided. The number in limbo awaiting outcomes is now greater than the total number of potential victims referred into the system in 2019, and 2020 has seen an even greater backlog.

Another area of concern is that convictions of those operating in the field of modern slavery remain low, with approximately only 67 cases across the UK in 2019, revealing impunity of offending running at over 99.4 per cent as a minimum.

My personal commitment

Being raised in London in a Catholic Irish immigrant family has greatly influenced my values and beliefs. My now demolished primary school in Edmonton, north London, had children from many faiths including Sikhism, Islam, Jehovah's Witnesses, Anglican denominations or those whose families identified as non-believers. Parents and children came from all over the world including the West Indies, Sri Lanka, India, Poland and Pakistan.

Weekly trips to catechism were the envy of others in the class, who saw the Catholics heading off to the nearby more salubrious modern school, in contrast to our Victorian building with the leaking roof and wood-burning stove, and which still had some outside toilets with an assembly hall off limits for fear the bell tower might fall through. None the less, I recall my time there with fondness and as happy.

My secondary education by Jesuits I felt brought a sense of humility along with determination, and for me a strong belief that justice should be equally available to all, especially the most vulnerable and marginalized in society. It was a strong foundation in what was to become a lifelong vocation.

During my career in the Royal Military Police, and then policing in London, the west Midlands and Devon and Cornwall, I saw many incidents and crimes where people were the victims of serious violence, abuse or exploitation. As a young constable I recall attending a convent in Tottenham where an elderly religious sister had been the victim of a street robbery when collecting her pension at a nearby post office. I recall her pain, both physical and emotional, but also her forgiveness to her attacker and her telling me she would pray for him. Less than a month later I again visited the same convent to see the same elderly sister reporting another street robbery. She still spoke with humility, but this time told me that she would never leave the convent again. Despite knowing it was impossible to prevent every crime, it did not stop me feeling guilty and responsible for what had happened to her. She died within a few months; I have no doubt she again forgave her assailant, something I would have found impossible to do.

I faced personal tragedy when my sister was killed in a car accident in County Limerick in Ireland, leaving behind two young daughters. My pain was immense, but to see my Mum and Dad's grief still haunts me to this day. At her funeral I spoke of solace knowing she was in a better place, something I genuinely believe.

Over three decades I saw thousands of situations where criminals inflicted suffering on others, abundantly so when leading London's human trafficking investigations. Seeing the scale of commercial exploitation was astonishing, yet responses were nowhere near commensurate to deal with the risk these crimes created for victims and communities. Legislation was available but there were irrational gaps preventing prosecutions, especially in cases of forced labour or servitude. Partnerships existed but could be conditional, often failing to meet the needs of victims, while criminal justice and remedy were rarely in the equation.

I began working with NGO partners and faith groups across London. All Souls Church in Langham Place created an initiative to reduce demand of trafficking across Westminster. In West London religious sisters accompanied police on operations, offering support and accommodation for victims. This partnership assisted in convicting several international organized crime groups of human trafficking offences.

In the run-up to the 2012 London Olympics, a strategy was introduced to provide pathways of support away from criminal justice intervention for women in street prostitution. The collaboration included police, healthcare professionals and anti-trafficking charities. This ran throughout the Olympic and Paralympic Games and was hosted by religious sisters in North London.

These relationships with NGOs and faith groups become more integrated into everyday policing activities. So successful was the West London project that the EU provided funding to enhance deployment over three London boroughs. Collectively this collaboration identified and supported many thousands of potential victims, leading to the disruption and conviction of traffickers in the UK and overseas, and significantly contributing to greater prevention of exploitation.

Interest in these activities travelled to my own parish in Hertfordshire, where I was requested to give a presentation on human trafficking; this was brought to the attention of the Catholic Bishops Conference of England and Wales, who asked that I provide them with an overview of the situation. Cardinal Vincent Nichols and Bishop Patrick Lynch were both shocked at the prevalence of this crime and were particularly influenced by a meeting with Sophie Hayes, a young British woman who had been trafficked to Italy from the UK. Her exploitation included being threatened at gunpoint, raped and sold into prostitution. So disturbed were they by this phenomenon that in May 2012 they organized a meeting attended by bishops, religious sisters, NGOs, government representatives and police. It was hosted by Cardinal Peter Turkson in Rome, where Sophie spoke eloquently and humbly of her life in exploitation. She showed no anger or malice but spoke of the need to protect others from the same fate. Although not a Catholic herself, she said:

> The Catholic Church has a huge role to play as there are 1.8 billion Catholics across the world, which is really pivotal to make sure that with all of their networks and all of their support we can really make this a hostile place for traffickers but also really support the victims of trafficking. (Hayes, 2012)

This meeting was followed by an audience with Pope Benedict XVI attended by myself and Sophie, where I surprisingly found myself shaking hands with the world's most recognized religious leader, who spoke to the crowds in St Peter's Square of the collaboration between police and Church in the UK.

To raise greater awareness and increased prayer, Bishop Patrick Lynch called upon his fellow bishops to support his notion for 8 February, the Feast Day of St Josephine Bakhita – herself a house slave – to be recognized as a day of prayer for victims of human trafficking. He won their unanimous support in England and Wales, followed by the USA, and it was later dedicated by Pope Francis as a global day of prayer.[20]

In April 2014, another much larger event was held at the Vatican. This brought together police, faith groups and civil society from across the world to promote the value of collaborating in fighting human trafficking, marking the establishment of the Santa Marta Group launched at the Pontifical Academy, Rome, by Pope Francis. Police chiefs, bishops, religious sisters, political leaders, including the then Home Secretary Theresa May, and representatives of civil society came together from 20 nations and committed to a declaration of collaboration to end human trafficking.

Pope Francis addressed the new Santa Marta Group,[21] and, giving his first ever media interview to a journalist, he said to Julie Etchingham:

It's an absolute shame. It's a crime against humanity. It's a form of slavery and as Christians, those who suffer are the body of Christ, the flesh of Christ. Humanity still hasn't learned how to cry, how to lament. We need many tears in order to understand the dimension of this drama. (Pope Francis, 2014)

Since the 2014 meeting I often reflect on these words, something I will return to later.

Membership of the Santa Marta Group has increased, and now over 35 countries participate, with regional chapters and programmes in Africa, Latin America, Asia, Australia, the USA and Europe. The Santa Marta Group is currently planning its next phase to focus on root causes, prevention and accountability, continuing to place human rights and dignity at the core of responses.

The seed was sown for the Santa Marta Group from a small meeting at the church hall of the Sacred Heart of Jesus and St Joseph, Ware, Hertfordshire, coincidentally the same parish where Thomas Clarkson,[22] an ordained Church of England deacon, first resolved to fight the transatlantic slave trade, having been awarded a literary award at Cambridge University for his Latin writings on the subject (Abolition Project).

The Santa Marta Group has blossomed from a meeting in a church hall into an international entity alongside many church groups providing sanctuary for the marginalized and exploited, rebuilding thousands of lives every day. This is evidence of how the reach and potential influence of the Church and faith should never be underestimated.

Resistance in history – never give up!

Arguably the most influential figure in fighting slavery is the British politician William Wilberforce, a deeply religious man who campaigned tirelessly on the importance of religion, morality and education. However, his historical world-renowned fight to end slavery was not welcomed by all, with many seeing it as detrimental to the British economy and its empire. One such denouncer was Lord Admiral Horatio Nelson, who wrote:

> I have ever been and shall die a firm friend to our present colonial system ... I was bred, as you know, in the good old school, and taught to appreciate the value of our West India possessions; and neither in the field or in the senate [House of Lords] shall their interest be infringed while I have an arm to fight in their defence, or a tongue to launch my voice against the damnable and cursed doctrine of Wilberforce and his hypocritical allies. (Quoted in Petley, 2018)

Wilberforce often felt overwhelmed by his adversaries but refused to give in, and one of his most famous quotes reflects his values: 'Let everyone regulate his conduct ... by the golden rule of doing to others as in similar circumstances we would have them do to us, and the path of duty will be clear before him' (Biography Online).

Has much changed since the days of the transatlantic slave trade? Nowadays modern slavery and trafficking is a crime in almost every country, whereas in Wilberforce's day it was an accepted business model and way of life. In today's complex web of slavery, it could not be policed as in the nineteenth century by a squadron of 25 ships of the British Naval fleet staffed by over 3,000 sailors. However, we need the same resolve, resourcing of agencies policing modern slavery, while also challenging and reforming root causes. Seeking out who is responsible, knowingly or through wilful blindness, whether an individual, business, multinational company, government, public official or any entity, is crucial. And with the same degree of integrity and tenacity of William Wilberforce and the so-called 'hypocritical allies', we need to bring accountability to those who benefit from the presence of this abomination.

What can faith groups and churches do? How can they respond in their communities and across their leadership?

There are already tens of thousands of people of belief across the world committed to fighting modern slavery and human trafficking. When starting to work on human trafficking preparation is essential, seeking a basic understanding of domestic and international legislation. While not everyone needs to be a lawyer, police officer or an expert, knowledge of the rules and governance is a basic need. Understanding legally binding instruments advocating for implementation of and establishing ways of measuring impact, and accountability, can assist in ensuring responses and activities are not fragmented, fragile, temporary or operate in isolation.

The 47 Articles of the Council of Europe Convention on Action Against Human Trafficking provided a template of what is necessary to address human trafficking, including the role of civil society.[23] The UK Modern Slavery Act places much of the convention into domestic law, but implementation remains patchy at best.

Awareness-raising to be able to identify the signs of modern slavery and trafficking is essential within faith communities. People who work with adults and children-at-risk are key in being able to identify exploited people. The following section highlights some of the signs of modern slavery.

Why are people trafficked? Things to know

Children, women and men are trafficked for a wide range of reasons, including:[24]

- Sexual exploitation
- Domestic servitude
- Forced labour, including in the agricultural, construction, food processing, hospitality industries and in factories

- Criminal activity including cannabis cultivation, street crime, forced begging and benefit fraud
- Organ harvesting.

How might you encounter a victim of modern slavery?

- A person may tell you about their experience.
- You detect signs that suggest a person may have been trafficked.
- They may be practising their faith in a church or other religious building and you recognize indicators.

Signs of trafficking in adults, children and young people include:

- A person being accompanied by someone who appears controlling, who insists on giving information on their behalf – even in a church.

Signs in a person include:

- Being withdrawn and submissive, seemingly afraid to speak to a person in authority and with the accompanying person speaking for them.
- Gives a vague and inconsistent explanation of where they live, their employment or schooling.
- Has old or serious injuries left untreated. Is vague and reluctant to explain how the injury occurred or to give a medical history.
- Is not registered with a GP, nursery or school and has no recorded history in the UK.
- Has experienced being moved locally, regionally, nationally or internationally.
- Appears to be moving location frequently.
- Their appearance suggests general physical neglect.
- They may struggle to speak English.

Signs in children and young people include:

- Having an unclear relationship with the accompanying adult.
- Going missing quickly (sometimes within 48 hours of going into care) and repeatedly from school, home and care.
- Giving inconsistent information about their age.

Signs in adults include:

- Having no official means of identification or possessing suspicious-looking documents.

What are the healthcare issues endured by trafficked people?

- Evidence of long-term multiple injuries from manual work or being prevented from accessing healthcare for minor injuries;
- Indications of mental, physical and sexual trauma;
- Sexually transmitted infections;
- Midwives have reported pregnant women making late bookings (over 24 weeks) for maternity care;
- Disordered eating or poor nutrition;
- Evidence of self-harm;
- Dental pain;
- Fatigue;
- Non-specific symptoms of post-traumatic stress disorder;
- Symptoms of psychiatric and psychological distress;
- Back pain, stomach pain, skin problems, headaches and dizzy spells.

Points to be aware of:

- Victims of trafficking can be prevented from revealing their experience due to fear, shame, language barriers and a lack of opportunity to do so. It can take time for a person to feel safe enough to open up.
- Err on the side of caution regarding age – if a person tells you they are under 18 or if a person says they are an adult,

but you suspect they are not, then take action as though they were under 18 years old: this assumption is contained in the Modern Slavery Act.

- Support for victims of human trafficking is available, but most important is to be aware of what is in your local area; services in local settings must be prioritized.

What do you do next?

In all cases for children, young people and adults:

- Do not raise your trafficking concerns with anyone accompanying the person.
- Ensure you address the immediate safety needs of the person. Do not put yourself at risk.
- Ensure the person is in a safe place or can be directed to a place of safety.
- React in a sensitive way that ensures the safety of the person.
- Think about support and referral.
- Try to use an interpreter (where possible) if translation is necessary.
- Do not use anyone accompanying the person as an interpreter. This applies to children, young people and adults.
- Try to find out more about the person's circumstances but do not pressurize them and do not start asking intrusive questions.
- When speaking to the person, reassure them that it is safe for them to speak.
- Do not make promises you cannot keep.
- Only ask non-judgemental relevant questions.
- Seek professional support. If the victim is a child the authorities must be informed.

Venues of trafficking

There is much information on the indicators of people who are trafficked, yet venues of potential trafficking can go unchallenged in plain sight on high streets, are accessible and reliant on consumers to keep them afloat. Prevention through compliance with existing regulatory standards including environmental, health and safety, tax compliance and National Insurance contributions can all be means to raise standards and stop exploitation at various premises – for example, at car washes, nail bars or other high-risk venues. There are also industries such as agriculture, construction, food processing and packaging where prevention can be improved through effective management of conditions in the workplace.

Conclusion

My personal experience in modern slavery has been wide-ranging, working with victims, prosecuting perpetrators, supporting NGOs and local communities across the world, collaborating with governments, influencing multilateral agencies, multinational companies and world leaders. I have visited over 40 countries and worked with at least another 20. I have seen extraordinary dedication, humility and compassion, and met many hundreds of survivors – some of whom have endured extreme trauma and exploitation, others who are indifferent to their situation, and some who can be adamant they are not trafficked or exploited, yet they are.

But the reason I commit to this work is summed up by some personal encounters that have shaped my views and driven my resolve – an undernourished seven-year-old, her education withheld, kept as a domestic slave in London. Or the 14-year-old Nigerian girl wrongly detained in a UK adult prison for a document offence under the control of her trafficker, with the authorities deciding she was a 26-year-old adult despite her physical appearance clearly proving she was a child. Her rape and trafficking went unnoticed, as did her trafficker – who sat only a few seats from her when she was arrested leaving the UK. Or the Syrian doctor and her husband and young son, living among 1,500 refugees in a Greek migrant camp, fleeing conflict having seen their loved ones perish. On arrival into the safety of Europe they experienced exploitation in forced labour. They spoke of how on their marriage and setting out in life together, they could never imagine this would be their destiny.

One of the most heart-wrenching meetings came with a 15-year-old Eritrean girl I met on the Italian island of Lampedusa. To avoid military conscription where she would have endured years of sexual abuse, her parents arranged for her to leave for Europe and travel to Sweden. They were heartbroken, but could not see any alternative in order to protect their precious child. Escorted on a route covering over 2,000 kilometres and crossing borders without incident, on arrival in Libya she was abandoned into a so-called 'connection house'. For the next three months she was raped several times every day, and sold into prostitution to the highest bidder. Eventually a seat was secured in a rickety boat destined for Italy, but she spoke of seeing tragedy on the voyage. Looking at her slight build and pleasant demeanour, I wondered, how *anyone* could treat a young girl like this, and what has happened to humanity? Some questioned her parents' decision, but I am so grateful that because of where I was born I never had to contemplate such choices to protect my teenage daughter.

In 2019 when the EU voted to end rescue missions in the very seas she crossed, I immediately thought of her and felt angry. It is this vote that could mean girls like her will not get protection. The view that rescue missions encourage more migrants to take dangerous routes is not only flawed, but immoral, and contrary to the very basis of the Universal Declaration of Human Rights.[25]

In 2015, when Alan Kurdi, aged three, was washed up on a beach in Turkey, the world stood by in shock. David Cameron said, 'Anyone who saw those pictures overnight could not help but be moved and, as a father, I felt deeply moved by the sight of that young boy on a beach in Turkey. "Britain is a moral nation and we will fulfil our moral responsibilities."' (Quoted in Dathan, 2015.) Irish Prime Minister Enda Kenny stated:

I think the picture was absolutely shocking ... Any parent could see that child in their own arms. Here's the body of a young boy, a life lost and washed up on a beach like driftwood. I think that picture more than any I've seen may shock political processes into taking action, both in terms of the stream of migrants and the causes that underlie that. (Quoted in Hand, 2015)

President Erdogan of Turkey had a telephone conversation with Alan's father in the days after the tragedy. Speaking of the loss of Alan, but also the loss of Mr Kurdi's wife and the suffering of another son who survived, Erdogan said, 'Those two babies were our children as much as they were your children. And your esteemed wife was our sister' (*Hurriyet Daily News*, 2015).

These and many more statements echoed across the world, but what has followed to address root causes to protect communities from those who use vulnerability to make money, whether in Europe, North Africa, South East Asia, or indeed any part of the world?

I return to the words of Pope Francis when he said of human trafficking: 'Humanity still hasn't learned how to cry, how to lament. We need many tears in order to understand the dimension of this drama' (Pope Francis, 2014).

When Alan Kurdi died, world leaders began to lament, to cry, showing an open hand of compassion. But what since? Decisions such as the withdrawal of rescue missions in the Mediterranean, the wrongful imprisonment of children and the absence of justice for victims of modern slavery, indicate humanity has not learned how to cry, to lament, and has swapped the open hand of compassion for a clenched fist of aggression. Were those tears in 2015 nothing more than crocodile tears and political posturing?

Church and faith groups can become the prodigy. Once we feel the pain and suffering and become angry about modern slavery, then our determination to end this abuse will be as strong as that of Wilberforce, bringing inner strength not to back down, to face the challenge head on, to a time when there is a clear delineation between those who support its existence and those who oppose it. Once we are clear who prospers and who looks the other way, we can challenge them and call to account their complicity.

This tragedy is created by humankind and can only be ended by humans acting with kindness. The argument often put forward is that there needs to be a compromise to achieve the 'greater good'. There is nothing good in modern slavery and human trafficking, so no compromises need be made; we need all-out efforts to end this vile abuse and serious crime.

The target is set in Sustainable Development Goal 8.7 to be achieved by 2030. Dedicated work is necessary to make the mission a reality, and not as a celebration, but so history can show that the twenty-first century was when people of goodwill, courage and determination used their time as temporary guardians of this planet to make a better world for generations to come. Ambitious though this may seem, the lives of 40 million souls are depending on it.

Bibliography

Abolition Project, 'Thomas Clarkson – Key Events', *Thomas Clarkson*, available from http://abolition.e2bn.org/box_59.html, accessed 23.02.21.

Biography Online, 'Quotes of William Wilberforce', available from www.biographyonline.net/politicians/quotes/william-wilberforce-quotes.html, accessed 17.12.20.

Church in Wales, 2019, 'Highlights', *Highlights of the Church in Wales' Governing Meeting*, available from https://churchinwales.contentfiles.net/media/documents/Highlights_-_September_2019.pdf, accessed 23.02.21.

Clewer Initiative, 'About Us', *The Clewer Initiative*, available from www.theclewerinitiative.org/about-us, accessed 17.12.20.

Dathan, M., 2015, 'Alan Kurdi', *Independent*, available from www.independent.co.uk/news/uk/politics/aylan-kurdi-david-cameron-says-he-felt-deeply-moved-images-dead-syrian-boy-gives-no-details-plans-take-more-refugees-10484641.html, accessed 17.12.20.

Gren-Jardan, T., 2020, 'It Still Happens Here: Fighting UK Slavery in the 2020s', London: Justice and Care, available from www.justiceandcare.org/wp-content/uploads/2020/07/Justice-and-Care-Centre-for-Social-Justice-It-Still-Happens-Here.pdf, accessed 14.10.20.

Hand, L., 2015, 'A young boy ... washed up on the beach like drift-wood', *Independent Ireland*, available from www.independent.ie/irish-news/a-young-boy-washed-up-on-beach-like-driftwood-taoise ach-describes-migrant-crisis-as-human-catastrophe-31500065.html, accessed 17.12.20.

Hayes, S., 2012, quoted from 'Victim of human trafficking praises conference', *Catholic News Agency*, available from www.catholic newsagency.com/news/victim-of-human-trafficking-praises-vatican-conference, accessed 17.12.20.

Hoogteijling, J., 2019, 'Safe Havens', *The Salvation Army International*, available from www.salvationarmy.org/ihq/ahteurope, accessed 17.12.20.

Hurriyet Daily News, 2015, 'If only you had stayed in Turkey ...', available from www.hurriyetdailynews.com/if-only-you-had-stayed-in-turkey-erdogan-tells-drowned-syrian-toddlers-father-88025, accessed 17.12.20.

In Communion, 2019, 'Fighting Modern Slavery and Human Traffick-ing as a Parish', available from https://incommunion.org/2019/10/22/fighting-modern-slavery-and-human-trafficking-as-a-parish/, accessed 5.01.21.

Minderoo Foundation, 2018, 'More than 136,000 people are living in modern slavery in the United Kingdom', *Walk Free Global Slavery Index*, 18 July, available from www.globalslaveryindex.org/news/more-than-136000-people-are-living-in-modern-slavery-in-the-united-kingdom/, accessed 14.10.20.

Petley, C., 2018, 'Lord Nelson and slavery: Nelson's dark side', *HistoryExtra*, available from www.historyextra.com/period/georgian/lord-nelson-slavery-abolition-william-wilberforce-dark-side/, accessed 17.12.20.

Pontifical Academies of Sciences and Social Sciences, 2014, *Joint Dec-laration of Religious Leaders*, available from www.pass.va/content/scienzesociali/en/events/2014-18/jointdeclaration.html, accessed 17.12.20.

Pope Francis, 2014, Responses to interview with reporter J. Etching-ham, 'An extraordinary meeting with Pope Francis', interview with J. Etchingham, *ITV News*, available from www.itv.com/news/2014-04-10/an-extraordinary-meeting-with-pope-francis, accessed 17.12.20.

Pope Francis, 2019, 'Address of His Holiness Pope Francis to Partici-pants at the International Conference on Human Trafficking', *Libreria Editrice Vaticana*, available from www.vatican.va/content/francesco/en/speeches/2019/april/documents/papa-francesco_20190411_con ferenza-trattadipersone.html, accessed 17.12.20.

René Cassin, 'Slavery and Trafficking', available from www.renecassin.org/category/slavery-and-trafficking/, accessed 17.12.20.

United Nations Association, UK, 'United Nations Day', available from https://una.org.uk/un-day-factsheet, accessed 17.12.20.

United Nations Department of Economic and Social Affairs, 'Targets and Indicators', *Goals 8*, available from https://sdgs.un.org/goals/goal8, accessed 17.12.20.

United Nations Treaty Collection, 2000, 'Protocol to Prevent, Suppress and Punish Trafficking in Persons, Especially Women and Children', *United Nations Treaty Series Online*, Penal Matters, vol. 2, ch. XVIII, available from https://treaties.un.org/doc/Treaties/2000/11/20001115%2011-38%20AM/Ch_XVIII_12_ap.pdf, accessed 17.12.20.

US State Department, 2020, *Trafficking in Persons Report*, available from www.state.gov/wp-content/uploads/2020/06/2020-TIP-Report-Complete-062420-FINAL.pdf, accessed 17.12.20.

Notes

1 www.ihrb.org, accessed 17.12.20.

2 www.ilo.org/global/lang--en/index.htm, accessed 17.12.20.

3 Referred to as the Trafficking Protocol or UN TIP Protocol.

4 www.coe.int/en/web/anti-human-trafficking/about-the-convention, accessed 17.12.20.

5 www.alliance87.org/the-alliance/, accessed 17.12.20.

6 www.fastinitiative.org, accessed 17.12.20.

7 https://afjn.org, accessed 17.12.20.

8 https://santamartagroup.com/partners/nigeria-benin-project-grow-edo/, accessed 17.12.20.

9 www.acan.org.au, accessed 17.12.20.

10 https://acrath.org.au, accessed 17.12.20.

11 https://ec-patr.org, accessed 17.12.20.

12 www.jrsuk.net, accessed 17.12.20.

13 www.aptireland.org/apt-act-prevent-trafficking/, accessed 17.12.20.

14 https://mecpaths.com, accessed 17.12.20.

15 www.medaille-trust.org.uk, accessed 17.12.20.

16 www.caritaswestminster.org.uk/bakhita-house.php, accessed 17.12.20.

17 https://care.org.uk, accessed 17.12.20.

18 www.coe.int/en/web/anti-human-trafficking/home, accessed 17.12.20.

19 www.gov.uk/government/collections/national-referral-mechanism-statistics, accessed 17.12.20.

20 https://cruxnow.com/church/2015/02/vatican-announces-a-day-of-prayer-against-human-trafficking/, accessed 17.12.20.

21 https://santamartagroup.com, accessed 17.12.20.

22 Refer to Clarkson, Thomas, *The History of the Rise, Progress, and Accomplishment of the Abolition of the African Slave-Trade by the British Parliament*, 2 volume set, Cambridge: Cambridge University Press, 2010.

23 www.coe.int/en/web/conventions/full-list/-/conventions/rms/09 0000168008371d, accessed 17.12.20.

24 Refer to the following NHS video regarding spotting the signs of modern slavery, www.youtube.com/watch?v=FxF4ByHXlsU, accessed 17.12.20.

25 www.un.org/en/universal-declaration-human-rights/index.html, accessed 17.12.20.

PART 2

Survivors' Stories

2

Stella's Story

Life in Colombia[1]

I was born in Colombia. I wanted to become a lawyer. I chose to do this because of what happened to my family, and I wanted to send my dad to prison. I was a lesbian, but I did not deserve what he did to me. That was why I wanted to become a lawyer, because of what was done to me for being a lesbian. I really wanted to get a degree and have my vendetta, and put my father away for the rest of his life because he took advantage of me. I wanted my revenge. He did whatever he wanted to do with me. He hurt me a lot. The worse thing is to be raped because you are a lesbian. That was bad. It ruined the rest of my life. It is something that remains with you for the rest of your life. How can someone be protected when someone hurts you? What I most needed, I didn't have. The pain and suffering that I have never goes away. Now I'm getting help from the psychologists and lawyers.

I was very happy to go to university, where I studied law. I've always been the top student, and I really wanted to become a top lawyer. But I failed at that. I had to finance the university course myself, and part way through my course I found out I had cancer. I had to pay for the treatment, for radiotherapy and chemotherapy. Where I come from, we have to pay for hospital treatment. I didn't have enough money to pay for both the university and the hospital costs. What I earned was not enough. I had to leave university because I didn't have any money to pay for it. I lost my job. There was no one to help me. After my father did what he did to me, I just left my family and never went back. That is when I really missed having a family. I was ill. I didn't have a job. I had no support.

Offer of employment

I used to go on Saturdays to a gay club. There were gay and transgender people there, and I met some who befriended me. After a while my new friends offered me a job in France. It sounded like I could earn some money and pay for my university career. I saw this open door and opportunity to go to France. I was very happy. I planned to stay there for six months and earn enough to fund my degree and to buy my return ticket to Colombia.

So I went with them to France and it was the worst thing I have ever done. Things didn't turn out the way I thought they would. The people don't let you understand fully what they are offering. They don't tell you straight what it is all about. Once I understood the situation, I tried to escape. But I didn't know the language, I didn't know where I was. They took away my passport. They wouldn't let me have a phone. The only person I was in contact with was my brother, and I really wanted to speak with him.

I was told to walk the streets as a prostitute. I said, 'No, I don't want to do that.' But there was no choice. It was either that or they would beat you to death. They would kill you. I had to. It hurts me to speak about it.

From 9 p.m. they would take us out until late. There was a pimp who would take us to a road; he would be in a car and guard us. If the police were around that was the end, and he took us away by car. Then in the morning, until 5 p.m., they would take us back to the house. At the house they would give us some clothing and condoms to put in our handbags. They would work out how many condoms we would use and therefore how much money we were supposed to hand in at the end of the day. Once we were back at the house, they would then work out how much we earned. They would only give us one bottle of water and sandwich. Who was I going to ask for help?

In the house where we were locked in, there were seven women and three transgender. We were all from South America. The door to the house was always locked, and we were monitored on a CCTV camera. We were kept by two Colombian men, Rodrigo and another man. They were partners and the main bosses. They would observe how much money we got from clients. If the clients gave us more, Rodrigo wanted that money too. Every girl had to make at least 300–400 euros per day. Of this, 70 euros went towards accommodation and then the rest were for expenses, and deduction of the air tickets for travel to France. Rodrigo made bags of money.

Rodrigo would threaten the girls, and sometimes they would disappear. We never knew if they had been killed. When he was high on drugs, he was able to do anything in a nasty way. He was capable of doing anything. If anyone refused a client for any reason, then once the client had gone he would beat us up. He would then rape us, saying: 'You didn't make money for me.' Rodrigo laid down the law. 'Do it, or I'll rape you', he would say. It was the same for all of us, women or trans.

I learned that I was in a big city, and I remember the street very well. We started there, but then moved addresses many times to other towns. I was in France for ten years and I just wanted to die. Because there is no way out. I just wanted to end it all. It's horrible.

Escape and prosecution

One day Rodrigo was notified that one of his contacts who delivered him cocaine had been stopped by the police in Italy. Rodrigo became scared thinking the police could connect him with the cocaine delivery, and because he was scared he made a mistake. He forgot that the key for the window of the house was on the table. When I saw it, I took the key and hid it, as the door to the house was always locked.

I told Marco, who was locked up with me. He was a gay Colombian friend. Rodrigo often threatened to kill Marco with a knife, because he didn't want to take cocaine and he didn't want to have sex without protection. When I told Marco about the key, he was scared and said: 'Put it back. If Rodrigo comes back, he will know it is you. He will kill you and me. He will kill us both before anyone survives.' But I said: 'I am going to escape. Come midnight, I am going to escape.' Marco was very scared. But I couldn't think of anything else but running away, of escaping.

Following the tip-off about the cocaine, there was a risk that the police would come to the house and so Rodrigo left the house. Around midnight, Marco said: 'Shall we tell the rest of the group, and then we escape together?' But I said: 'No, just you and me, or they will kill us.' As everyone else went to sleep that night, I sneaked through the darkness and opened the window. First Marco went out through the window and then I followed him.

It was strange because we didn't know where we were. It was dark. There was countryside. We didn't know where to go and it was cold. We walked all night. At some time after 7 a.m., we met a lady. We were tired and dirty. The lady asked: 'What happened?' I said: 'We have run away from a prostitution house and we would like to go to the police.' The lady explained to us how to get to the police station. We went in that direction and asked a couple more people. When we arrived, we found the police station was closed as it was still very early in the morning. We went to a train station and found a police officer. We explained we had escaped from a prostitution house and I wanted to report the people holding us. More police officers arrived and we told them our plight. They took us to a police station where we stayed all day and night. We told our story and, with the help of an interpreter, they took a statement.

I had to tell them about Rodrigo. I wanted to report that piece of shit. He used to beat Marco. He would drug the girls and beat them. We informed the police about the houses. We also gave them Rodrigo's telephone number. After a month of surveillance, the police raided the four houses at the same time. Everyone in the houses was found and freed. They also found cocaine. It was all over the newspapers. Rodrigo was arrested, and the judge gave him nine years in France. I was so happy he'd been caught. The Colombian partner escaped to Colombia.

Marco found out that he was HIV+ and went to Madrid to receive treatment. After that I was informed by the police that he went back to Colombia to his family. There was nothing else he could do, as the illness was too advanced.

I couldn't believe that I was free. I was out. I was alive. I could walk. I had my life back. The police gave me accommodation, but they did not support or help me. As I could not get a proper job in Italy, because of what I went through, I could only get cash-in-hand jobs, cleaning and domestic jobs. I was happy for a couple of years in France. From what I understand, French law is not right. The French authorities did not help me. I thought they would help me get a proper job, but they didn't. The police were always telling me: 'You have to get a contract.' In the end they deported me.

When I went back to Colombia, I chose to go back to a different city from where I was born. When I arrived there I hoped the police would help, but they gave no help or support. There were some desperate moments. I did not know where to go. I didn't know anybody. I had no money. I was homeless and would just walk around all day. I was lucky as I used to sleep on the beach with other homeless people.

In this city I ran into Luca, who was part of Rodrigo's set-up. He used to find the houses, as they were always moving us around. I had seen him stabbing a girl in France, he was a very nasty guy. He was doing voodoo. He was killing chickens. He would threaten us with that. We were scared as I had run into him. He wanted to get even. He said to me: 'You have to pay for what you did in France.' I said: 'No, that is done and dusted.' He pushed me on the floor and snatched my handbag and left. The handbag had my passport in it. I was left only with the clothes I was wearing. I went to the police and told them everything. I wanted him to be put away because he destroyed a lot of people's lives, including mine. I had nothing to lose. Eventually Luca went to prison. He was sentenced to eight years.

Both Rodrigo and Luca have recently been released. Inside

me, I have such fear. I am worried they are going to find me and kill me. No one can understand how I feel. I'm very surprised to learn these people have been set free. I had the courage to report them to the police, but they freed them. Can anyone explain to me where is the law? It is unjust. Ultimately you can pay your way out. It is corruption. People who have been trafficking human beings are now released. I am of course worried, because of the injustice.

Running to freedom

A new opportunity came along. I needed a way out, so I went. There was a Venezuelan girl who had been working at the same place as me in France. She had started a new life and was now married and had children. Her husband does not know about her past, or mine. They were living in Switzerland. I told her my story. She sent me money for the ticket and told me to come to her house. When I left Colombia, I flew to London and had a stop-over on the way to Switzerland. In Switzerland, immigration wouldn't let me in. They told me I needed a visa to stay. They sent me back to London, and I arrived there in August 2016. In London, they put me in a detention centre and asked me questions. I was too ill and too weak. I didn't want to explain a lot of these things. I was there from August to November.

It is only recently that I have been able to speak about these things. It's not easy to talk about it. Inside I feel bitter. It burns inside of me. The psychologist is helping me open up. I shared my story and was identified as a victim of trafficking. I was then given a temporary place in a shelter, before I was moved on to Ella's safe home. I'm very happy to be here at Ella's.

What helps me every day is I can go to the park. I feel free. I feel good about it. I don't feel like I'm in prison. Just to be able to run has helped. I recently completed a 10 km race. I haven't got words to explain how good I felt when I finished the 10 km. The T-shirt that I was wearing said 'Stop Human Trafficking'. It was very important to me. I've been a victim.

When I run, it feels like I'm free. I have my life in my hands, I can do whatever I want. I feel the air on my face, and that I'm free. The fact that I achieved 10 km, it was my first time. I want to do more 10 kms, and I am getting ready for my next 13 km race. Nobody is going to stop me. I have the will to live. To study. I want to carry on running. I want to become a lawyer, as I always dreamt about it. My aim is to jail those people. I swear to God.

Note

1 Names and locations have been changed to protect identities. Stella is a survivor of modern slavery and at Ella's, a home for exploited women. With thanks to Ella's for supporting Stella in telling her story.

3

Richard's Story

Recruitment[1]

I first met him in Manchester, in a homeless hostel. I was in my mid-twenties. A notice came over the announcement system: 'If anyone is interested in a job in Austria, come to reception.' I went down to reception and met him. He had a suit on and presented himself politely. He asked: 'Do you have a passport? Can you drive?' 'Yes', I replied. The job would be ground-work and tarmacking. He offered me 900 Austrian schillings a day with accommodation paid for. I jumped at the chance. I had no reason to disbelieve what he was saying, and I didn't think twice about it. I was young and naïve, so I left the hostel and went with him. I didn't know anything about Irish travellers at that time.

I was born and brought up in the Manchester area. I had a fantastic childhood. All the fields and farms. I didn't do very well at school – bottom of the class – and when I left school I couldn't get a job. I had nowhere to stay as I had an argument with my dad. Nothing could have been worse for me at that time, and I ended up at the homeless hostel. If I hadn't been in the hostel, I wouldn't have met him.

We travelled to Austria, where I thought I'd be put up in a hotel. Instead, we arrived at an old car park with lots of caravans. It then dawned on me that this wasn't a normal company. There were people from different parts of the UK who had been recruited like me – our caravans were on one side, and the posh caravans of the travellers were on the other side. I stayed in a battered old touring caravan with skylights and windows missing and the wind blowing through the windows. In Austria in February it was cold. We had a gas bottle until it ran out. I only

had a sleeping bag to keep warm. There was no TV or enter-
tainment. I had to try to scrape together my own money to buy
a radio to entertain myself at night. I was sharing the caravan
with a couple of guys who had been recruited from a homeless
hostel in Barrow, Cumbria. Recruiting from homeless hostels
was a very popular way of getting workers. They would also
recruit a lot of Polish workers as they could pay them less.

The tarmac years

Sometimes we would work 6.30 a.m. until 8 p.m., Monday to
Friday. We'd go in a tarmac truck to do a job. There was no
breakfast or food and we had to work until the job was finished.
It was hard work and very physically demanding, especially
with no food. I only got through it because I was young and fit.
I had to work fast because if the tarmac got cold, it got hard
like concrete and they couldn't use it. It was all about speed.
We used wooden rakes and wheelbarrows – like something off
the Flintstones cartoon. Like 'Carry On' tarmacking. On the
wagon there would be 30 tons and we only had wheelbarrows
to get it off. Nine wheelbarrows to a ton. Two hundred and
seventy wheelbarrows. The work was very dangerous. Trying
to tip a full wheelbarrow of tarmac was very heavy. If I stopped
to try to have a cigarette or food, they would shout at me. I'd be
threatened and told I'd be beaten with a shovel. My back even
aches now, years later, from all that bending down and raking
tarmac the whole day.

   For payment, I would get different amounts. Often I would
work all day and not get paid, because they didn't get paid.
They would say: 'The man's not paid me, the job's no good,
so I'm not paying you.' So I would be stood there starving,
covered in tarmac, dirty, tired as a dead dog. I'm nearly laughing now because it was that bad. And I wouldn't get a penny
for it. That's the height of frustration. You're always guessing,
whether they had been paid or not. When I wasn't paid, I felt
bad. But I would think tomorrow would be a better day, that I
would be paid. I had to keep positive and motivated.

Having worked long hours during the week, on a Saturday I would drive the tarmac truck ten to twelve hours to a new location for work. I wouldn't get paid for that. I was conned really. I'd work all year and have a few schillings, and when I changed it back to pounds I hardly had anything for the year abroad. That was frustrating. After a year's work I had about 4,000 Austrian schillings, which was about £300. As I made friends with others who had been recruited like me, the weeks and months flew by. And then the next year came around.

I have to ask myself, why did I stay with them so long? One reason is I am a vulnerable person. I wasn't very good at school. Job opportunities weren't very good. I was always thinking at the back of my mind: 'If I go back to England, I'll be on the dole and on benefits.' So I thought, this is better than being on the dole. At least there's a chance of getting some money and doing some work. That's what kept me going. Another challenge was I had never been abroad before in my life. It wasn't very nice being stuck hundreds and hundreds of miles abroad with no money to get back. I didn't know what decisions to make.

For the first ten years I was mostly in Austria, with some work in Sweden and the Netherlands. I worked for four different people. For each, I was told I had to work for them, or I was threatened. They were big people and there was a lot of them. I was on my own. It's not worth taking the chance. They used to say, 'I own you', like a piece of furniture. One guy sold the tarmac truck to another guy and he said to me: 'Because I bought the wagon, you come with the wagon. You are part of the deal.' So that's how I came to be working for another person. I came with the wagon. I was like a spare wheel. It's bad, you know, but that's the truth. I just accepted it. I would think that things would get better. I kept carrying on working with them. I had no choice. They were very aggressive, saying: 'I'm telling you, you've got to work for me.' I would be threatened. And so I left. They said they would kill me. My family were threatened, which makes things even worse. I was scared. So I went to work for different people. My mental health wasn't very good. I still suffer with my mental health now.

It was extremely tiring. The only time off I had was on

Sundays. Sometimes I would go to an Austrian church. In other countries where I worked, I would also go to church on a Sunday morning. In the afternoon, I might go for a walk. I had no holiday leave, that wasn't even discussed. You were like a robot. You had to work no matter what. I've not had a holiday since I was with my mum and dad. The last holiday was 28 years ago. I went up to Scotland, and rented a cottage in the north of Scotland. I'm 47 now.

Sometimes we would come back to the caravan site in Yorkshire for Christmas. After the first year I had built their trust in me. They then allowed me to go home for Christmas to be with my mum and dad, and would then pick me up in January. I never told my parents what was happening. I don't know why. I thought to myself, I'd told them I was going abroad working for a company. I thought it was a good thing. I tried to stick with that. My dad didn't like me working with them. My mum didn't mind. She thought if I was happy, then she was happy. My mum even invited one of them into the house and made them a cup of tea. They were as good as gold. That's their trick, their con. My dad kept saying to me years later that I should get a proper job. He then found out who I was working for. He used to say: 'Stop working for that gang, you'll get yourself into trouble.' He was right.

The tar 'n' chip years

For the second half of the 20 years, they had a special tar 'n' chip truck. It had a tank behind the cab for the liquid tar and there was a container for chippings. We went to Spain and all over Europe doing tar 'n' chip. In a way it was easier work, as the truck does a lot of the work. But I had to do preparation of the ground. Lots of sweeping and shovels. Often they would have a job ready, but sometimes there would be no job. I would be parked on an industrial estate, in the middle of nowhere. The worst thing was being left all day in the wagon at the industrial estate. I'd be cracking up from boredom and starving from hunger. In the winter my feet and hands would be freezing. I wouldn't be able to work on the wagon or hold the nuts and bolts. But if they got a job, they would phone me and be like maniacs. I had to work like lightning. It was a nightmare. That happened for years.

They were conning people. The sticky tar was expensive to buy – 1,500 euros for one ton. A tank would hold three tons. They would buy half a tank and then fill the rest with water. It would save a lot of money, but the tar would lose its stickiness. Sometimes the Austrian police would stop us for different reasons, to check paperwork, or if they had a complaint about bad work. They would talk with me, but they never asked if I was OK. All they thought about were the Austrian people. Were they getting ripped off? Were they getting good work? They weren't bothered about me. They would see us being mistreated, but they weren't bothered. They would drive on. In them days it was totally different; things like modern slavery weren't discussed.

On a Saturday morning from 9 a.m. to 1 p.m. I would have to clean the wagon. I could see my reflection out of the bodywork. They used to say: 'If your truck's clean, you won't get pulled over by the police.' That's why I used to make it so clean. I would have the cleanest truck out of all the trucks. When I used to go to the quarries, they would say: 'That's a clean truck.' It might seem sad to you this, in a way, but it used to make me so proud. I was so brainwashed. Sometimes I would cheat, and I would pay the Polish men out of my own money to clean it.

That yellow wagon nearly killed me stone dead. The brakes failed twice. They were very dangerous times. The cab/tractor unit wasn't built to have the heavy trailer body behind it, so the brakes weren't designed for it. They went completely about three times coming down a mountain. On one occasion, I was going down a mountain just outside Frankfurt. The wagon went around a bend and on to two wheels. It seemed to stay like that for a lifetime. I don't know if it was God. I am a bit of a religious person. It seemed to take a lifetime, but it fell back down on to its four wheels. I thought I was dead. Scared is not the word. I'm not saying there's another being that saved me, but how I survived them three occasions, I still don't know.

Maybe somebody else was deciding: 'Should I be kept alive, or should I not?' Trying to save me for better days maybe.

During these later years we stayed on and off at a caravan site in Kent. I had an old caravan in a yard. It wasn't very nice. The skylight used to leak, and it was cold. There was a little electric fire that didn't keep the caravan very warm. You would have children throwing rocks at the caravan. It felt very scary at times, being surrounded by two to three hundred travellers. Sometimes the boss would come back from the pub and threaten to beat me up. I'd have my door locked, and he would nearly rip the door off its hinges. It wasn't nice. He was a massive fella. He would threaten me. There were periods when I didn't have much food. Sometimes they would do me an English breakfast and dinner at night, then there were times when I got nothing. Some days I only had a sandwich to eat. I was told by one of the travellers who came to pick me up: 'Richard, you've lost about two stones.' He went mad, and he was a traveller himself. The times they were good to me were very few. Sometimes the police would come on to the caravan site, but they never used to see me. I was hidden away in a little caravan. If only they knew.

In the later years, they took out a load of vehicles in my name: tarmac trucks, cars, vans. They weren't returned. Companies and the police in Austria were chasing me left, right and centre. I'm still receiving bills and fines from these. I spent two years in the Netherlands, where I was frogmarched down to an office. They opened up a company in my name with my passport. I had no choice. If there was a problem with the company, I would get into trouble. They kept their names out of it. The companies didn't pay tax and did shoddy work. If anyone phoned up and complained about work, the authorities would look for me.

Freedom and the future

In 2014 I was arrested by the Dutch police relating to a job we did. The company had been set up in my name. I was sentenced to four months in a Dutch prison. In a way I had already been in prison by working for them. They had me in chains, because I couldn't go anywhere. I was scared. The travellers abandoned me and fled to Austria. All they care about is money, but it turned out to be a blessing in disguise. If they hadn't got me locked up in the Netherlands and left me, I would still be working for them. I thank God because that was the last I saw of them. After four months I had to make my own way back to the UK. I ended up homeless.

I came to Essex, because that's where I had my best friend. He had also worked for the travellers, and I knew he would let me sleep on his sofa. It was the only option I had until the homeless hostel would take me when I was on benefits. But even after the travellers were out of my life, there were still after-effects. Eight months after being free in the UK there was a knock on my door. It was the police and they said: 'You're being arrested on a European arrest warrant.' I had been made to transport items that I did not know were illegal. I was sentenced to a further 13 months in prison in England and Denmark for their crimes. The log-book of the van transporting those goods was registered in my name.

I spent 13 months in Wandsworth prison and a Danish prison. I'm not the type of person to be put among a whole lot of not very nice people. It will take me a long time to get over that. The police know all about what I went through. I talked with them about it. Those I worked for are multi-millionaires. They're not bothered about the police – the amount of run-ins they've had with the police over the years. There's nothing the police can do to them. It's pointless. When I got out of the Danish prison, I made my way back to the UK and I became homeless again. I had to do it all over again.

During the last few years my memory has gone downhill. It's so frustrating. I can't recall all the bad things they've done to me. I'll see something and it will trigger a memory, an event, or something that happened to me. I still suffer with my mental health now. I don't know what to do with my days. I've got to do something. I need to get away desperately. I walk around every day. I want to do something. I want to see my family, my sister.

I constantly worry and look over my shoulder. I don't want to see them again or bump into them. That's very hard, but it's getting easier as time goes on. They are still looking for me, phoning my friend and asking: 'Where is he?' How long are they going to try and contact me? They've done enough damage to me without adding on top of that.

I have been scared of trying to get a normal job. I've been put out of society. People ask: 'Where have you been for over 20 years?' It's not easy. I've been on universal credit for a while and I don't know how much chance there is of me getting a job. Another big after-effect is because they didn't pay income tax or National Insurance contributions, I'll get no pension. I was outside of the UK for so long.

A year after finding a room with the homeless charity, I got my first flat. It feels fantastic to have my own place. I'm nearly 50 years old. Normally people have lived in many places before they reach 50. My hope for the future is to get healthier and live for a while longer. I'd like to get a part-time job, to get my flat sorted. My mum and dad passed away. But when I do go up-above, I hope to see my mum and dad again.

The most helpful thing in recovering is the help I've received from the church and other people within the community. They tried to make it as easy as possible. I appreciate my story being told. It might help put a stop to these people recruiting more people. It might stop others ending up as victims and being abused. Hopefully, more people will help put an end to it.

Note

1 Names and locations have been changed to protect identities.

4

Amna's Story

Life in India[1]

I was born into a poor family in India. My father worked away from home to support the family, so I lived with my mother and younger brothers. My mother was strict and I was married very young. Society is sadly not equal for women in India. As I am a girl, I was not allowed to make my own decisions and choose my own life. I was pulled out of school once I got married. I became engaged at 13 years of age and married at 16.

After only seven days of marriage my husband was violent to me. He slapped me across the face and I became very scared of him. The physical violence continued and it affected everything. I felt so sad. I was expected to cook and clean, but I was so young and still learning. As I was scared of him, I made mistakes all the time. This didn't help my relationship with my husband. I told my mother what was happening. I hoped for her support, but she told me that 'This is what marriage is like. Find a way to manage it.'

My life was focused on doing housework. I felt stuck, and at times I wanted to die. I was forbidden from going into town or talking to the neighbours. My neighbours were unhelpful and watched everything I did. They would report back to my mother, influencing her. My mother was more concerned about what people thought than how I was doing as her daughter. People beyond my family would not talk to me. I'm not sure why. It was like they were scared of interacting with me. But this didn't stop them gossiping and reporting what I did and how I behaved.

At home I was treated like a servant. It was as if I was only there to cook, clean and have children. My husband behaved so well and nicely when other people were around. When it was just us together, he would push my head and pull my hair. Occasionally he mistreated me in front of his parents, telling them not to tell anyone. They followed his request.

Pregnancy and financial pressure

As soon as I was married, my in-laws put a lot of pressure on me to have children. They wanted me to have four or five boys. At first, I didn't know I was pregnant. I was never educated to know that when my period stopped, I was pregnant. I miscarried my first pregnancy. The miscarriage made everything worse. My in-laws blamed me and were so angry with me. I was locked in a room and repeatedly told: 'The first child is very important.'

They waited for me to fall pregnant again, keeping track of my period dates. When I did become pregnant, they became even more strict with me. I was still expected to keep up with the demanding chores, including hand-washing all the clothes. I was stressed. When I went to see a doctor, I was informed that my body was weak. I was scared and wanted to talk to somebody, but who could I tell? Who would listen to me? I could not even tell my mother. My first son was born when I was 17.

My in-laws were happy that a son had been born. However, this did not satisfy them as they continued to put pressure on me for more children. My second son was born when I was 18 years old. My life focused on looking after my sons and doing housework.

Although my in-laws wanted me to have many children, they tricked me into having an abortion. It is believed that if a pregnant woman's blood pressure is 160/130, then she is pregnant with a girl. When my blood pressure was at that level, I was put to sleep and when I woke up I was no longer pregnant. This happened three times. My in-laws forced me to have three abortions. They only wanted me to have boys.

I was so weak. My body looked like a skeleton and I had pain everywhere. I begged my mum to help me. I wanted to have an operation that would prevent me from having any more pregnancies. For once she listened and agreed to help. But this caused a big family fight. I was so distressed and ill that after nine months they found out that I could no longer become pregnant anyway.

You may ask why I stayed with my husband. As a woman in India, divorce is not easy. To make matters worse, my father-in-law is a lawyer. He is a well-known and respected man. A divorce would have been impossible.

My husband could not find work and his reputation was affected by only having fathered two children. People were laughing and thinking badly about our family. My husband's father was proud and would not let him get a factory job, thinking that he deserved a better job. In the course of our marriage my husband only worked for one year. He changed jobs four or five times with excuse after excuse. He would tell me: 'The timing was not right [because he] struggled to tolerate the work environment.' Financially, things became really difficult.

Even though my parents were poor, my mother would try to help. They struggled to support themselves and my brothers. My mother would buy clothes for my children. She tried to give me money, but I was too proud to accept anything from her. She would therefore hide money in our house.

My husband decided that he would find a higher class of job in a different country, as we needed the money. I was told I would go with him without my children. I didn't want to leave them – I was so worried about them. They told me we would be gone for one month and then I could come back. Little did I know that the family just wanted to use me. Thinking I was only leaving India for a short trip, we set off and arrived in the UK.

Life in the UK

When we arrived in the UK we stayed with people my husband knew. One month came and went, and I expected to return to India. I was told: 'There is no money for you to go back to India. If you want to return you need to work to earn the money for the flight.' I was desperate and would cry, telling my husband that I wanted to go home to my children.

My husband found me a job with a family just outside London. He would not get a job himself. He told me: 'Now is the time for working. When you make money, you can go back.' I went to live with the family who I worked for. I was only allowed to leave and visit my husband one or two days a month. I had to do all the chores in a certain time. They did not treat me well and expected me to work all the time. I felt like they were torturing me. After two years I went to work for a second family in London. I was able to get the job because I had developed a good reputation as a trusted and hard worker.

If I did something my husband did not like, he would slap me. He would get so angry and beat me. He told me: 'You can make more money from prostitution.' If a man sat next to me on a bus he would say: 'Why don't you sit on his lap?' I felt so dirty. My husband really wanted me to sleep with other men for money. He told me: 'You can work only at night. You would need no other job.' But I refused to become a prostitute, and I remained working for families.

I found out my husband was cheating on me. I was so miserable. I had no one to turn to and was never allowed to make any friends. After four years in the UK, I told my mum everything that had happened. She did not believe me and told me: 'Your husband is a good man.' The community in London also believed he was a good man. But he was manipulative and used me. I started to have problems with my employer because my husband told them bad things about me.

I did not understand the law or how the visa system worked. No one explained anything to me. I thought if I had a visa, I could go to any country and work. I didn't know what the law was. After one year I managed to get some knowledge about the visa system and realized with horror that I was illegal and my passport was no good. After this discovery, things became worse.

I then went to work with a third family, and this family was even worse. They caused me so many problems. The family told me that if I didn't do as they wanted, they would call the police and tell them that I was an illegal immigrant. As I did not have a valid visa, every day the pressure increased. I knew I was in the country illegally. The woman made problems and issues out of everything. She even made threats against my family.

The houses I had to clean were large, with four to five bedrooms. I would work all day, from 5 a.m. in the morning until 10 p.m. Sometimes I was not able to eat anything. Once, as they were moving house, they made me pack up their entire house by myself. I worked from early in the morning carefully packing items, until 1 a.m. I was also expected to be a childminder to my employer's two children 24 hours each day, seven days a week.

The family's son was so rude to me. Once he put his hands around my throat. I felt sad as I did everything for these families. I was scared all the time by the way they spoke to me and the threats they made. They controlled me through fear. I wanted to find another job as I was struggling under the pressure. They paid me money but it was always late. This made my husband angry and he made me look bad to other people. He controlled me. I eventually managed to leave this third family.

After six years in the UK I found a new job by myself. I trusted this family – however, they treated me badly too. The woman was so clever. She would play mind games with me. She had a newborn and went to Pakistan, leaving me to care for the child. She said she would return after ten days but did not come back for two and a half months. Her husband was in the house with me but did nothing. I had to do everything 24 hours a day.

I wanted to leave this family because they did not pay me for the work. They tricked me and treated me badly. There were times I did not even eat because I was told I could not touch the food. I went back and forth on trying to leave, but I became attached to their children. I missed my own children in India. It was hard emotionally. I also had no idea how I would survive as an illegal immigrant in the UK without working for a family. The woman convinced me not to leave. I was so confused.

After one year of working for that family, immigration officers came to their house at 6 a.m. one morning and found me there. When immigration arrived, they took me to the police station. I was so worried that I would be arrested. But instead, I was entered into the National Referral Mechanism (NRM) because of my experiences and taken to a safe house run by the Medaille Trust.

First experience of safety

Life is so confusing. Even now that I am safe from my husband and the families who exploited me, my circumstances are still uncertain. My immigration status is up in the air. I spend so much time thinking about all I've been through and worrying about the future. I do not know what it feels like to be happy.

The thing I want the most is to be reunited with my children. It is so complicated. They are with my in-laws. My husband told me that my children would not speak to me if I stopped sending money back to India. I do not know if it is their choice not to talk to me, or if they are being controlled by my in-laws. I have not heard from my eldest son for nine months. It hurts that I have not seen my children for eight years. I have so many things to sort out, but I hope one day my children can join me in the UK.

Being in the safe house is the first time in my life that I have felt safe. Everyone I trusted in my life has let me down. I find it hard to trust anyone anymore. My life has so many complications and uncertainties. I have had counselling, which is helping. I have also begun developing my skills by volunteering in a local charity shop. I have found support. I now feel free, but I need my children with me.

Note

1 Names and locations have been changed to protect identities. Amna is a survivor of modern slavery residing at a safe house run by the Medaille Trust. With thanks to the Medaille Trust in supporting Amna in sharing her story.

PART 3

Listening to Survivors and Emerging Theologies

5

Real People, Real Lives:
Biblical Perspectives on Modern
Slavery and Human Trafficking

MARION L. S. CARSON

Introduction: the stories

In Part 2 of this book, Richard, Stella and Amna tell their stories. Richard became homeless after a row with his parents. Young, naïve and vulnerable, he was trafficked abroad, forced to do hard physical work and to live in broken-down caravans, often without payment and even food. His traffickers knew the tools of coercion and control: threatening violence, sending him mixed messages and withholding necessities. After years of being told that he is a non-person, Richard now believes it to be true. Having gone through cycles of homelessness, slavery and imprisonment, he has become a displaced person, reliant on soup kitchens and homeless charities.

Stella is from Colombia. Unable to afford both university fees and medical bills, she became homeless and jobless. She too found herself trafficked abroad, forced to work as a prostitute and under constant threat of beatings and rape. Stella and a friend managed to escape and tell their story to the police, but finding work was difficult, and she became homeless again. She is now in the UK, where she is recognized as a victim of human trafficking, and is living in a safe house. She wants to go back to university.

Amna is from a poor family in India, and was married at 16. Her husband was violent, and his family put her under intense pressure to give birth to boys, even tricking her into aborting girls. He brought her to the UK illegally, without her children, and when she refused to work in prostitution he forced her to work as a domestic servant. Although technically employed, she was ill-treated and was not always paid. Amna was discovered by the authorities and is now in a safe house, away from her husband. She has not seen her children for eight years.

I have not met Richard, Stella or Amna. But I feel I know them, for in the course of my work as chaplain at Glasgow City Mission in Scotland I meet many who have been through similar experiences. As I sit with them, sharing a meal, drinking tea and hearing their stories, I can see the fear and sadness in their eyes. For some, 'mental defeat' has taken over – they believe that they are non-persons, that there is no hope (Ehlers and Boos, 2000).

In the UK, we are well placed to help victims of trafficking. We can enlist the help of social workers, housing officers and charitable organizations to ensure that these victims receive safe accommodation as well as financial, medical and psychological help (Hemmings et al., 2016). The City Mission can also provide safety and community for people who, although no longer enslaved, remain vulnerable, for they are deeply traumatized by their experiences of coercion, violence and sexual abuse – often, like Stella, from childhood onwards.[1]

As chaplain, it is my role to bring spiritual comfort to victims of human trafficking and it is natural that I should look to the Bible to help me. However, as is well known, the Bible does not overtly question the existence of slavery, and in many cases supports it. So what can the Scriptures say to victims of human trafficking? What words of comfort can they bring? What, if anything, do they have to say about the injustice of slavery and the personal suffering it causes? These are questions with pastoral concerns at their heart. But we need also to ask a broader question. What does Scripture have to say about a Christian response to the continued existence of slavery in the world today? Much of this chapter will assess the biblical material that directly addresses the subject of slavery. Taking lessons from the antebellum abolitionist debate, we will see that there are voices in the canon of Scripture that challenge dominant cultural views and provide rich material with which to speak into people's lives (Carson, 2017). We will also, however, consider how Scripture might help the Church respond to the continued existence of slavery in general. Drawing on Paul's teaching in the letter to the Galatians, we will ask: what is a biblically informed response to human trafficking?

Slavery in Scripture and some lessons from the Abolitionism debate

How might Scripture speak into Richard's experience? When we look for passages that speak directly about slavery, we soon run into a problem. The Bible does not share our twenty-first-century Western assumption that it is wrong to enslave another human being. Rather, the practice is endorsed in the legal codes:

> As for the male and female slaves whom you may have, it is from the nations around you that you may acquire male and female slaves. You may also acquire them from among the aliens residing with you, and from their families that are with you, who have been born in your land; and they may be your property. You may keep them as a possession for your children after you, for them to inherit as property. These you may treat as slaves, but as for your fellow Israelites, no one shall rule over the other with harshness. (Lev. 25.44–46)

According to this, not only was it acceptable for the ancient Israelites to take foreign slaves when they went to war with neighbouring nations, God commanded that it should be so, and the captives were to be considered as property. According to one law code it was acceptable to beat your slaves provided you didn't injure or kill them (Exod. 21.20–21). Foreign slaves were used in national building projects (e.g. 1 Kings 9.22; 2 Chron. 2.17–18; 8.7–9), and in mines and foundries (1 Kings 5.13–15), and Nehemiah enlisted 'men and their servants' to build the Jerusalem wall after the return from the exile (Neh.

4.16–22). The moral rights and wrongs of slavery are never discussed; it is simply assumed to be a part of life.

In the New Testament, too, slavery is accepted as the norm. Even Jesus, who tells stories about masters and slaves in his parables, does not address the morality of slavery. In fact, his use of slavery as a metaphor for discipleship could be taken as an implicit acceptance (Mark 13.33–37; Luke 12.35–38). Paul too speaks of believers as slaves (1 Cor. 7.22; Rom. 1.1; 6.22; Gal. 1.10; 2 Cor. 6.2–4), and never condemns slavery. Worse still, we find passages like this: 'Let all who are under the yoke of slavery regard their masters as worthy of all honour, so that the name of God and the teaching may not be blasphemed' (1 Tim. 6.1).

And in Colossians:

Slaves, obey your earthly masters in everything, not only while being watched and in order to please them, but whole-heartedly, fearing the Lord. Whatever your task, put your-selves into it, as done for the Lord and not for your masters, since you know that from the Lord you will receive the in-heritance as your reward; you serve the Lord Christ. For the wrongdoer will be paid back for whatever wrong has been done, and there is no partiality. (Col. 3.22–25)

According to these texts, there is nothing wrong with slavery. Slaves should obey their masters, accept their situation and await their reward in heaven. If we apply these passages directly into our contemporary world, Richard should respectfully have done what his captors said, and accepted his lot as God's will.

It is to be hoped that no Christian would interpret these texts in this way, or use them to argue the case for slavery. How-ever, we do need to acknowledge that, historically, verses like these have been used to support slavery. In the years prior to abolition, when their way of life came under threat, these texts were grist to the slave holders' mill. The fact that Abraham, Jacob and Isaac had slaves was proof that slavery was con-sidered divinely ordained. One American clergyman, the Revd Fred Ross, argued on the basis of Leviticus 25.44–46 that it was

God's will to bring slaves from foreign countries (Ross, 1857).[2]
Thornton Stringfellow, an American Baptist pastor, argued
that to end slavery would be tantamount to 'moral hatred' of
the laws of God (Elliott, 1860, pp. 459–91). 1 Timothy 6.1
was used to teach slaves that they should not question their
lot, but obey their masters. A catechism for slaves, written by
Elias Neau for the Anglican Society for the Propagation of the
Gospel in Foreign Parts in 1704, illustrates this point:

> Who gave you a master and a mistress?
> God gave them to me.
> Who says you must obey them?
> God says that I must.
> What book tells you these things?
> The Bible. (Callahan, 2006, pp. 31–2)

To be sure, some were uneasy about slavery, but could not
bring themselves to support abolition on the grounds that there
was no direct command for this in the Bible. One such was
Charles Hodge, principal at Princeton Theological Seminary.
Hodge believed in the good treatment and education of slaves,
and felt that slavery was not part of the divine plan. However,
since neither Jesus nor Paul called for freeing the slaves he concluded that abolition must be against the divine will (Hodge,
1836). Although Hodge should be considered anti-abolitionist
rather than pro-slavery, his highly influential view undoubtedly
contributed to the perpetuation of the suffering of many (Noll,
1983).

These slavery texts should cause us to ask questions, and
their use by pro-slavers in the abolitionist debate should provoke alarm. On this evidence, it is hard to see how Scripture can
be used to speak into the lives of those who have experienced
slavery. Thankfully, however, these texts represent only one
strand of thinking regarding slavery within the canon. There
are other voices that, sometimes subtly, sometimes clearly,
challenge the cultural norms of the times that they represent
and uphold (Brueggemann, 2013). In the Hebrew Scriptures,
these voices are represented by the teaching that *all* men and

women are made in God's image (Gen. 1.27). They are to be found in narratives that subtly subvert the idea that slaves are worthless and unimportant. For example, Abraham's slave is faithful to Yahweh and ensures that Rebekah becomes his master's wife (Gen. 24). The story of Joseph tells of a victim of human trafficking who became politically powerful and acted with integrity (Gen. 37—50). Naaman's slave-girl (2 Kings 5) is astute and spiritually aware. These stories accord slaves great dignity, and any idea that only the powerful can hear the voice of God is shrewdly undermined. Above all, this voice of freedom is heard in the Exodus narrative, which would become the central narrative of Hebrew self-understanding, recited in poetry and song. It became the basis of those laws that advocated the better treatment of slaves (Exod. 20.2; 21.20, 26; Deut. 7.6–11; 8.11–20), and the seven-year Jubilee (Lev. 25.8–13).

The prophets continually hark back to this theme; Amos and Micah are horrified at the existence of debt slavery in society. Just as God had released the Hebrews from injustice and oppression, so they too should treat others with justice and mercy. Moral decline in the land stemmed from forgetting that Yahweh had brought them out of Egypt (Amos 2.10; 3.1; 9.7; Hos. 13.4–6; Micah 6.2–8). Jeremiah strongly objected when the Jubilee was ignored (Jer. 34.12–16). In Isaiah, Yahweh will bring about a new, peaceful Exodus (Isa. 43.16–21; 51.9–11), and Israel will bring liberation to all nations by means of her example. All human divisions will ultimately break down (Isa. 24.1–3; 49.1–6; 50.4–9; 52.13—53.12). In Wisdom literature, despite a general acceptance of slavery and that people should know their place in society (Eccles. 10.5–7; Prov. 19.10; 30.22), slave owners are urged to treat their slaves sensibly (Prov. 30.10). In Job 31.13–15, the just treatment of slaves is seen as a natural part of an ethical life.

In the New Testament, the pattern continues. In the highly stratified Graeco-Roman world, it was accepted that slaves were non-persons with no civic rights – despite the fact that some could have considerable influence in the households in which they worked. To advocate the abolition of slavery would have made little sense in such a world (Horsley, 1998, p. 58).

Rather, continuing in the Hebraic prophetic tradition, Jesus protests about corrupt and complacent religious leadership (e.g. Matt. 23.27). He preaches a kingdom of love and justice in which religious and political power have no currency at all. At the very start of his ministry, Jesus reads from the scroll of the prophet Isaiah in the synagogue and declares to those present that this Scripture has been fulfilled:

> The Spirit of the Lord is upon me,
> because he has anointed me to bring good news to the poor.
> He has sent me to proclaim release to the captives
> and recovery of sight to the blind,
> to let the oppressed go free,
> to proclaim the year of the Lord's favour. (Luke 4.18–19)

The message is clear: Jesus is on the side of those who are oppressed and enslaved in society. In his letter to the slave-owner Philemon, Paul makes the revolutionary statement that Onesimus and his master are now spiritual brothers. In 1 Corinthians 7.21, Paul even tells the slaves in the church that, if possible, they should seek their freedom – but that this should not be the focus of their ambitions. In both these epistles, it is clear that, for Paul, social status is a matter of indifference for believers – all are spiritually equal in the *ekklēsia*. Moreover, the apostle speaks of Jesus taking the form of a slave in order to bring about God's purposes in the world (Phil. 2.5–11). In Revelation 18.13, the trade in human beings is seen as one of the iniquities of the greedy Roman Empire.

For the early abolitionists, these voices of equality and freedom were fundamental to the campaign against slavery. In particular, the so-called 'Golden Rule' came to encapsulate the idea that slavery was incompatible with the will of God. In 1688, the first written protest against slavery in North America was sent to the monthly meeting of the Germantown Pennsylvania congregation of Mennonite Quakers: 'There is a saying, that we should do to all men like as we will be done ourselves; making no difference of what generation, descent or colour they are' (Morgan 2005, p. 370). For Granville Sharp, one of the first British abolitionists, the Golden Rule was the 'sum and substance of the whole Law of God', and it trumped the laws that had been used to prop up slavery for so long (Sharp, 1776, pp. 20–1).

While Christian theologians hesitated because they could find no scriptural instruction to abolish slavery, the abolitionists heard the redemptive voices, and acted upon them. The Golden Rule became the yardstick against which pro-slavery texts should be measured. And while pious slave-holders were instructing their slaves that Scripture said they should obey their masters, the slaves themselves were finding comfort and strength from the biblical teaching that all men and women are made in the image of God. Slaves also saw the Exodus narrative as their own story, and took strength from the promise of liberation for God's people (Callahan, 2006; Raboteau, 2004).

The biblical texts that inspired the abolitionist campaign two centuries ago, and spurred the enslaved on to resistance, continue to motivate Christians to work against slavery today, and can bring comfort to those who, like Richard, have been denied their freedom. When we learn to listen to the voices that speak of freedom, equality and love, rather than those that uncritically reflect the cultural norms of their time, the message of Scripture regarding slavery becomes clear: exploitation of human beings is contrary to the will of God. All men and women are equal in God's sight, and may not be considered the property of others. All are loved by the God who leads his people into freedom.

Women, sexual exploitation and Scripture

But what about Stella? Not only has she been enslaved, she has been forced to work in prostitution. She has been subject to sexual and emotional trauma, time after time, day after day, and threatened with violence if she does not comply. Surely Scripture will have a word of compassion for her? Here again there are problems. According to the law codes, while prostitution is not outlawed, women who work as prostitutes are deemed impure. They bring shame upon their families, the sanctuary, and indeed the nation as a whole (Deut. 23.18; Lev. 19.29; 21.7, 9, 14). If the daughter of a priest works in prostitution, she must be burned to death (Lev. 21.9). Widows and divorced women may have no alternative way of supporting themselves, but if they become involved in prostitution they are to be shunned. On the other hand, the men who buy their services are never condemned, never prohibited from doing so, but merely advised that buying sex is unwise (Prov. 23.27–28; 29.3).

The message that prostitutes are unclean and dangerous is reinforced by the use of prostitution as a metaphor for disobedience against God. The phrase 'playing the whore' is a metaphor for idolatry (e.g. Exod. 34.15–16; Isa. 1.21; Jer. 2.20), or for greed (Isa. 23.15–17), and in Ezekiel (16.23) prostitution is a metaphor for unfaithfulness to God that should be punished severely. A similar idea is found in the New Testament, in the book of Revelation. In chapter 17, Babylon (which represents the Roman Empire) is described as 'mother of whores and of earth's abominations' (17.5). She must be punished, made 'desolate and naked' (17.16). Of course, the language in these passages is metaphorical – these are not real prostitutes. But it is hard not to hear a message that women in prostitution are considered to be filthy, impure, lustful and greedy and that they should be subjected to terrible, degrading punishment. It is hard not to conclude that God hates prostitutes.

As in the case of slavery, however, when we dig deeper we find more compassionate perspectives. Two stories cleverly subvert the societal norms that denigrate women in prostitution. In Genesis 38, Tamar, deprived of her right to Levirate marriage (which was intended to continue the family line), dupes her father-in-law Judah by pretending she is a prostitute, and becomes pregnant as result. When this is discovered, Judah pronounces that Tamar should be put to death; however, when he realizes that he is the father and that he has been tricked, he declares that Tamar is more righteous than he is. Because of her action, the family line will continue. In the story of Rahab (Josh. 2), Israelite soldiers, charged with spying out the land of Canaan, head for her brothel, and the king finds out that they are there. Rather than hand them over, Rahab hides the soldiers in the roof space of her house, telling them that the Canaanites fear them because they know God guides them. She receives their assurance that her family will be kept safe, and helps the men escape. Thus, victory for Israel is ensured; Rahab and her family are rewarded by being allowed to live in Israel (Josh. 6.15–25).

In the Gospels, women in prostitution are seldom mentioned. The common belief that Mary Magdalene and the woman who anoints Jesus' feet (Matt. 26.6–13; Mark 14.3–9; Luke 7.36–50; John 12.1–8) are prostitutes is the invention of the medieval Church and cannot be substantiated from the text itself (D'Angelo, 1999). On two occasions, Jesus refers to prostitutes as examples of people whom religious leaders class as shameful outsiders (Matt. 21.31; Luke 15.30). He does this, however, not to add to their shame but as part of his objection to the view that those who consider themselves religiously and morally pure are favoured by God. He does not, as the Church would later do, single out women in prostitution as special cases. Moreover, in Matthew 1, both Rahab and Tamar are honoured as ancestors of Jesus, and Rahab is commended for her faith (James 2.25; Heb. 11.31).

In Paul's first letter to the Corinthians something quite remarkable happens. There, the apostle instructs men who are believers not to buy sex (1 Cor. 6.15) – this in a world in which it was considered quite normal for men to visit brothels and bathhouses. For the first time in the biblical literature, men are challenged to control their sexual behaviour. The double standards that characterize the world at large have no place in the Church.

Unfortunately, Christians have been slow to hear the redemptive voices with regard to prostitution. The idea that prostitutes are unclean and should be kept away from society has been influential throughout most of Christian history, and continues to be so in many settings today. It underpinned the kind of treatment that women in prostitution received at the hands, for example, of the 'Magdalen laundries', whose aim was to correct the women and help them leave their lives of sin (Mahood, 1990). The double standards illustrated in the

Tamar narrative – that women who engage in prostitution are to be shunned, while men may use their services with impunity – are still common. Often, women who have escaped from sex trafficking find themselves rejected, and many churches are reluctant to become involved in reaching out to the women at all, let alone allow them to attend their services (e.g. Brock and Thistlethwaite, 1996, p. 235). These experiences compound their terrible sufferings. It therefore is incumbent upon us to introduce women who have been victimized in commercial sexual exploitation to the redemptive voices in Scripture and help them to hear these messages for themselves. They need to hear of Jesus' love for them, his hatred of the religious hypocrisy that so often compounds their shame and suffering, and the scriptural challenges to sexual double standards that pervade every culture.

Amna managed to avoid sexual exploitation, and the stigma attached to it. But she was, in effect, enslaved by her husband. 'Find a way to manage it', her mother said, when she told her about the violence in her marriage. Amna's life opportunities were severely limited, childbearing was a duty, and she was exploitable precisely because she is female. How can Scripture speak to her? In the Old Testament, women are the property of the husband (Exod. 21.3, 22; Deut. 22.19; Prov. 31.11), who may sell them on if they wish. Wives are listed alongside animals in legal codes (Exod. 20.17; cf. Deut. 5.21), and considered to be of less worth to a husband than children (Deut. 29.11). They can be divorced (Deut. 24.1) if they displease their husbands. Women, on the other hand, do not have the right to divorce. There are accounts of women suffering horrific abuse for which the perpetrators are not condemned (e.g. Judg. 19). Women may be bought as sex slaves (Exod. 21.2–11). There is pressure to bear children: fertile wives are associated with blessing and righteousness (Ps. 128.3), and infertility is a punishment from God (Hos. 9.14). In the New Testament, women are said to be inferior to men, on the grounds that they were created second (cf. 1 Cor. 11.2–6; Eph. 5.23; 1 Tim. 2.9–25), and wives told to be submissive to their husbands. In 1 Timothy 2.15, women are said to be saved through childbearing.

From these texts, there does not seem to be much to offer as comfort to women who, like Amna, find themselves abused and enslaved in marriage. However, as before, there are alternative voices that subtly challenge the idea that women are inferior to men (Meyers et al., 2001). In the Old Testament, there are examples of good marriages and kind husbands (Hannah and Elkanah in 1 Samuel 1), women may be powerful (Deborah in Judges 4—5) and there are several female prophets (Miriam in Exodus 15 and Huldah in 2 Chronicles 34.22). In the legal collections we see moves towards more just treatment of women. While women could be bought as wives, they could not be sold as slaves (Exod. 21.11; Deut. 21.14), and the Jubilee law applied to women slaves as well as men (Deut. 15.12–17). Stories of women such as Tamar and Ruth tell of women showing up male foolishness (Sharp, 2009, pp. 84–124). In the New Testament, as well as flouting the purity laws (Matt. 9.20–22; Mark 5.25–34; Luke 8.43–48), Jesus refuses to collude in a culture that sees women in general as second-class citizens. He treats women as equals, and challenges cultural double standards and religious purity laws (Matt. 9.20–22; Mark 5.25–34; Luke 8.43–48). He puts limits on the rights of men to divorce their wives (Matt. 19.8; Mark 10.5–10). Women are among the first to recognize who Jesus is (the woman at the well in John 4.4–26) and Mary Magdalene is the first witness to the resurrection (Mark 16.9; John 20.14). There are examples of influential women in the early Church (Rom. 16), and whether or not these women have children is not deemed worthy of mention.

Women who, like Amna, have been exploited precisely because they are women need to hear that in God's sight they have dignity and worth, that men and women are equal, and no one, male or female, has the right to abuse them in any way. Pastorally, we can teach them that the idea that women are inferior to men, although prevalent in many cultures, is undermined throughout Scripture – in particular, by Jesus himself. We can encourage them to learn to become free from – and challenge – the cultural forces that stifle their voices and keep them in subjection, and help them to begin to develop and use the gifts God has given them.

Christian responses to modern slavery

We have seen that there are strands of tradition in the biblical canon with regard to slavery and exploitation that reflect the cultural norms of their times, and voices that represent the gradual development of new ways of thinking. We have seen that there is, throughout the canon of Scripture, a redemptive impulse that challenges the accepted values of society and culminates in the coming of Christ to set free the captives and oppressed (cf. Webb, 2001).

Based on this reading of Scripture, how should Christians respond to the fact that slavery still exists? First, following the example of the abolitionists, for whom the Golden Rule was so important, we can take part in the efforts to rescue and minister to those who are its victims – treating others as we would want to be treated ourselves. We can speak the voice of love into the lives of those who, like Richard, Stella and Amna, have been traumatized by years of exploitation. We can provide for their basic needs, welcome them into our communities, help them to recover from the trauma of their experiences, and to re-build their lives. We can campaign for perpetrators to be brought to justice.

Like the prophets, we can protest against the injustices and greed that are the causes of slavery in the first place, and proclaim that all men and women are created equal in God's sight. We can teach that the objectification of human beings is unacceptable. We can become involved in lobbying groups that bring modern slavery to the attention of law-makers and politicians. We can find out which companies are using exploited labour, boycott their goods, and make this known to others. We can raise awareness of human trafficking, and educate vulnerable young people who are at risk of exploitation. With regard to commercial sexual exploitation we can help reduce demand by reaching out to those who buy sex, bringing the love of God into their lives (Bales, 2007; Miles and Foster Crawford, 2014).

Of course, many Christians throughout the world are involved in ministries whose express aim is to end human trafficking and care for the victims. However, if our study of the biblical perspectives on slavery and prostitution and the way they were interpreted during the abolitionist campaign teaches us anything, it is that there is a tendency for the people of God to allow strong cultural and religious forces to drown out the voices of love and redemption.[3] Today, I believe, we are no different. It is true that we are no longer in an age in which Christians think slavery is acceptable, but slavery still exists. Its root causes are many and complex – poverty, lack of job opportunities, globalization, capitalism, gender, racial and religious inequality – and these must be tackled by political means (Enrile, 2018, pp. 51–70). But at a far deeper level it is human greed, and lust for power and self-gratification, that exploit the vulnerable, and if Christians are to be a prophetic voice for change we have to examine ourselves. How far do our communities embody the redemptive impulse of Scripture, and how far do they reflect the accepted cultural norms that underpin and contribute to inequality and the exploitation of human beings? We must ask ourselves these questions, for we cannot protest about injustice and inequality while allowing it among ourselves.

A community marked by freedom

In large part, our self-examination requires us to think about our attitude to money and possessions. Are Christians driven by the love of money or the love of God? Material poverty has many complex causes; human greed perpetuates it and exploits the poor for its own gain. The prophets have much to say about this, as does Jesus himself. His words on the matter are stark – you cannot serve both God and mammon (Matt. 6.24). We Christians have to be honest about our own failings in this matter and learn how to become communities in which mammon is kept well under control (Welby, 2016). But the causes of human trafficking cannot be reduced to economic factors. Attitudes towards race, gender, religious affiliation and social status also have a large part to play, and we must examine ourselves with regard to these too.

Here, we can learn from the letter to the Galatians in which

Paul tackles a problem of one group trying to impose its customs and practices on the whole community. A group of 'Judaizers' – Jewish believers who were insisting that Gentile converts should adhere to Jewish practices such as circumcision and food law observance – were, in Paul's opinion, attempting to keep the Church under a 'yoke of slavery' (Gal. 5.1).[4] They were putting religion before simple faith in Christ. Not only that, they were insisting that everyone must be like them – with the implication that they believed themselves to be superior to those from pagan backgrounds. Paul, on the other hand, understood religious and cultural background to be of little or no consequence in the community of believers. In baptism (Gal. 3.27) all become equal – for all are one in Christ Jesus. Thus, he can say: 'There is no longer Jew or Greek, there is no longer slave or free, there is no longer male and female' (Gal. 3.28).[5]

Paul, of course, is primarily concerned with the immediate problem of the Judaizers, and the relationship between Jewish and Gentile believers. But he does not limit his message of freedom to ethnic/religious matters; he includes social and gender distinctions too. In Christ (see also 1 Cor. 12.13; Col. 3.11), believers are released from cultural and religious constraints with regard to race/religion, status and gender that limit their freedom in Christ. Society in general may be characterized by such dualities, but in the new creation those who are baptized are united in Christ. It is important to note what Paul is *not* saying, however. He is *not* saying that all differences are erased. He *is* saying that attitudes towards social status, racial difference and gender roles need to be re-evaluated in the light of allegiance to Christ (Horrell, 2005, pp. 124–9; Collins, 2019). He is *not* saying that cultural and religious custom and practice should be abolished altogether (Jewish believers may choose to continue with their practice if they wish), or that the law itself is obsolete (Gundry Volf, 1997). He *is* saying that they should not be allowed to become the dominant factors in the life of the community, for when they do they can easily take priority, with the result that the ability to serve one another in love (Gal. 5.13) becomes inhibited.

Paul insists that the Galatians should be free from the 'curse of the law', for obedience to it can become self-serving and idolatrous, and love, mercy and justice can become secondary concerns. The curse of the law is that the need to fulfil its demands can become tyrannical. The curse of the law is to induce the fear of freedom. In antebellum America, pro-slavers and anti-abolitionists had to be freed from precisely that – they had to be freed from prioritizing their own interests (social, financial and even theological), and from absolving themselves of moral responsibility. Freedom in Christ is to be prepared to ask how our cherished assumptions and beliefs measure up against the law of love.

Throughout its history the Church has wrestled with the problem of recognizing when adherence to cultural and religious custom and practice might be jeopardizing spiritual freedom, and the abolitionist debate is a case in point. No doubt the Church will continue to struggle in this way. Moreover, how we understand what it means to live in a world in which social, cultural and religious distinctions do matter, while being members of a new creation in which such things are ultimately meaningless, will always require wisdom and humility. We must never cite Galatians 3.28 glibly, or use it as a blunt instrument to serve our own purposes (Horrell, 2017). However, if we are to be credible advocates for social justice, if the Christian community is to pose any challenge to the unjust systems that give rise to slavery and perpetuate it, we must at least be seen to be open to the discussion of these matters. We must work towards self-awareness regarding our prejudices, acknowledge our own weaknesses, and be willing to tackle injustice and inequality within our communities. In other words, we must be willing to take the log out of our own eye before taking the speck out of others' eyes (Matt. 7.4). We must ask ourselves when and if religious and cultural presuppositions might be undercutting our freedom in Christ. We must not cling to our dearly held beliefs and thereby collude in the injustices that cause suffering to millions, however indirectly.

Conclusion

It takes courage for victims of modern slavery to tell their stories. We are indebted to Richard, Stella and Amna for sharing theirs with us. They have so much to teach us, and they challenge us to examine our response to the suffering to which they bear witness. As a chaplain concerned with the pastoral care of victims of modern slavery, I have been asking how Scripture can speak into their lives. At first sight, this is problematic. Many texts uphold the idea that it is acceptable to enslave and exploit another human being. However, as the Quakers and slaves in antebellum America knew, there are other voices within Scripture that challenge long-accepted ideas, and if we – like them – listen to the voices of redemption within the canon, we find much that can bring hope into the lives of trafficked men and women.[6]

Following the guidance of the Quakers, we can use the Golden Rule as the yardstick against which to measure those voices that could be employed to perpetuate the exploitation of human beings. Indeed, when we consider the whole canon of Scripture, we see that its overarching trajectory is one of redemption. As the antebellum slaves well knew, the God of the Exodus is the same God whose Son took on the form of a slave, pronounced freedom for the captives and urged us to live our lives by the law of love. It is this 'redemptive impulse' that offers hope for victims of modern slavery, and demands that Christians join in the work of setting the captives free.

However, Stella and Amna's stories remind us that there are related problems that must be addressed. Many biblical texts teach that women are inferior to men and that their roles should be circumscribed – a notion that supports and perpetuates the exploitation of women throughout the world. Still others teach that prostituted women are shameful and worthy of punishment – an idea that underpins the cruel treatment of women who have been caught up in commercial sexual exploitation. Here again, the yardstick of the Golden Rule and redemptive, subversive voices of Scripture – not least the example of Jesus himself – speak truth in the face of injustice, and offer comfort and hope for the future.

There is much in Scripture, then, that can speak into the experience of victims of human trafficking. But the redemptive impulse of Scripture also urges us to follow in the footsteps of the Old Testament prophets and Jesus himself, and work to prevent the exploitation of vulnerable people. Christians are involved in this effort at all levels. However, if our message of love, freedom and equality is to have integrity, we need to examine ourselves. How far do our communities model what we are advocating for the rest of the world? How different are our values from those of the prevailing cultures in which we live? Are we serving God or mammon? How far are cultural and religious ideas regarding race, class and gender hindering our ability to love one another? Do we really believe that among the baptized there is 'no longer Jew or Greek, there is no longer slave or free, there is no longer male and female'? If we are honest, we must admit that we still struggle in these areas. So while it is entirely right that we speak out about modern-day slavery, care for its victims, and work to tackle its causes, we must also be willing to acknowledge and address the injustices and inequalities that exist in our own communities. For if we are to be credible voices against modern slavery and help bring about its abolition, we need to set our own house in order first.

Bibliography

Bales, K., 2007, *Ending Slavery: How We Free Today's Slaves*, Berkeley, CA: University of California Press.

Brock, R. N. and Thistlethwaite, S. B., 1996, *Casting Stones: Prostitution and Liberation in Asia and the United States*, Minneapolis, MN: Fortress Press.

Brueggemann, W., 2013, *Truth Speaks to Power: The Countercultural Nature of Scripture*, Louisville, KY: Westminster John Knox Press.

Callahan, A. D., 2006, *The Talking Book*, New Haven, CT: Yale University Press.

Carson, M. L. S., 2017, *Human Trafficking, the Bible and the Church: An Interdisciplinary Study*, London: SCM Press.

Collins, A. Y., 2019, 'No longer "male and female" (Gal 3:28): ethics and an early Christian baptismal formula', *Journal of Ethics in Antiquity and Early Christianity* 1, pp. 27–39.

D'Angelo, M. R., 1999, 'Reconstructing "real" women from Gospel literature: the case of Mary Magdalene', in Ross Shepherd Kraemer and Mary Rose D'Angelo (eds), *Women and Christian Origins*, New York: Oxford University Press, pp. 105–49.

Ehlers, A., Maercker, A. and Boos, A., 2000, 'Post traumatic stress disorder following political imprisonment: the role of mental defeat, alienation and perceived permanent change', *Journal of Abnormal Psychology* 109(1), pp. 45–55.

Elliott, E. N. (ed.), 1860, *Cotton is King, and Pro-Slavery Arguments*, Augusta, GA: Pritchard, Abbott & Loomis.

Enrile, Annalisa V., 2018, *Ending Human Trafficking and Modern-Day Slavery: Freedom's Journey*, Thousand Oaks, CA: Sage Publications, pp. 51–70.

Farley, Melissa (ed.), 2003, *Prostitution, Trafficking and Traumatic Stress*, Binghamton, NY: Haworth Press, pp. 33–74.

Fung, Ronald Y. K., 1988, *The Epistle to the Galatians*, 2nd rev. edn, Grand Rapids, MI: Eerdmans.

Gundry Volf, J. M., 1997, 'Christ and gender: a study of difference and equality in Gal. 3.28', in C. Landmesser, H.-J. Eckstein and H. Lichtenberger (eds), *Jesus Christus als die Mitte der Schrift. Studien zur Hermeneutik des Evangeliums*, Berlin/New York: Walter de Gruyter, BZNW 86, pp. 439–77.

Hemmings, S., Jakobowitz, S. and Abas, M., 2016, 'Responding to the health needs of survivors of human trafficking: a systematic review', *BMC Health Services Research*, doi:10.1186/s12913-016-1538-8.

Hodge, C., 1836, *View of the Subject of Slavery Contained in* The Biblical Repertory *for April, 1836 in which the Scriptural Argument, It is Believed, Is Very Clearly and Justly Exhibited*, Pittsburgh.

Horrell, D. G., 2005, *Solidarity and Difference: A Contemporary Reading of Paul's Ethics*, London: T & T Clark, pp. 124–9.

Horrell, D. G., 2017, 'Paul, inclusion and whiteness: particularizing interpretation', *Journal for the Study of the New Testament* 40(2), pp. 123–47.

Horsley, R. H., 1998, 'The slave systems of classical antiquity and their reluctant recognition by modern scholars', *Semeia*, 83/84, Slavery in Text and Interpretation, pp. 19–66.

Mahood, L., 1990, *The Magdalenes: Prostitution in the Nineteenth Century*, London: Routledge.

Meyers, C., Craven, T. and Kraemer, R. S. (eds), 2001, *Women in Scripture: A Dictionary of Named and Unnamed Women in the Hebrew Bible, the Apocryphal/Deuterocanonical Books and the New Testament*, Grand Rapids, MI: Eerdmans.

Miles, G. and Foster Crawford, C. (eds), 2014, *Stopping the Traffick: A Christian Response to Sexual Exploitation and Trafficking*, Eugene, OR: Wipf & Stock.

Morgan, K., 2005, *Slavery in America: A Reader and Guide*, Edinburgh: Edinburgh University Press.

Nanos, M., 2002, *The Irony of Galatians: Paul's Letter in First-Century Context*, Minneapolis, MN: Fortress Press.

Noll, M. A., 1983, *The Princeton Theology 1812–1921: Scripture, Science and Theological Method from Archibald Alexander to Benjamin Breckenridge Warfield*, Grand Rapids, MI: Baker.

Raboteau, A. J., 2004, *Slave Religion: The 'Invisible Institution' in the Antebellum South*, 2nd edn, Oxford: Oxford University Press.

Rogerson, J. W., 2016, *According to the Scriptures? The Challenge of Using the Bible in Social, Moral and Political Questions*, London: Routledge.

Ross, F. A., 1969 (1857), *Slavery Ordained of God*, Miami, FL: Mnemosyne.

Sharp, C. J., 2009, *Irony and Meaning in the Hebrew Bible*, Bloomington, IN: Indiana University Press.

Sharp, G., 1776, *Law of Liberty or Royal Law by which All Mankind Will Certainly Be Judged!*, London: B. White and E. and C. Dilly.

Stringfellow, T., in Elliott, E. N. (ed.), 1860, *Cotton is King, and Pro-slavery Arguments*, Augusta, GA: Pritchard, Abbott & Loomis, pp. 459–91.

Thiselton, A. C., 2006, 'Canon, community and theological construction', in C. Bartholomew et al. (eds), *Canon and Biblical Interpretation*, Grand Rapids, MI: Zondervan, pp. 24–7.

Webb, W. J., 2001, *Slaves, Women and Homosexuals: Exploring the Hermeneutics of Cultural Analysis*, Downers Grove, IL: InterVarsity Press.

Welby, J., 2016, *Dethroning Mammon: Making Money Serve Grace*, London: Bloomsbury Continuum.

Notes

1 On the trauma experienced by victims of sex trafficking in particular, see Melissa Farley (ed.), 2003, *Prostitution, Trafficking and Traumatic Stress*, Binghamton, NY: Haworth Press, pp. 33–74.

2 Ross believed that slavery would one day be ended, but upheld the institution in his own day.

3 On the need for discernment in using the Bible for social, ethical and pastoral questions today, see John W. Rogerson, 2016, *According to the Scriptures? The Challenge of Using the Bible in Social, Moral and Political Questions*, London: Routledge.

4 Most scholars hold the view that agitators are believing Jews, but there are dissenting voices. For an overview of the debate, see Mark

Nanos, 2002, *The Irony of Galatians: Paul's Letter in First-Century Context*, Minneapolis, MN: Fortress Press, pp. 110–92.

5 The phrase 'male and female' is most likely to be an allusion to Genesis 1.27. See Ronald Y. K. Fung, 1988, *The Epistle to the Galatians*, 2nd rev. edn, Grand Rapids, MI: Eerdmans, p. 175.

6 On the idea of multiple voices in Scripture, see Anthony C. Thiselton, 2006, 'Canon, community and theological construction', in Craig Bartholomew et al. (eds), *Canon and Biblical Interpretation*, Grand Rapids, MI: Zondervan, pp. 24–7.

6

Learning from the Church's Role in the Transatlantic Slave Trade in Responding to the Exploitation and Trafficking of People Today

GALE RICHARDS

In 2016, when I took up my role as a minister of a city-centre Baptist church in Cambridge, I never imagined that I would encounter people fleeing modern slavery. I have encountered survivors as I supported people newly arrived in the UK, and as I supported people experiencing homelessness.

But I have come to recognize that the support I have offered survivors is rooted in part in my understanding of what it means to be enslaved, as someone who is a descendant of victims and survivors of the transatlantic slave trade. I was born in England to Jamaican parents of the so-called '*Windrush* generation' that came to Britain in the 1960s, at a time when Jamaica was still a British colony. My childhood was framed by hearing stories told by my mum and her peers about Jamaican national heroes rising up against slavery imposed by ruling British authorities.

The story of one of those Jamaican national heroes, Sam Sharpe (a Baptist deacon), over the years has come to influence the way I approach ministry. In particular, through my personal involvement in sponsored projects and exchange trips between Jamaican and British Baptists, from 2012 to 2015.

It is an experience of supporting one young woman, 'V', fleeing a quasi-domestic exploitation situation[1] early on in my role as a minister in Cambridge that has led me to reflect on the following question: how might Baptists' involvement in the abolition of slavery in British colonies inform the global movement against the exploitation and trafficking of people today? Two answers have emerged: the importance of doing theology from below; and the significance of relationships being forged between opposing Christian communities, for liberation.

Before addressing each of these themes, I begin by sharing first the story of the young woman, 'V', fleeing a quasi-domestic exploitation situation, and then the story of Sam Sharpe leading a revolt against slavery.

'V's story

I was born into a large family in Cameroon, and I was raised in a house with nine siblings and with all the different generations together. I remember life feeling calm as a child. I would go fishing with my cousins and have fun recreating scenes from TV programmes and films.

Deep down, I have always been drawn to England even though France was the preferred destination for the majority of people where I am from. The attraction comes from the connections we have from the colonial past.

I left Africa for France in April 2004, in the middle of the school year when my mum married a French man. It was a big shock, seeing so many white people and so few black people. It was like another world, and I had to adapt quickly.

I believe God created me with a love for England and a love of all that is 'British'. My desire from a young age was to learn English for a future life in England. I discovered a way to get to England to learn English, and that was to become an au pair for a host family. Before leaving for England in 2017, I asked God to help me choose the right host family. I asked him to help me find a Christian host family whose faith is in Jesus Christ, the Lord.

While browsing an au pair internet site I came across a family based in England who stated that they followed the Christian faith. I felt this was answered prayer, and it led me to begin conversations with them. I had a good Skype interview with them and I felt sure this was the host family for me, so I flew to England to be their au pair.

On my arrival I was very well received by the host mother and one of the children. The host father was away on vacation with their other children. I met him and the other children about a month later when they got home.

We agreed the terms of my appointment for the year ahead. I was to get the children ready for school, take them to school and pick them up after school. This would also include me washing and ironing their uniforms and laying them out for them. I was also to help keep the kitchen clean. This was a great help to the host parents, who had full-time professional jobs.

I like helping others, it's as if it is in my DNA. At times the host mum would be away for up to three days at a time attending conferences. She had peace of mind knowing that I was taking care of the children. I was also getting to learn about another culture, so I was happy too.

Every Wednesday (the host mum's day off from work) I volunteered at a local charity shop to help me practise my English. There I had a great experience as I met wonderful, funny people, and spent time out of the house. Spending time with other young adults helped me a lot.

My host family regularly led prayer meetings and Bible discussions in their home for members of their church. I went to two of them, but when I saw these same individuals at church they ignored me.

My host family read the Bible to their children every night before they went to bed. They played Christian music at home and every Sunday they went to church where they sang, danced and worshipped Jesus Christ.

As time went by, I realized my needs did not matter to them. When I first arrived, I noticed how dirty their house and garden was so I agreed to help with cleaning them up. I simply wanted to help. However, that voluntary help turned into them ordering me to continue to do all the cleaning. This was what my list of daily tasks had become:

- Make the children's breakfast.
- Get the children ready for school (uniforms, hair and packed lunches).
- Take the children to school.
- Clean the house (dust, vacuum, etc.).
- Load the washing machine (including handling others' soiled underwear), and put clothes outside to dry.
- Iron.
- Sometimes cook the evening meal.
- Pick the children up from school.
- Prepare an after-school snack for the children.
- Help the children with their homework.
- Ensure all the children had a wash before bedtime.
- Manage the children's mealtimes.
- Ensure the children brushed their teeth.
- Read the Bible to the children.
- Wash the dishes.

It was non-stop from morning until night.

This experience in the house with this family has deeply marked me. They were supposed to be Christians yet they had no regard for my needs. My great disappointment was that as a Christian you are supposed to be self-sacrificing, share with people, show people love, but they showed me none of this.

The family saw their worth as linked to their social position, and they seemed to think they were superior to me. I saw this in the way they ordered me to do things and refused to listen to my protests.

I started to see the host family as giving the outside world the impression they were good, caring Christians – but they were like Pharisees in their hearts. Christians by name, but not in their hearts.

It was a painful experience for me living with them, and I cried a lot when I was alone in my room. However, the experience also helped reveal to me what it really means to have a heart for God. I grew in my love for God. I grew in my faith and confidence in God. It is in the challenging times that God can catch our attention. I fell in love with God in that house.

The problems really began a couple of months into my time there when I asked the family if I could attend an English language course. This was something I had talked to them about before I took up the post: the importance of me having time to go to English classes. I had been doing a good job taking care of their children so I thought this would not be a problem, but it was.

My relations with the family deteriorated as the months went by because I felt cheated. I kept insisting on being able to attend the English classes but they would not listen to me or allow me to go. On one rare occasion when I did manage to get myself to an English lesson, I met another au pair. I discovered from her the amount of free time au pairs usually have, and how much weekly pocket money au pairs are usually paid. That meeting opened my eyes to how my host family was exploiting me. I had lived such an isolated life with this family, and not felt I could share with my family back home in France what I was going through.

I grew weary of my host family's treatment of me. When I eventually said to them that I only wanted to take care of the children now because I felt I was being exploited, I was told to pack my bags and leave. I had to pack my suitcases in the middle of the night. I naively believed that Christians would not behave in this way. So I found myself in a foreign country with nowhere to go. I had no idea what to do.

I decided to go to the charity shop I had been volunteering at when it opened, to ask one of the workers there if they knew where I could find a place to stay. She told me to go to the nearby church, which was known for helping people in need.

It was a Saturday morning and the church was open for its weekly English lessons. The volunteers assumed I had come to register for the English lessons, but I explained I needed help and someone told the pastor who was there. He told me to join one of the lessons, and that after the class she would help me find a bed for the night.

She listened to my story and was able to find me somewhere nearby to stay for the next few nights. I chose to worship at the church the next morning and evening. They gave me a warm welcome and were very caring and encouraging. I saw the love of Jesus in them. This was very different from the church I had been going to with my host family each Sunday, where I went unnoticed. In that church, when I tried to say hello to someone they looked at me as if I was a thief.

The pastor didn't just help me find a bed for a few nights, she also helped me find a new host family to be an au pair for. I am pleased to say that this family showed me respect and welcomed me into their family. They showed a genuine interest in my needs instead of trying to mistreat and exploit me like the previous family. I stayed with them for a few months, which was nice and helpful, but after all I had been through I no longer had the same desire to live in England. I felt God was telling me to go back to France.

I eventually returned to France, found a job, and began the next stage of my life. I am full of expectations and I especially know that I am in the team of Jesus Christ.

I want to conclude with this quote from Michelle Obama: 'Success isn't about how much money you make, it's about *the difference* you make in people's lives.'

The story of Sam Sharpe leading a revolt against slavery

> If you have any love for Jesus Christ, to religion, to your ministers, or to those friends in England who have helped you build this chapel, and who are sending a minister for you, do not be led away. God commands you to be obedient; if you do as he commands you, you may expect his blessing, but if you do not, he will not do you good. (Hinton, 1847, pp. 118–19)

These words were spoken by William Knibb on 27 December 1831 at Salter's Hill chapel, Jamaica. He had been sent as a Baptist missionary from England to Jamaica seven years earlier. On 27 December 1831, Knibb was urging enslaved black Christians to abandon their plans to claim their freedom through a 'sit-down strike' over the Christmas period. He knew they were mistaken in believing that the king in England had granted them their freedom. He told them that he was pained that they were refusing to work for their owners, and told them he loved their souls, as he appealed to and encouraged them to go back to work for their owners. The following day Knibb told some of the enslaved people in the city of Falmouth to risk their lives in protecting their masters' property, as it became clear some of the enslaved intended to turn what was supposed to be a peaceful 'sit-down strike' into a violent protest.

Letters Knibb sent back to England show his dislike of the brutality of the slavery regime, and his commitment to offering religious instruction to the enslaved. Yet he adopted a clear stance that it was God's expectation that the enslaved should serve their slave masters, until such time as they were granted their freedom. He saw it as their Christian duty.

The man behind the plans Knibb sought to thwart was Sam Sharpe, a black Baptist deacon. Sharpe had been a beneficiary of the 'class system' that Baptist missionaries like Knibb operated (Gardner, 1873, pp. 360–1). This system entailed a number of class leaders (that is, enslaved black people) being developed by the missionaries to undertake pastoral tasks. This meant that when a missionary was absent the class leaders were able to take the lead within the life and mission of the Church, which included them having some freedom to shape and take worship services.

Sharpe is recorded as gathering enslaved black people and declaring on the authority of the Bible that the 'whites had no more right to hold black people in slavery, than the black people had to make the white people slaves' (Bleby, 1853, p. 116). He is believed to have been inspired by texts such as Matthew 6.24, 'No one can serve two masters', in articulating his belief that the very structures of slavery were contrary to the will of God and the Christianity he understood and practised (Reid-Salmon, 2012, p. 28).

It is hard to reconcile the differing views of Knibb and Sharpe. Yet Knibb's stance was more progressive than those of many of his contemporary white ministers from the different Christian denominations in Jamaica. Many of them were also uneasy about the brutality of the slavery regime, but not the structures of slavery itself. However, Sharpe did not feel that individuals such as Knibb went far enough in supporting the enslaved, and believed there was no expectation from God that he should serve his slave master in the interim; indeed, he is recorded on the day of his execution as saying: 'I would rather die upon yonder gallows than live in slavery' (Bleby, 1853, p. 116).

The differences in the theological outlooks between Sharpe and Knibb perhaps lay in their different faith journeys.

Sam Sharpe's theological outlook as a black Baptist was in part a product of the groundbreaking work of black American Baptist missionaries, who first went to Jamaica in the early 1780s – men such as George Liele, Moses Baker and George Gibb. They worked among the enslaved Black people in Jamaica, reportedly urging them to seek their individual freedom. This was complex work because there were many restrictions on black people practising their faith in Jamaica at that time. George Liele went as far as to draft and adopt a church covenant that garnered certification from the government and enabled his fellow black preachers to practise their Christian faith. The covenant included the article: 'We permit no slaves to join the Church without first having a few lines from their owners for good behaviour' (Erskine, 1981, p. 43). This in effect meant they agreed to keep the status quo, which included an understanding that Christianity permitted people to hold slaves.

The extent to which Liele adhered to the spirit of that covenant is questionable (Reid-Salmon, 2012, p. 109), for it is hard to imagine Liele totally abandoned the convictions he revealed in his earlier sermons. These sermons included one he preached on Romans 10.1, in which he compared the plight of Africans enslaved in Jamaica to the plight of Israel enslaved in Egypt. It was a sermon that led to Liele's imprisonment because it included him urging the enslaved to seek their freedom, which was against the law.

Knibb's faith journey included the instructions he received through the Baptist Missionary Society (BMS) in Britain, the body responsible for sending him as a missionary to Jamaica. BMS gave its missionaries instructions that included:

as a resident in Jamaica, you have nothing whatever to do with its civil and political affairs, and with those you must never interfere ... The gospel of Christ, you will know, so far from producing or countenancing with a spirit of revolt or insubordination, has a directly opposite tendency ... (Reid-Salmon, 2012, p. 43)

This was somewhat at odds with the kind of preaching Liele was imprisoned for – namely, advocating that the enslaved seek their freedom.

Black Baptists such as Sharpe would have been exposed to the preaching of Liele and his contemporaries for more than 20 years before BMS missionaries arrived in Jamaica. BMS sent its first missionary, John Rowe, to Jamaica in 1814, in response to a request from Moses Baker for support from British Baptists. Baker recognized the need for help in resourcing the growing black Baptist gatherings he and others had established over the 20 years or so they had been in Jamaica. However, Baker and others were limited in what they could do without the help of white British Baptists, given the restrictions on black people practising their Christian faith at that time.

It is perhaps not surprising, then, that Knibb failed in his efforts to thwart the plans of Sam Sharpe and others to revolt, given their different theological outlooks.

The revolt led by Sharpe thus took place and has been described as 'the most widespread and greatest of all enslaved peoples' revolts' to take place. It involved no less than 60,000 people and an estimated 600 people lost their lives, many of them executed by the ruling British government of the day (Reid-Salmon, 2012, p. xvi).

It was just one year after the revolt that the Slavery Abolition Act 1833[2] was passed, abolishing slavery throughout much of the British Empire. According to national British archives' records, some 3.1 million Africans had already been forcibly transported across the Atlantic Ocean between 1662 and 1807, to British-owned colonies in the Caribbean, to work as slaves on plantations. Many more millions were also transported from

Africa to British-owned colonies in North America to work as slaves during that period.

In the aftermath of the revolt led by Sam Sharpe, and the mass executions that followed, white ministers and missionaries from the non-conformist church traditions (such as William Knibb, a Baptist) were arrested, but later released. Ruling authorities felt that the non-conformist way of operating church was responsible for inciting the revolt (Reid-Salmon, 2012, p. 25). Sam Sharpe, after all, may have learnt to read through the schooling that British Baptist missionaries set up for the enslaved, which in turn enabled him to read the Bible for himself. He was given religious instruction and assigned the role of a Baptist deacon, which gave him some leadership responsibilities for others, and therefore influence over them. This level of influence garnered him the titles within the enslaved community of 'Daddy Sharpe', 'Ruler Sharpe' and 'preacher to the rebels' (Reid-Salmon, 2012, p. 2).

While Knibb had originally tried to thwart the revolt, in its aftermath – as he was personally threatened and violently pursued by plantation owners – he changed his stance. In his dealings with the plantation owners it became clear to him that they wanted to stop the enslaved receiving any form of religious instruction. That led Knibb to conclude that the only way forward was to challenge the system of slavery itself. Accordingly, he left Jamaica for England in April 1832 to become one of the leading campaigners for the abolition of slavery.

Despite the campaigning of key figures like Knibb, the passing of the 1833 Act by the British Parliament was by no means a foregone conclusion, and perhaps the terms of the Act shed some light on this. The Act provided for a £20 million pay-out, worth billions of pounds in today's money, to the registered slave owners of the freed slaves. This payment was to compensate slave owners for the loss of their slaves as 'business assets'. The Act also required the black women, men and children freed from slavery to work an unpaid apprenticeship for their existing slave masters on their existing plantations. The British government stated that the apprenticeship scheme was designed to enable the freed slaves to learn how to live as free people.

This scheme was supposed to last between seven and twelve years, depending on the age and skills of the enslaved person. However, it was brought to an end in 1838, as freed slaves and abolitionists protested against the brutality being experienced by those still working on plantations.

William Knibb's and Sam Sharpe's collective efforts serve as a powerful motif of the Church's involvement in the abolition of slavery in the Caribbean and other British colonies. Two Christians, one free, one enslaved, two different theological outlooks, both playing key roles in the abolition story.

It is a motif that has in turn shaped my response to individuals like 'V' fleeing quasi-domestic exploitation today, and might usefully inform the global movement against the exploitation and trafficking of people: it is a motif that points to the importance of doing theology from below and the significance of relationships being forged between opposing Christian communities for liberation. These two themes will be considered in turn.

Doing theology from below

The term 'doing theology from below' is being used to describe the act of understanding the nature of God, in part through reading Scripture from the social location of those living on the underside of society. An early example of this kind of approach can be found in the first Baptist church on English soil. One of the leaders of that church, John Murton, argued that he and his congregation were well placed to hear and respond to the voice of Christ in Scripture, in a way the author intended or envisioned. This was because, like Christ and his disciples, they too were living on the underside of society, as the 'poor and despised of the world' (Murton, 1621, p. 11).

Murton described their experience of being prevented in English law from freely practising their Christian faith in a Baptist way as follows:

Our miseries are long and lingering imprisonments for many years in divers counties of England, in which many have died and left behind them widows, and many small children: taking away our goods and others the like, of which we can make good probation; not for any disloyalty to your majesty, nor hurt to any mortal man our adversaries themselves being judges; but only because we dare not assent unto, and practise in the worship of God, such things as we have not faith in because it is sin against the Most High. (Murton, 1621, p. 2)

Almost two centuries later in the British colony of Jamaica, a theme of doing theology from below is apparent once again. This time it is through the preaching and teaching of black American Baptist missionaries in Jamaica, people such as George Liele. They chose to read Scripture from their social location – namely, from the margins of society as former slaves. In doing so, Liele was able to correlate the experiences of the enslaved in Jamaica with the experiences of the people of Israel being enslaved in Egypt. Sam Sharpe grew up in a black community that was most likely exposed to that kind of teaching. Sharpe himself went on to read Scripture from his social location. In doing so, he identified those supporting slavery as individuals seeking to serve 'two masters', God and wealth, which Christ in Matthew 6.24 had warned was impossible. He further deduced that those enslaved had an obligation to change society in Jesus-like ways, to enable God's will to be done, including speaking truth to power and revolting against policies and structures, to liberate the oppressed.

V's story also has a theme of doing theology from below as she gradually correlated the stories of Pharisees behaving in ways Christ disapproved of, with her host family exploiting her. The implications of making that correlation and responding in a Christlike way involved her being willing to put at risk dreams she had held since childhood about living in England. She had always seen England as the place that offered the kind of study, job and standards-of-living opportunities that her African country of birth did not, and she longed for them. She had tasted some of these opportunities in France, but saw greater ones in

England. It was not easy for her to put her dream of living in England at risk, to offer a Christlike challenge to her host family exploiting her, but challenge them she did.

The next question 'V' had to consider was what more she was willing to risk in order to stay in England, once her host family demanded she leave their house. Initially she asked strangers she came across if they knew of a place she could sleep for the night. As a young woman on her own on the streets in a foreign country, she was vulnerable. It is, after all, not unknown for traffickers or unscrupulous landlords and business owners to target people experiencing homelessness. Her ultimate decision to approach the charity-shop worker she knew about finding a place to stay may well have saved her from a plight far worse than the one she had fled. That charity worker sent her to the local church known for supporting people experiencing homelessness, and that church was able to help her find somewhere safe to stay, and influence the future trajectory of her life.

The church in the process of helping her was able to expose her to ways of consciously doing theology from below. Not much more than 24 hours after her fleeing a quasi-domestic exploitation situation, she chose to attend the church's 'Extremes'-themed Communion service, where extracts of Martin Luther King Jr's 'Letter from Birmingham Jail' 1963 were explored. In this letter Martin Luther King Jr, like Sam Sharpe before him and George Liele before Sam Sharpe, embodied a way of doing theology from below. The sections of the letter explored concerned Martin Luther King Jr's response to being called an extremist by white clergy:

> But though I was initially disappointed at being categorized as an extremist, as I continued to think about the matter I gradually gained a measure of satisfaction from the label … Was not Jesus an extremist for love: 'Love your enemies, bless them that curse you, do good to them that hate you, and pray for them which despitefully use you, and persecute you.' Was not Amos an extremist for justice: 'Let justice roll down like waters and righteousness like an ever flowing stream.' (Martin Luther King Jr, 1963)

These extracts from the letter show Martin Luther King Jr reading Scripture from his social location. In doing so, he was able to correlate the actions of the Civil Rights Movement he was leading with the actions of Christ, and Old Testament prophets like Amos. Like Sam Sharpe before him, he saw the oppressed as having an obligation to change society in a way that enables God's will to be done. This included responding in Christlike ways of speaking truth to power and revolting against policies and structures, in order to liberate the oppressed.

'V' benefited from being exposed to consciously doing theology from below, which helped her grow in her confidence that God did not mean for her to return to a life of exploitation. Her story of a quasi-domestic exploitation situation, at the hands of a wealthy Christian family, did also beg the question of how they reconciled what they were doing to her with their faith.

The words of Knibb when urging black Baptists not to revolt perhaps provides some clues. He referred to loving their souls while urging them to be obedient and not be insubordinate. Did Knibb not love their bodies just as much? Was he influenced by Neo-Platonic dualism in his thinking? Did 'V's wealthy Christian host family share a similar theological outlook?

Many have written about the legacies of Neo-Platonic philosophies that influenced the early Church (Reddie, 2019, p. 48). It was an approach that separated the human spirit and human flesh, and saw them as in opposition to each other. It provided a basis by which the Church could justify disregarding the mistreatment of physical human bodies, in the short or long term. It underpinned an understanding of spheres of the sacred and secular, and regarded only the sacred sphere as the concern of the Church. This understanding also had a lasting influence on readings of Pauline Epistles that required slaves to offer their loyal obedience to their masters (no matter how harsh their treatment of them), as a necessary act of faithfulness to God.

Knibb's words discouraging the enslaved from revolting, as well as the BMS instructions to missionaries, collectively echo Neo-Platonic readings of Pauline epistles. BMS had encouraged Knibb to have nothing to do with Jamaica's civil and political affairs, on the basis that the gospel of Christ did not produce or countenance a spirit of revolt or insubordination (Reid-Salmon, 2012, p. 43).

'V's story also suggests a possible Neo-Platonic dualism influence in her host family's thinking. She confirms that over time she identified her host family as perceiving their rituals of going to church, praying and reading Scripture at home as their 'worship of God'. In contrast, they regarded their treatment of her as a separate matter. She correlated this with them behaving like 'Pharisees'. This was based on them being concerned with appearing to be deeply religious people to the outside world, while hiding their mistreatment of her. However, she also references them as seeing themselves as superior to her and seeing her as their servant. This latter point of them viewing her as a servant could be coupled with them seeing God as expecting servants to show loyal obedience to the masters of the house they live in (even if the master's treatment of them is harsh).

The theological outlook of both William Knibb and 'V's host family suggest that legacies of Neo-Platonic dualism in the early Church may well still need to be addressed in churches today – particularly if churches are to effectively play their part in tackling the exploitation and trafficking of people. One of the ways this might be done is by enabling more Christians, and more congregations, to engage in approaches to doing theology from below.

The story of the 200-year-plus partnership between Jamaican and British Baptists provides examples of how this might be addressed. It is to that 200-year story I now turn in exploring the potential of partnerships being forged between opposing Christian communities, with the goal being liberation.

Partnerships between opposing Christian communities for liberation

The passing of the Abolition of Slavery Act 1833 did not mark the end of British and Jamaican Baptists working together. In 2014, Jamaican and British Baptists marked the bicentenary of their partnership in mission. This partnership has its roots in a black man, Moses Baker, who was not free to preach, appealing to BMS for support, and BMS sending John Rowe to help in 1814. BMS later sent others, such as William Knibb. The relationship withstood disagreements, such as the opposing views of Knibb and black Baptists like Sam Sharpe regarding the 1831 revolt. Knibb, in the aftermath of the revolt, changed his stance as he began to see things more from the point of view of the enslaved, and went on to be a leading campaigner for the abolition of slavery.

It was noted during the bicentenary celebrations in 2014 that the relationship between Jamaican and British Baptists had been 'forged through years of slavery, colonization, and the arrival of the *Windrush* from the Caribbean to Britain' (Jamaican and British Baptists Together, 2014).

One of the products of this enduring relationship between Jamaican and British Baptists was the establishment of the joint Sam Sharpe Project in 2012, for education, research and community building. The project states in relation to Sam Sharpe:

> He remains a witness to the principle of 'liberation from below': that is, true liberation comes when those who are oppressed or marginalized participate in making their own freedom and justice, rather than simply having it granted to them by those who have power and authority. This is what the Project identifies as the 'legacy' of Sam Sharpe today. (Sam Sharpe Project, 2012)

One of the streams of the project is the holding of an annual Sam Sharpe lecture. The lecture series' stated aim is to seek to explore subjects such as mission, race, class and neocolonialism in unpacking the legacy of Sam Sharpe.

In 2019, the lecture was delivered by Professor Verene Shepherd, on the theme of 'Women in Sam Sharpe's Army: Repression, Resistance, Reparation'. During the lecture she made the case for reparations being paid to all those impacted by the horrors of colonialism, including the legacies of the transatlantic slave trade.

Her call for reparations was framed within the Caribbean Community (CARICOM) action plan for reparations. This had its origins in discussions on the issue of Reparations for Native Genocide and Slavery, initiated at the Conference of Heads of Government of CARICOM in July 2013, in Trinidad and Tobago.

The conference led to the forming of a regional CARICOM Reparations Commission (CRC) with the following mandate to:

> Establish the moral, ethical and legal case for the payment of Reparations by the Governments of all the former colonial powers and the relevant institutions of those countries, to the nations and people of the Caribbean Community for the Crimes against Humanity of Native Genocide, the Trans-Atlantic Slave Trade and a racialized system of chattel Slavery. (CRC, 2013)

The CRC went on to assert among other things that European governments created the legal, financial and fiscal policies necessary for the enslavement of Africans; defined and enforced African enslavement as in their 'national interests'; refused compensation to the enslaved with the ending of their enslavement, while compensating slave owners at emancipation for the loss of legal property rights in enslaved Africans.

Shepherd's call for reparations, in the context of the ongoing partnership between Jamaican and British Baptists in mission, challenged British Baptists to join with Jamaican Baptists and beyond, in lobbying the British government to substantively respond to the call.

In seeking to respond to that call there is potential for churches (including the ones that help individuals like 'V') to join the campaign for reparations. These reparations might include things like debt cancellation, so that countries can redirect debt repayments towards generating more of their own study and work opportunities. These reparations might also include making changes to British migration policies to provide additional overseas living and working experiences. These opportunities could be open to people from the countries Britain sourced African people from, or relocated African people to, during the transatlantic slave trade. There are already favourable migration schemes (for example, Youth Mobility Scheme) open to residents of former British colonies such as Australia, New Zealand and Canada. Additionally, reparations might include changes to British border control policies. This might include ensuring there are safe routes open for people seeking asylum, including people from countries in Africa and the Caribbean, as places Britain exploited during the transatlantic slave trade.

'V', in sharing her story, spoke of many like her born in Cameroon who sought safe and legitimate living and working experiences in France and England. It is also notable that Cameroon is one of the African countries that had people forcibly removed and enslaved in British colonies as part of the transatlantic slave trade. It is also a country that is in part both a former British colony and a former French colony, and it finds itself currently experiencing internal conflict as it navigates the complexities of this legacy. This conflict is in turn leading to some within the English-speaking regions of Cameroon seeking asylum in Britain. In the process of seeking asylum in Britain it does not seem inconceivable that some of them could be vulnerable to being exploited or trafficked both here and abroad – particularly as I reflect on my engagement with people like 'V', as well as other known cases of people from parts of Africa being exploited and trafficked en route to and in Europe.

Conclusion

In conclusion, Baptists' historic involvement in the abolition of slavery in the Caribbean and other British colonies serves as a powerful motif for today's global movement against the exploitation and trafficking of people. It is a story rooted in the 200-year-plus relationship forged between Jamaican and British Baptists, a story that began with Moses Baker, a black American missionary in Jamaica, reaching out to English Baptists.

While black Baptists like Moses Baker, George Liele and Sam Sharpe doing theology from below had a different theological outlook from the English Baptists sent by BMS, their collective efforts combined hastened the abolition of slavery in the Caribbean and other British colonies. In the course of the journeying together, Knibb and others came to see – as Sam Sharpe and other black Baptists had previously seen from their social location – the need to challenge the system of slavery, not just the brutality of it.

Today, as some call for the global Church to work together on a movement against the exploitation and trafficking of people in the present, I pray that there will be more opportunities to do theology from below, and to forge relationships between opposing Christian communities, for liberation.

Bibliography

Bleby, H., 1853, *Death Struggles of Slavery: Being a Narrative of Facts and Incidents, which occurred in a British Colony During the Two Years Immediately Preceding Negro Emancipation*, London: Hamilton, Adams, & Co.

CRC (CARICOM Reparations Commission) Mandate, 2013, available at https://caricomreparations.org/about-us/, accessed 16.10.20; https://caricomreparations.org/caricom/caricoms-10-point-reparation-plan/, accessed 16.10.20.

Erskine, N. L., 1981, *Decolonizing Theology: A Caribbean Perspective*, New York: Orbis Books.

Gardner, W. J., 1873, *History of Jamaica*, London: Elliot Stock.

Hinton, J. H., 1847, *Memoirs of William Knibb*, London: Houlston & Stoneman.

Jamaican and British Baptists Together, 2014, Bicentenary Celebrations, available at www.baptist.org.uk/Groups/233776/Bicentenary.aspx, accessed 16.10.20.

King Jr, Martin Luther, 1963, Letter from a Birmingham Jail, available at https://kinginstitute.stanford.edu/king-papers/documents/letter-birmingham-jail, accessed 16.10.20.

Murton, J., 1621, *A Most humble supplication of many the King's Maiesties loyal subjects ready to testifie all civil obedience, by the oath as the law of this realm requireth and that of conscience; Who are persecuted onely for differing religion contrary to divine and humane testimonies*, available at https://quod.lib.umich.edu/e/eebo2/B07159.0001.001/1:1?rgn=div1;view=fulltext, accessed 16.10.20.

National Archives, Caribbean Histories Revealed – Slavery and negotiating freedom, available at www.nationalarchives.gov.uk/caribbeanhistory/slavery-negotiating-freedom.htm, accessed 16.10.20.

Reddie, A. G., 2019, *Theologising Brexit: A Liberationist and Post-colonial Critique*, Abingdon: Routledge.

Reid-Salmon, D. A., 2012, *Burning for Freedom: A Theology of the Black Atlantic Struggle for Liberation*, Kingston: Ian Randle Publishers.

Sam Sharpe Project, 2012, Sam Sharpe project rationale, available at www.samsharpeproject.org, accessed 16.10.20.

Shepherd, V., Sam Sharpe Lecture 2019, 'Women in Sam Sharpe's Army: Repression, Resistance, Reparation', available at www.youtube.com/watch?v=qU7la-zbhsM, accessed 16.10.20.

Youth Mobility Scheme visa (Tier 5) eligibility criteria, available at www.gov.uk/tier-5-youth-mobility/eligibility, accessed 16.10.20.

Notes

1 The term 'quasi-domestic exploitation' situation is used to acknowledge that 'V's story lacks the clear use of violence or threats to prevent her leaving the house, and the withholding of her identity documents, that would normally meet the definition of enslavement.

2 A response to a freedom of information request on 31 January 2018 confirmed that the British government used £20 million to fund the Slavery Abolition Act 1833. In 1833, this was equivalent to approximately 40 per cent of the Government's total annual expenditure, available at www.gov.uk/government/publications/slavery-abolition-act-1833, accessed 16.10.20.

7

Towards a Liberation Theology of Modern Slavery: Emerging Grassroots Responses to Exploitation

DAN PRATT

Introduction

Richard, who tells his story in Part 2 of this book, attended 57 West's[1] community café, and it was here, over a period of a year, that he first shared his story. 57 West is a church rooted among the rough sleeping community of Southend-on-Sea, Essex. It offers a community café during the week, and at weekends holds church services for the homeless, vulnerably housed and those who have complex needs. Other stories emerged from vulnerable men at 57 West: of being approached outside churches, night shelters or charities with offers of employment, accommodation and food. Places where vulnerable people congregated were being targeted in order to recruit them for labour. Individuals were promised payment for long hours of hard work. Payment, however, wasn't always forthcoming. Sometimes these vulnerable individuals were able to leave their exploiters after a week or two. In other cases, the exploiters coerced, controlled and threatened the vulnerable individuals, forcing them to stay for years at a time. In Richard's case, he was held captive for 20 years.

As a church, 57 West grappled to understand these stories and experiences. These narratives of suffering raised questions about how our church and community should and could respond. This cycle of reflection and action was organic, growing gradually, in conversation, with those who had suffered and experienced exploitation. Here, we will highlight some of this journey.

Drawing on first-hand experiences with survivors of modern slavery, the chapter starts to develop a liberation theology of modern slavery. Employing the pastoral cycle of 'seeing, judging and acting', we follow this cycle: first, by journeying with survivors of modern slavery; second, by looking at local community responses to modern slavery; and, finally, by examining wider faith community responses to modern slavery.

The chapter explores how the experiences of survivors can inform and develop the Church's response, witness and discipleship, and how churches can engage in community mobilizing and activism in order to find local solutions to local problems and exploitation. Examples are given of how local solutions can include developing community partnerships in order to confront injustice and exploitation. The chapter concludes by highlighting how liberation theology can inform church responses in order to pursue the goal of slavery-free communities and justice.

Towards a liberation theology of modern slavery

In order to develop a liberation theology of modern slavery, this section highlights the emergence of contextual and liberation theologies. Schreiter notes a 'shift in perspective' in global theology, which first came to the world's attention in the 1950s in parts of Africa and Asia, where there was 'a growing sense that theologies being inherited from the older churches of the North Atlantic community did not fit well into these quite different circumstances' (Schreiter, 1985, p. 1). The detrimental effects of Christianity and imperialism have been noted by various writers (Stanley, 1990; Walls, 2002), and the authenticity of what had been viewed as universal theology and concepts came into question. New questions asked within Africa and Asia could not be answered by traditional frameworks of theology (Schreiter, 1985, p. 3). Localized and contextual theologies emerged that focused on the study of life in relation to Scripture and the Christian tradition. These contextual theologies were viewed as 'theologies that show greater sensitivity to context' (Schreiter, 1985, p. 6).

Bevans notes that classical theology conceived theology as having two theological sources: Scripture and tradition. However, contextual theologians push beyond this, arguing that in actuality what makes theology contextual 'is the recognition of the validity of another *locus theologicus*: present human experience' (Bevans, 2002, pp. 3–4).

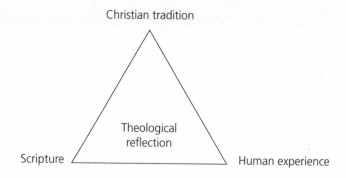

Christian tradition

Theological
reflection

Scripture

Human experience

Figure 1 Bevans's three sources of theological enquiry (2002, p. 4).

Bergmann helpfully defines contextual theology:

> By contextual theology we mean a Christian interpretation of life that is conscious of its circumstances. Contextual theology constitutes a reflection on experiences and expressions of the living and acting God in his/her multi-shaped revelations of the world. (Bergmann, 2003, p. 16)

This emphasis upon context as a source in the theological enquiry, along with Scripture and tradition, has been an important development within contextual theology (Schreiter, 1985, p. 2; Bergmann, 2003, p. 16). Indeed, Bevans argues that there is no such thing as 'theology', stating there is only contextual theology: 'feminist theology, black theology, liberation theology, Filipino theology, Asian-American theology, African theology, and so forth' (Bevans, 2002, p. 3).

One of the earliest contextual theologies was that of liberation theology, emerging in Latin America from the 1960s onwards. Largely Roman Catholic progressive theologians began to theologically challenge the socio-political and economic status quo.[2] God's preferential option for the poor and the theme of justice became key concepts within liberation theology (Gutiérrez, 1973). This placed the poor centrally within the theological process. God was seen as dwelling with the poor in the midst of their sufferings and was perceived to be explicitly interested in their needs. Justice is therefore seen as a central task of liberation theology.[3]

In practice, liberation theology's preferential option for the poor became rooted in the basic church communities within Latin America. Liberation theologians, educators and priests helped shape these basic church communities (CEBs – an acronym formed from their Spanish title, *Communidades Ecclesiales de Base*), which consisted of 'persons at the lowest echelons of society, the poor, the labourer, the marginalized' (Boff, 1970, p. 26). These communities formed in many countries in Central and South America. As of 2007, it was estimated there were 80,000 CEBs in Brazil alone (Rohter, 2007).

The initial dynamism of liberation theology was from Latin America, but parallel movements also emerged in Africa, Asia, Europe and North America. Rowland writes concerning these movements: 'Not all of these are called liberation theology. Contextual theology is a term now widely used to designate theological reflection which explicitly explores the dialogue between social context and Scripture and tradition' (Rowland, 1999a, pp. xiii–xiv). Indeed, Latin American liberation theology and its method of critically analysing the context and experiences of people has been influential in the emergence of other contextual theologies, such as black theology (Cone, 1969); feminist theology (Ruether, 1992; Gebara, 2003); Asian liberation theology (Wielenga, 1999); Hispanic liberation theologies (Costas, 1992); *Mujerista* theology, arising from Hispanic Women in the USA (Isasi-Díaz, 1990), gay and lesbian liberation theology (Hill and Treadway, 1990), African-centred, black British liberation theology (Reddie, 2003, p. 221) and Jewish theology of liberation (Ellis, 1992).

As these theologies emerge out of liberation struggles, the concepts of liberation theologies have direct import for developing a liberation theology of modern slavery. Paris writes: 'each liberation theology claims not only to have emerged out of some liberation movement but to have as its goal the enhancement of that struggle' (Paris, 1992, p. 134). Indeed, liberation approaches to contextual theology are noted as turning the 'focus [of theology] to situations of suffering and oppression that demand redress' (Turpin, 2014, p. 153). The stories from Richard, Amna and Stella give glimpses of liberation movements that echo those of thousands of survivors of modern slavery. A potential liberation theology of modern slavery is to stand alongside those who have not been free, and to enhance the cause of their struggle.

In kindly sharing their stories, Richard, Amna and Stella give permission for theology's attention to turn towards their suffering, and that in turn demands redress. Their stories can, and should, help catalyse responses from churches and faith communities. Indeed, the many untold stories of others, already engaging with faith communities through food banks, night shelters, crèches and drop-in centres, can help local churches and communities respond to the exploitation happening on their doorsteps. In practice, how can churches, faith groups and communities develop wider responses to localized exploitation? The CEBs within Latin America implemented a community mobilization model through utilizing the *pastoral cycle*.

The pastoral cycle

Within Latin America, the CEBs utilized a problem-solving pedagogy. This was rooted in Freire's *Pedagogy of the Oppressed* (1996), in which illiterate people literally 'learn to "read" their lives with acuity' (Boys, 1989, p. 139). This grassroots pedagogy found its expression through the influential *pastoral cycle* (Figure 2). Juan Luis Segundo's *The Liberation of Theology* (1976) took the work of Roman Catholic priests in Europe, and applied and refined it to the South American context through the pastoral cycle. Father Joseph Cardijn, a Belgian priest, encouraged Catholic workers and students to engage in careful theological analysis of their situation by asking them to 'see, judge and act' upon their experiences (Green, 2009, p. 18). Boff notes that the threefold pedagogy of seeing, judging and acting reveals how liberation theology's central emphasis on justice, and hope for the poor, was outworked in the basic ecclesial communities (Boff, 1997, pp. 109–10).

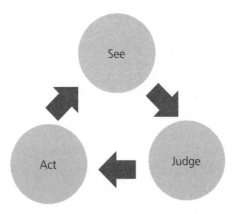

Figure 2 The pastoral cycle.

The pastoral cycle's historical and continued success enabled facilitators and participants within the education process to engage in a *praxis* approach to education[4] (Wijsen, Henriot and Mejia, 2005). Praxis became an important concept within liberation theology, emphasizing the need for unity between theory and practice; reflection and action[5] (Boff, 1987). Contrary to the Roman Catholic Church's teaching, Gutiérrez emphasized praxis over doctrine, promoting a circular relationship between orthodoxy and orthopraxis (1973). Orthodoxy is seen to be only achieved through orthopraxis; right belief is therefore achieved through right action. Liberation theology's emphasis on praxis was central to the success of the CEBs within South America. It permitted a greater freedom for the biblical text to dialogue with the contextual situation for the purpose of liberation (Mesters, 1992).

The pastoral cycle (*see, judge, act*), will now be explored and then applied to contexts of modern slavery. First, participants 'see' their contextual reality. The hermeneutical starting point of both liberation theology and critical pedagogy is the socio-cultural struggle of individuals. Participants are encouraged to 'see' as they exist in exploited or oppressed communities by wider socio-political practices.[6]

Second, participants 'judge' their contextual reality. To judge is to critically reflect on what is seen. Within liberation theology, judging is a 'critical reflection on human praxis – the praxis engaged in by men and women in general and Christians in particular – in light of the practice of Jesus and the exigencies of faith' (Boff, 1970, p. 14). Consequently, there is a 'fusion of horizons' (Gadamer, 1979) as Scripture and Christian tradition interact with contextual reality.

Finally, participants are encouraged to 'act'. Through the dialogical hermeneutic interplay between contextual reality and the Christian tradition, liberating theologies are developed in order to finally act. Within the CEBs, 'acting' urged participants towards what they hoped for in the present, to struggle for a more just and peaceful society.

The success of liberation theology's theological basis, as well as the pastoral cycle's education process within these CEBs, encouraged theologians from outside South America to take note and apply principles from their praxis model to other contexts.[7] The following section will explore how contextual theologies of liberation can help resource localized church and community responses to exploitation and modern slavery within the UK.

Through utilizing the pastoral cycle within 57 West's church service and community café, participants (as individuals and in groups) were encouraged to analyse their experiences, through seeing, judging and acting. Freire's emphasis on finding 'generative themes' from participants' lives within the process places experiences at the centre of the pedagogical process (Freire, 1996). Various themes, such as unemployment, homelessness and inclusion, were explored. When individuals shared stories of exploitation, both through one-to-one and group sessions, the pastoral cycle aided reflection. When appropriate, the pastoral cycle was employed with those who had experienced exploitation. The cycle was not a one-time process. Through continual movement within the cycle, it enabled our understanding and actions in response to emerge and develop. For the purposes of this chapter, this will be demonstrated through employing the cycle three times.

The pastoral cycle, phase one: journeying alongside survivors

Phase one: seeing

In the same way as within Latin American liberation theology, seeing involves exploring the *lived experience* and context of participants, especially within oppressive contexts.[8] Boff writes, 'liberation theology's starting point is the anti-reality, the cry of the oppressed' (Boff, 1997, p. 109).

As mentioned at the beginning of this chapter, in Chapter 3 we were introduced to Richard, who spoke about his experience of being recruited for labour exploitation:

> I first met him in Manchester, in a homeless hostel. I was in my mid-twenties. A notice came over the announcement system: 'If anyone is interested in a job in Austria, come to reception.' I went down to reception and met him. He had a suit on and presented himself politely. He asked: 'Do you have a passport? Can you drive?' 'Yes', I replied. The job would be ground-work and tarmacking. He offered me 900 Austrian schillings a day with accommodation paid for. I jumped at the chance.

In a context of vulnerability, of being in a homeless hostel, a place that should have been safe and secure, Richard was recruited for labour and subsequently exploited. He highlights how easy it was for an exploiter to make contact with him, and then recruit him, with offers of employment, accommodation and travel. But Richard was deceived about the nature of the job and accommodation: 'We travelled to Austria, where I thought I'd be put up in a hotel. Instead, we arrived at an old car park with lots of caravans. It then dawned on me that this wasn't a normal company.' Richard was also deceived about the payment, having been promised 900 Austrian schillings a day: 'Often I would work all day and not get paid ... So I would be stood there starving, covered in tarmac, dirty, tired as a dead dog.'

When wondering why Richard didn't leave his exploiters, he helps us to understand the complexity of the situation. He says:

> I have to ask myself, why did I stay with them so long? One reason is I am a vulnerable person ... I kept carrying on working with them. I had no choice. They were very aggressive saying, 'I'm telling you, you've got to work for me.' I would be threatened. And so I left. They said they would kill me. My family were threatened, which makes things even worse. I was scared.

Richard is aware that his exploiter's control over him includes his own vulnerability, their aggression towards him, and the threats he and his family received.

Over months and sometimes years of developing trust with other homeless or vulnerable individuals, others shared some of their stories of exploitation. These often involved labour exploitation, but sometimes there were also stories of sexual exploitation, domestic exploitation and forced criminality.

Phase one: judging

Alongside listening to stories of those from our community, including Richard's, several leaders and volunteers from the church and community café attended local workshops to help us understand more about exploitation and modern slavery.[9]

The UK's Modern Slavery Act defines modern slavery as when a 'person holds another person in slavery or servitude and the circumstances are such that the person knows or ought to know that the other person is held in slavery or servitude' (Modern Slavery Act, 2015). Human trafficking is defined as when a person arranges or facilitates the travel of another person with a view to that person being exploited.

Although the experiences of Richard and others were distinct, there were common characteristics. These characteristics were part of what the UN highlights as three consistent elements in the trafficking in persons:

1 **The Act** (What is done)
  Recruitment, transportation, transfer, harbouring or receipt of persons.

2 **The Means** (How it is done)
  Threat or use of force, coercion, abduction, fraud, deception, abuse of power or vulnerability, or giving payments or benefits to a person in control of the victim.

3 **The Purpose** (Why it is done)
  For the purpose of exploitation, which includes exploiting the prostitution of others, sexual exploitation, forced labour, slavery or similar practices and the removal of organs. (UN)

Through Richard and others seeing and sharing their experiences, the judging part of the pastoral cycle ensues. This involves a process of *problem-posing* (Freire, 1996), where participants are encouraged to not only 'see' but 'judge' what is going on around them, as well as what is being carried out by them.[10] This involves what Boff writes concerning liberation theology as a 'critical reflection on human praxis' (Boff, 1970, p. 14). Through discussion, individuals 'develop their power to perceive critically the way they exist in the world' (Freire, 2003, p. 65). Critical reflection upon experiences is a skill that needs nurturing.

Richard was exploited for 20 years. During that time he was treated as an object. His humanity and worth were denied.

> They used to say, 'I own you', like a piece of furniture. One guy sold the tarmac truck to another guy and he said to me: 'Because I bought the wagon, you come with the wagon. You are part of the deal.' So that's how I came to be working for another person. I came with the wagon. I was like a spare wheel. It's bad, you know, but that's the truth. I just accepted it.

Following years of control and being told that he was 'owned', like an object, Richard is honest in saying he 'just accepted it'. He experienced what Martin Buber (1970) refers to as an 'I/It' relationship. The exploiter, 'I', views Richard 'like a spare wheel', an object, an 'It'. This follows a subject/object, master/slave relationship. Having escaped his captors, and being able to live freely within the community, Richard found himself having to re-frame his identity and think critically about who he is in light of his past and present experiences. For Buber, the antithesis to an 'I/It' relationship is an 'I/Thou' relationship. The 'I' doesn't objectify the 'It', but rather acknowledges the other person as a 'Thou', an equal, as a living relationship. Rather than 'power over', the 'I/Thou' reflects a relationship of 'equality with'.

To transition to experiencing relationships as equal, and 'I/Thou' rather than 'I/It', is by no means easy for Richard. In trying to adapt into society and community, he struggles to integrate into a 'normal job', and the sense of otherness, disconnectedness, 'of being put out of society' lingers.

But what does Scripture and theology have to say about Richard's and others' experiences? Latin American liberation theology develops a theology of God's 'preferential option for the poor'. Boff writes: 'liberation theology's starting point is the anti-reality, the cry of the oppressed, the open wounds that have been bleeding for centuries' (Boff, 1997, p. 109). It highlights how Scripture shows that God is especially concerned with, and close to, the poor and vulnerable within society. This is based on using a 'liberatory hermeneutic' and reading of Scripture. For example, the biblical prophets and the apostles called for the children of Israel and the Church to care for the most vulnerable within society – the orphan, the widow and the foreigner (Isa. 11.4; 58.6–8; Zech. 7.8–10; Luke 4.18–19; James 1.27).

Boff notes: 'The preferential option for the poor is rooted in the very nature of God. Being drawn to the oppressed and unjustly impoverished comes from the depths of God's being. An offense against them is an offense against the nature and glory of God' (Boff, 1988, p. 124). Boff continues: 'the option for the poor, against their poverty and for their liberation, has constituted and continues to constitute the core of liberation theology. To opt for the poor entails a practice; it means assuming the place of the poor, their cause, their struggle, and at the limit, their often tragic fate' (Boff, 1997, p. 107).

Through walking alongside Richard and others, it became clearer to our church and leadership that their struggle and cause was becoming our struggle and our cause. This period of judging and critical reflection convicted us of the need for action. It became no longer possible only to talk or preach. This interplay between Richard's experiences and Scripture and the Christian tradition helped us understand that action was required.

Phase one: acting

To be able to act with Richard and others, their immediate needs were our concern. When we first met Richard, he was sleeping on a sofa in his friend's house and walking several miles each day to access soup kitchens. Richard was aware and anxious that his exploiters were trying to find him: 'I constantly worry and look over my shoulder. I don't want to see them again or bump into them. That's very hard … They are still looking for me, phoning my friend and asking, "Where is he?"'

Maslow's hierarchy of needs (1943) describes five levels of need to show how humans partake in behavioural motivation. At a basic level, there are physiological needs such as food, water, warmth and rest, as well as safety needs, such as security and personal safety. For Richard, it was essential that these needs were met. Leonardo Boff writes: 'The rights of the poor are spoken of as the rights of God. The rights in question are prioritized: first come the right to life and the means of life – food, health, housing, employment, education ...' (Boff, 1970, p. 27).

For our church, action involved walking alongside Richard to find a safe place for him to stay, where his exploiters wouldn't know where to find him. As Richard didn't want to access statutory or safe-house support, local third-sector pathways and options were explored. As a church with limited resources, we weren't able to solve these problems ourselves. Our role involved advocating for Richard and helping him access local services and pathways. Only after Richard accessed unemployment and housing allowance was he able to obtain accommodation through a homeless charity in a shared house. Additional furniture and household goods were sourced to help him be more comfortable. A local community fund was accessed to enable Richard to go on holiday for a few days as well as visit his family, who he hadn't seen for several years.

According to Maslow (1943), following basic needs are psychological needs. These include belonging and love needs, including the need for intimate relationships and friends, as well as esteem needs, including prestige and a feeling of accomplishment. Richard started to make connections with a couple of other men within the church who also accessed the community meals.

Although other community support services were highlighted, Richard and others we worked with didn't feel comfortable engaging with them. Through the church, pastoral care was offered on a bi-weekly basis, in the form of a coffee, walk and chat. These were valuable times, where Richard was able to talk through concerns and achievements as he adjusted to life in the community.

In contrast to the exploitation, it was essential that relationships with Richard and others were modelled on equality and togetherness, reflecting an 'I/Thou' relationship rather than 'I/It'. This was rooted in the understanding that all are created in God's image, with intrinsic value and dignity. McFadyen highlights the importance for individuals to be autonomous agents, while being in relationship. He promotes a theory of the human nature of individuality 'as a sedimentation of interpersonal relations which is intrinsically open to others as to God' (McFadyen, 1990, p. 24). For McFadyen, individuality refers to the capacity to be an autonomous centre of action and communication, to be a separate and independent individual (p. 23).

This view of personhood as a 'sedimentation of interpersonal relations' can be seen through the African Xhosa understanding of Ubuntu, where 'a person is a person through persons' (Villa-Vicencio, 1999, p. 169). Villa-Vicencio notes that identity is found in the presence of the Divine, who is present in others. This is outworked in relationship with others who are, in the African sense, a community that includes and unites (p. 70). As persons open themselves to act with others and relationships are 'sedimented', they and those with whom they have relationship are changed. Trust and openness grew over time between Richard and those of us in the church community, as we grew in our individuality and interdependence.

The pastoral cycle, phase two: local community responses to modern slavery

Phase two: seeing

Conversations with local charities, churches and faith groups highlighted that they had, and were encountering, individuals who had experienced similar forms of exploitation through being recruited, transported, deceived, controlled and exploited for the purposes of labour exploitation, sexual exploitation, domestic servitude or forced criminality. Many of these individuals, like Richard, did not want to interact with the police or statutory services. Fear and distrust of authorities were often stopping vulnerable people from accessing the help they needed.

Local police figures indicated 25 incidents of modern slavery in 2018 and 43 incidents in 2019. These statistics only reflect the victims the police had identified. Within our community, larger numbers of potential victims of slavery were evident.

Other local faith groups and charities had encountered individuals who had experienced exploitation, but were quietly seeking to get their lives back together. Others had recently escaped from exploitative situations and came to third-sector organizations as the first place for help. Some individuals were still experiencing exploitation and accessing local services at the same time. Seeing that exploited individuals were engaging with faith communities and third-sector organizations raised questions about how we could support those victims, as well as equipping charities to respond.

In talking with faith groups and charities, it was becoming clearer that they were targeted by potential exploiters in order to recruit victims for the purposes of exploitation. Richard highlights how, years before, he was recruited from inside a homeless hostel. Several churches and charities in our area had noticed people in vans stationed outside their food banks or night shelters. These individuals would engage with the clients, offering them jobs, money and accommodation. It was apparent that would-be exploiters still made direct contact with at-risk people in places where they find safety and shelter.

The scale of the local exploitation became more apparent. This picture was reinforced by recent reports indicating that 100,000 to 136,000 people were exploited by modern slavery within the UK (Gren-Jardan, 2020; Minderoo Foundation, 2018). This is equivalent to 2.2 people per 1,000 population being kept in some form of modern slavery. Therefore, within the borough of Southend and its population of 184,000, there are an estimated 405 people kept within modern slavery.

Phase two: judging

Critical awareness within the CEBs was encouraged through Freire's *conscientization* (1996). This process 'represents the *development* of the awakening of critical awareness' (Freire, 1973, p. 19). For us, conscientization involves critically thinking about what is happening to vulnerable people within our community, and how our church within the area could respond. This begins with Christian communities understanding their nature and mission. Only after revealing and challenging 'inherited assumptions' can new, more valid premises for faith claims and actions be appropriated.

David Bosch, in his seminal *Transforming Mission* (1991), highlights: 'The *missio Dei* is God's activity, which embraces both the church and the world, and in which the church may be privileged to participate' (Bosch, 1991, p. 391). This view of God's invitation for the Church to join in his existing work in the world breathes new life into the Church's reason for being.

Drawing on liberation theology, Bosch notes that an integral part of *missio Dei* is 'mission as liberation' (Bosch, 1991, p. 432–47). This has direct import into our faith community's response to modern slavery, as God invites us into Jesus' mission of setting the captives free (Luke 4.18). A theology of liberation, however, is not to be spiritualized. Within liberation theology, Christ is viewed as the *liberator* from sin and oppression,[11] who brings what Boff terms *integral liberation* (Boff, 1970, p. 25; 1989, pp. 59–60).

Integral liberation is viewed as God's salvific plan for the world. Boff writes that this salvation has been seen concretely in the process of integral liberation in various mediations – 'economic (liberation from hunger), political (liberation from marginalization), cultural (liberation from illiteracy and ignorance), pedagogical (liberation from depersonalizing dependency), and religious (liberation from sin as rejection of God and God's historical project)' (Boff, 1970, p. 19).

Consequently, there was a need for our church to respond to God's invitation of joining him in setting the captives free and working towards integral liberation within our community.

Phase two: acting

Through seeing the extent of local forms of exploitation as well as gaining an understanding of *missio Dei* and integral liberation, the church leaders developed more valid premises for faith and action, which were then encouraged within the faith community. Plans developed to start a localized anti-slavery partnership – one that would bring together various community stakeholders, including churches, faith groups, charities working with vulnerable people, as well as the police and local council.

With funding from the Essex Police, Fire and Crime Commission helping to initiate the Southend Against Modern Slavery (SAMS) partnership, I continued my role as a Baptist minister at 57 West part-time, and was released to minister 50 per cent of my time as co-ordinator of the newly emerging SAMS. This new role was viewed as part of my vocation as a minister, in serving the community.

In order to establish the partnership, community organizing has been essential. Citizens UK, who organize communities to act together for power, social justice and the common good, state: 'Community Organizing is based on the principle that when people work together they have the power to change their neighbourhoods, cities, and ultimately the country for the better' (Citizens UK).

Listening is a key part of community organizing, to explore concerns and develop strategies to improve communities. Through initiating the SAMS partnership, a listening exercise involved many one-to-one meetings with those working among at-risk individuals, including faith groups, charities and statutory bodies and police. This was an opportunity to 'see' and 'judge' more clearly how exploitation through modern slavery impacted our community and to explore how we could transform it. The mapping of stakeholders ensued through identifying local resources and noting gaps. Through an assets-based approach, potential partners highlighted what they could bring to the table. Local forms of exploitation needed to be solved by local solutions and through mobilizing the whole community.

A partnership approach would enable us to create a stronger response than if we were working independently.

In May 2018, the SAMS partnership had its first meeting, held within the community café of 57 West. Some 30 organizations were represented, including ten churches and faith groups, several charities working with vulnerable people, the University of Essex, the Citizens Advice Bureau, the homeless winter night shelter, local and regional police, the local council, as well as other active citizens. We unanimously passed a resolution to support the establishment of the anti-slavery partnership to work towards a 'Slavery-Free-Southend-On-Sea'. Quarterly partnership meetings were planned, with work in between ongoing. The SAMS partnership agreed to focus on four initial objectives.

First, partnership development, through stimulating multi-agency partnership work across the third sector, law enforcement and statutory bodies. This has enabled us to map existing support for victims of modern slavery and to learn from best practice. We have also learnt from the best practice of other locations and partnerships within the UK.[12]

Second, raising awareness has included a variety of approaches – such as posters and leaflets being distributed in the community to raise specific-awareness campaigns. For example, on the World Day Against Trafficking we partnered with a local street artist and Project 49, a charity that supports individuals with special needs, to create graffiti street art for Southend high street. The artwork made an impact locally as well as having local and national press coverage.

Through training from Essex Police and the Clewer Initiative, we developed a 'Spotting the Signs of Modern Slavery' workshop. This was to help faith groups and third-sector organizations to learn about: forms of modern slavery and local impact; identifying the signs/indicators of modern slavery; and how to respond and safeguard potential victims. In two years of running these workshops, 1,230 local people have participated in them. In addition, 16 community leaders have subsequently undergone the 'train-a-trainer' workshops to enable them to run these awareness workshops through their networks and organizations.

Resilience workshops were undertaken with those at risk of

being recruited for modern slavery. These included workshops with homeless people as well as disadvantaged children and teenagers, and individuals newly arriving from other countries who were seeking employment.

Third, the objective of safeguarding those at risk through developing safeguarding practices. This has included developing a safeguarding booklet developed for faith groups and charities, to help them think through their safeguarding practices. In partnership with the local council, SAMS has co-developed and co-delivers a training package specifically for charities and third-sector organizations. The training helps charities to work towards 'slavery proofing' their organization through appointing champions, and ensuring their safeguarding policies and pathways include victims of modern slavery.

The final objective is acting through catalysing community action. Although all the activities above involve action, we are developing focused actions in being proactive in seeking out and caring for those who are hidden and exploited.

A community intelligence lead is employed one day a week to work in partnership with local organizations and law enforcement. This lead is a retired detective chief inspector and part-time local church minister. Two areas have been focused on. First, 14 car washes within the borough, known to be high risk for potential exploitation, have been mapped. Volunteers have been trained to visit these car washes and collect data.

Second, potential online escorts linked to brothels in Southend are being mapped through identifying escorts advertising on public websites. They are then contacted by a trained operative to identify any information about their circumstances and services offered. The intelligence is then submitted on a 'partner information form' to Essex Police. From a recent brothel raid by the police, a potential victim of modern slavery was identified and safeguarded. From both activities, in the first year alone, 33 separate incidents of intelligence were recorded; some provide a local picture; and some incidents are passed on to law enforcement.

In addition, SAMS is starting to develop more robust care offered to survivors of modern slavery. This would be for individuals like Richard, who don't want to engage with the National Referral Mechanism (NRM), the government's safeguarding mechanism, or other statutory support services. People such as Richard have been keen to explore freedom on their own terms. This often involves accessing local services such as charities for the homeless, food banks and so on. Support would also be offered to survivors who are settling within the community, having accessed the safe-house support of the NRM.

With charity funding, a part-time survivor care co-ordinator will provide support intervention for survivors, through linking them with support networks, including volunteer support. In collaboration with partners, the co-ordinator will help survivors navigate local survivor care pathways, identify blockers and problem-solve.

In addition, the co-ordinator will co-ordinate, recruit, train and manage three tiers of volunteers to meet regularly with survivors:

1 Mentors to provide help relating to education and employment opportunities, including CV and other skills-related advice;
2 Practical helpers who can assist with practical needs such as obtaining a bike, finding English classes etc;
3 Befrienders who will help to reduce social isolation, encouraging community interaction.[13]

The pastoral cycle, phase three: wider faith community responses to modern slavery

Phase three: seeing

Keya regularly attends our local church. She appears shy, nervous and scared. The family she works for drops her off at the door and collects her exactly one hour later. This doesn't allow her to interact with people. In brief conversations it becomes clear that Keya is not paid properly for her work and is not allowed out of the house without permission. The two sons in the house ridicule her. She is unable to leave because she must pay off a small debt to the family, who built her and her disabled husband a small house in India. The debt would take years to pay off. It was a shock to those of us in the church who came to know Keya over her time with us that this situation was happening yards from our own homes.[14]

This story was shared by a local church minister whose church had regularly welcomed a victim of modern slavery to their church services. Talking with other church ministers, it became clear these weren't isolated cases. This led the Eastern Baptist Association,[15] with over 170 churches in the east of England, to conduct a survey among its churches relating to modern slavery and trafficking. The survey indicated that out of the 47 churches taking part, 19 per cent of them had knowingly encountered victims of modern slavery. These encounters had often been in their grassroots work or serving the community. There will be more churches who had unknowingly served victims through their church services, food banks, crèches, night shelters and other community activities. But why were so many victims/survivors of exploitation accessing services from churches?

The charity Hestia interviewed 12 survivors of modern slavery who had experienced homelessness, asking them: 'Where would a survivor of modern slavery who is experiencing rough sleeping go to seek help?' Only four out of the twelve would go to the police, with one person stating they 'would be too scared of police', and another saying 'that they'd been in trouble with the police before, and they'd be too frightened'. None out of the 12 would go to the council for help, with one person explaining they 'would be too scared of being deported', and another asking: 'How would I know I could trust them?' (Hestia, 2019, p. 10). All interviewees indicated they would approach a church, mosque or other religious organization for help (pp. 9–10).

In the same report, interviewees were questioned regarding what they thought were the barriers stopping survivors of exploitation who became homeless from seeking help. All indicated that 'fear was a barrier'. Other barriers included lack of information, poor English, low self-esteem, mental health issues, shame, mistrust, and fear of deportation (Hestia, 2019, p. 10). Hestia concludes their report by stating that: 'Faith organizations and grass-roots and homelessness charities are significantly more accessible to survivors of modern slavery who are sleeping rough than existing statutory pathways' (p. 14).

Phase three: judging

Latin American liberation theology helps with viewing Scripture through a liberatory lens. For example, Jesus' preaching of the 'kingdom' or 'reign of God' (Gutiérrez, 1973; Boff, 1974) gives focus to what Boff calls a 'utopian hope':

> The Kingdom of God expresses man's utopian longing for liberation from everything that alienates him, factors such as anguish, pain, hunger, injustice and death, and not only man but all creation. The Kingdom of God is the term used to convey the absolute lordship of God over the world stricken and oppressed by diabolic forces. (Boff, 1974, pp. 80–1)

Through employing a liberatory hermeneutic, in seeking transformation according to the utopian hope of God's kingdom, there is a turning away from sin and selfishness and a turning to God. Gutiérrez notes: 'To sin is to deny loving God and others' (Gutiérrez, 1998, p. 115).

For the Church, therefore, following Christ as liberator, integral liberation includes what Gutiérrez states as 'a demand for the transformation of the historical and political conditions in which men [and women] live' (Gutiérrez, 1974, p. 74). The extensiveness of modern slavery not only within the UK, but around the world, demands for the Church to engage politically. Societal transformation towards peace and justice will not happen through disengagement. Rather, the Church in joining in *missio Dei* works towards bringing the principles of God's reign to earth, just as Christ taught his followers to pray: 'Your kingdom come ... on earth as it is in heaven' (Matt. 6.10).

Gutiérrez writes, 'solidarity with the poor implies the transformation of the existing social order. It implies a liberating social praxis: that is, a transforming activity directed towards the creation of a just, free society' (Gutiérrez, 1974, pp. 59–60). As others note within this book (Blyth and Findlay in Chapter 8), exploitation of vulnerable people relates to not only traffickers but also unjust political and business policies that keep the poor marginalized and the vulnerable open to exploitation. The reign of God functions as the grounds of social critique or prophetic criticism, judging unjust social, political and economic structures as well as cultural arrangements (Nuhumara, 2002, p. 210). The Church consequently not only responds to the most vulnerable encountered, it also develops a prophetic voice calling for injustice to end and the exploitation of the most vulnerable to cease.

Phase three: acting

Discovering that nearly one in five churches has knowingly encountered victims of modern slavery, the Eastern Baptist Association (EBA) established a part-time role of anti-slavery co-ordinator. The role was to help resource churches respond to local exploitation and to explore how churches could advocate for change.

In partnership with the Clewer Initiative, the EBA held three summits in Chelmsford, Norwich and Cambridge, with the intention of raising awareness and developing partnership work. Along with the support and intention of key community stakeholders, anti-slavery partnerships are emerging in both Norwich and Chelmsford.

The anti-slavery work is expanding within wider Baptist and Free Church networks, through the catalysing and development of the Together Free Foundation.[16] Together Free is an emerging Free Church-led initiative partnering with churches, faith groups and communities seeking to end modern slavery and exploitation. In addition to organizing national conferences, resources for churches have been developed, including a 'Modern Slavery and Safeguarding Guide' for churches.[17] The aim is that more churches and faith groups will be able to identify and safeguard potential victims of modern slavery, such as Richard and Keya. It also raises questions about how church and faith groups can be empowered to welcome survivors to find safety, refuge and belonging.

Together Free is supporting localized anti-slavery initiatives to emerge and is currently incubating the SAMS partnership, and seeking to catalyse the Chelmsford Antislavery Partnership (CASP).

Having seen the impact of the SAMS partnership, senior community safety officers from Chelmsford City Council are seeking to replicate the community-led partnership within Chelmsford. At the end of 2020, some 35 individuals from a wide range of partner agencies representing both statutory and voluntary organizations within Chelmsford agreed to seek funding and appoint an anti-slavery co-ordinator to take the work forward. Local priorities and an action plan would be developed and agreed.

Conclusion and recommendations

Survivors' stories, such as Richard's, told with permission, have been central to critical reflection in order to promote action and response. These grassroots responses to exploitation and modern slavery have been catalysed by walking alongside survivors such as Richard. Indeed, as Bosch notes, 'The poor were no longer merely the *objects* of mission; they had become its *agents* and bearers' (Bosch, 1991, p. 436). Although the term 'the poor' is somewhat condescending, there is truth in the statement that Richard has become an agent and bearer in the mission of partnering towards a slavery-free society. From this work, several recommendations for churches and faith groups are made.

First, to encourage faith communities to 'see' suffering and exploitation around them. 'I'/'Thou' relationships can be fostered with those experiencing exploitation. Time, care and mutuality can nurture relationships of trust. Openness for a 'sedimentation of relationships' can be encouraged, where subject–subject give and receive, and will be transferred in the process.

Second, to resource faith communities so they are able to 'judge', using theological, biblical and sociological resources. Liberation readings of the Bible and Christian tradition will help inform, inspire and provoke faith communities to act. Sociological resources can help churches understand more about modern slavery, exploitation and the issues their communities face.

Third, to encourage faith communities to 'act'. Each faith community will respond differently according to their context and what is 'seen' and 'judged'. Partnering with what others are doing locally and regionally is a good first step, to explore what can be brought to the table in order to partner towards a slavery-free community.

Fourth, to release and encourage those with skills in faith communities to serve those who are exploited. There are many people with skills relevant to partnering towards slavery-free communities. These include food-bank staff, volunteers at homeless shelters, nurses, teachers and social workers. They should be empowered to view their roles as vocations, in which they participate in *missio Dei*.

Fifth, according to Maslow's hierarchy of need (1943), following basic and psychological needs, there are self-fulfilment needs and self-actualization through achieving one's full potential, including creative activities. Faith communities can journey with survivors through exploring how they can journey towards self-actualization. For those survivors who are Christians, this can be through encouraging them to find their vocation through participating in *missio Dei*. For survivors of other faiths or none, faith groups can find alternative ways to help them reach their full potential. All should adhere to the Human Trafficking Foundation's 'Survivor Care Standards', including to 'not engage in proselytization' (2018, p. 21). It is essential that survivors do not experience any pressure, coercion or control from faith groups.

Finally, faith communities can be a refuge community of

support for survivors of modern slavery. Victims have often been isolated and mistreated for many years at a time. Faith communities can model healthy relationships, where people are loved, accepted and are given space and time to come to terms with their trauma. Sacrificial love should be at the heart of the Church's identity and mission. It is in this sacrificial love of God and neighbour that myriad other ways could be found to serve and be in community with those who have experienced exploitation.

Through drawing on resources from liberation theology, including 'God's preferential option for the poor', 'Christ the liberator', 'integral liberation' and the 'reign of God', grassroots theologies in the form of reflection and action have emerged. Contextual theology is emerging and, as Bergmann notes, is an 'interpretation of Christian faith, which arises in the consciousness of its context' (2003, p. 4).

It is this consciousness of local exploitation that can enable churches to find new ways to be, and to serve through employing the pastoral cycle. These contextual theologies are provoking questions regarding how local churches engage in *missio Dei* within their communities in order to bring about God's reign.

Although more robust support could have been given, Richard generously states: 'The most helpful thing in recovering is the help I've received from the church and other people within the community. They tried to make it as easy as possible.' Richard ends his story by saying: 'I appreciate my story being told. It might help put a stop to these people recruiting more people. It might stop others ending up as victims and being abused. Hopefully, more people will help put an end to it.'

Bibliography

Bergmann, S., 2003, *God in Context: A Survey of Contextual Theology*, Aldershot: Ashgate.

Bevans, S., 2002, *Models of Contextual Theology*, rev. edn, New York: Orbis Books.

Boff, C., 1987, *Theology and Praxis: Epistemological Foundations*, New York: Orbis Books.

Boff, L., 1970, *When Theology Listens to the Poor*, San Francisco, CA: Harper & Row.

Boff, L., 1974, 'Salvation in Jesus Christ and the process of liberation', in C. Geffré and G. Gutiérrez (eds), *Theology of Liberation: Liberation and Faith*, London: Concilium, pp. 78–91.

Boff, L., 1980, *Jesus Christ Liberator: A Critical Christology of our Time* (trans. P. Hughes), London: SPCK.

Boff, L., 1988, *Trinity and Society*, trans. P. Burns, London: Burns & Oates/Search Press Ltd.

Boff, L., 1989, *Faith on the Edge: Religion and Marginalized Existence*, San Francisco, CA: Harper & Row.

Boff, L., 1997, *Cry of the Earth, Cry of the Poor*, New York: Orbis Books.

Bosch, D. J., 1991, *Transforming Mission: Paradigm Shifts in Theology of Mission*, New York: Orbis Books.

Boys, M. C., 1989, *Educating in Faith: Maps and Visions*, San Francisco, CA: Harper & Row.

Buber, M., 1970, *I and Thou*, New York: Charles Scribner's Sons.

Citizens UK, 'What is Community Organising?' available from www.citizensuk.org/about_us, accessed 23.01.21.

Cone, J. H., 1969, *Black Theology and Black Power*, New York: Seabury Press.

Costas, O. E., 1992, 'Hispanic theology in North America', in L. M. Getz and R. O. Costa (eds), *Struggles for Solidarity: Liberation Theologies in Tension*, Minneapolis, MN: Fortress Press, pp. 63–74.

Ellis, M. H., 1992, 'Jewish theology of liberation: critical thought and Messianic trust', in L. M. Getz and R. O. Costa (eds), *Struggles for Solidarity: Liberation Theologies in Tension*, Minneapolis, MN: Fortress Press, pp. 75–95.

Freire, P., 1973, *Education for Critical Consciousness*, London: Sheed & Ward.

Freire, P., 1996, *Pedagogy of the Oppressed*, trans. M. Ramos, new edn, London: Penguin Books.

Freire, P., 2003, 'Pedagogy of the Oppressed', in A. Darder, M. Baltodano and R. D. Torres (eds), *The Critical Pedagogy Reader*, London: RoutledgeFalmer, pp. 57–68.

Gadamer, H.-G., 1979, *Truth and Method*, 2nd edn, London: Sheed & Ward.

Gebara, I., 2003, 'A feminist theology of liberation: a Latin American perspective with a view toward the future', in F. Segovia (ed.), *Toward a New Heaven and a New Earth: Essays in Honour of Elisabeth Schüssler Fiorenza*, New York: Orbis Books, pp. 249–68.

Green, L., 2009, *Let's Do Theology: Resources for Contextual Theology*, London: Bloomsbury.

Gren-Jardan, T., 2020, *It Still Happens Here: Fighting UK Slavery in the*

2020s, London: Justice and Care, available from www.justiceandcare. org/wp-content/uploads/2020/07/Justice-and-Care-Centre-for-Social-Justice-It-Still-Happens-Here.pdf, accessed 14.10.20.

Groome, T., 1991, *Sharing Faith: A Comprehensive Approach to Religious Education and Pastoral Ministry*, San Francisco, CA: Harper.

Gutiérrez, G., 1973, *A Theology of Liberation, History, Politics, and Salvation*, trans. C. Inda and J. Eagleson, New York: Orbis Books.

Gutiérrez, G., 1974, 'Liberation theology and proclamation', in C. Geffré and G. Gutiérrez (eds), *Theology of Liberation: Liberation and Faith*, London: Concilium, pp. 57–77.

Gutiérrez, G., 1998, 'Liberation Theology and the Future of the Poor', in J. Rieger (ed.), *Liberating the Future: God, Mammon and Theology*, Minneapolis, MN: Augsburg Fortress, pp. 96–123.

Hestia, 2019, *Underground Lives: Homelessness and Modern Slavery in London*, October 2019, available from www.hestia.org/Handlers/Download.ashx?IDMF=7c01ce39-fded-468f-bca3-6163ed16844e, accessed 22. 02. 21.

Hill, A. C. and Treadway, L. 1990, 'Rituals of healing: ministry with and on behalf of gay and lesbian people', in S. B. Thistlethwaite and M. P. Engel (eds), *Lift Up Every Voice: Constructing Christian Theologies from the Underside*, San Francisco, CA: Harper & Row, pp. 231–44.

Human Trafficking Foundation, 2018, Survivor Care Standards, available from https://static1.squarespace.com/static/599abfb4e6f2e19ffo48494f/t/5bcf492f104c7ba53609aebo/1540311355442/HTF+Care+Standards+%5BSpreads%5D+2.pdf, accessed 27.01.21.

Isasi-Díaz, A. M., 1990, 'The Bible and *Mujerista* theology', in S. B. Thistlethwaite and M. P. Engel (eds), *Lift Up Every Voice: Constructing Christian Theologies from the Underside*, San Francisco, CA: Harper & Row, pp. 261–9.

Maslow, A. H., 1943, 'A theory of human motivation', *Psychological Review* 50(4), pp. 370–96.

McFadyen, A. I., 1990, *The Call to Personhood: A Christian Theory of the Individual in Social Relationships*, Cambridge: Cambridge University Press.

Mesters, C., 1992, 'The use of the Bible in Christian communities of the common people', in C. Cadorette, M. Giblin et al. (eds), *Liberation Theology: An Introductory Reader*, New York: Orbis Books, pp. 42–55.

Minderoo Foundation, 2018, 'More than 136,000 people are living in modern slavery in the United Kingdom', *Walk Free Global Slavery Index*, 18 July, available from www.globalslaveryindex.org/news/more-than-136000-people-are-living-in-modern-slavery-in-the-united-kingdom/, accessed 14.10.20.

Modern Slavery Act, 2015, available from www.legislation.gov.uk/uk pga/2015/30/part/1/crossheading/offences/enacted, accessed 25.01.21.

Nuhamara, D., 2002, 'The Significance of Critical Theory and Liberation Theologies for Religious Education for Social Transformation',
unpublished doctoral dissertation, Richmond, VA: Union Theological
Seminary and Presbyterian School of Christian Education.

Paris, P. J., 1992, 'The character of liberation ethics', in L. M. Getz and
R. O. Costa (eds), *Struggles for Solidarity: Liberation Theologies in
Tension*, Minneapolis, MN: Fortress Press, pp. 133–40.

Reddie, A. G., 2003, 'Developing a black Christian education of liberation for the British context', *Religious Education* 98(2), Spring,
pp. 221–38.

Rohter, L., 2007, 'As Pope heads to Brazil, a rival theology persists', *New
York Times*, 5 July 2007, available from www.nytimes.com/2007/05/07/
world/americas/07theology.html?pagewanted=1&ei=5089&en=34f
757c655dbef9f&ex=1336190400&partner=rssyahoo&emc=rss,
accessed 20.05.11.

Rowland, C., 1999a, Preface, in C. Rowland (ed.), *The Cambridge
Companion to Liberation Theology*, Cambridge: Cambridge University Press, pp. xiii–xv.

Rowland, C., 1999b, 'Introduction: the theology of liberation', in C.
Rowland (ed.), *The Cambridge Companion to Liberation Theology*,
Cambridge: Cambridge University Press, pp. 1–16.

Ruether, R. R., 1992, 'Feminist theology and interclass/interracial solidarity', in L. M. Getz and R. O. Costa (eds), *Struggles for Solidarity:
Liberation Theologies in Tension*, Minneapolis, MN: Fortress Press,
pp. 49–61.

Schreiter, R. J., 1985, *Constructing Local Theologies*, New York: Orbis
Books.

Segundo, J. L., 1976, *The Liberation of Theology*, trans. J. Drury (orig-
inal version 1975), New York: Orbis Books.

Sobrino, J., 2005, 'Foreword: faith, justice, and injustice', in F. Wijsen,
P. Henriot and P. Mejia (eds), *The Pastoral Circle Revisited: A Critical
Quest for Truth and Transformation*, New York: Orbis Books, pp. ix–
xxii.

Stanley, B., 1990, *The Bible and the Flag: Protestant Mission and British Imperialism in the Nineteenth and Twentieth Centuries*, Leicester:
Apollos.

Sutcliffe-Pratt, D., 2018, *Covenant and Church for Rough Sleepers*,
Occasional Papers, vol. 14, Oxford: Centre for Baptist History and
Heritage.

Turpin, K., 2014, 'Liberationist practical theology', in K. A. Cahalan
and G. S. Misoski (eds), *Opening the Field of Practical Theology: An
Introduction*, Lanham, MD: Rowman & Littlefield, pp. 153–68.

UN, Office of Drugs and Crime, *What Is Human Trafficking?* available
from www.unodc.org/unodc/en/human-trafficking/what-is-human-
trafficking.html, accessed 9.12.20.

Villa-Vicencio, C., 1999, 'Liberation and reconstruction: the unfinished agenda', in C. Rowland (ed.), *The Cambridge Companion to Liberation Theology*, Cambridge: Cambridge University Press, pp. 153–76.

Walls, A. F., 2002, *The Cross-Cultural Process in Christian History*, New York: Orbis Books.

Wielenga, B., 1999, 'Liberation theology in Asia', in C. Rowland (ed.), *The Cambridge Companion to Liberation Theology*, Cambridge: Cambridge University Press, pp. 39–62.

Wijsen, F., Henriot, P. and Mejia, P. (eds), 2005, *The Pastoral Circle Revisited: A Critical Quest for Truth and Transformation*, New York: Orbis Books.

Notes

1 The author's *Covenant and Church for Rough Sleepers* (Sutcliffe-Pratt, 2018) outlines the story and theological journey of being church in the midst of rough sleepers.

2 Refer to Boff, 1970, 1989; Gutiérrez, 1973, 1974; Segundo, 1976.

3 Boff, 1997, p. 107; Rowland, 1999b, p. 5.

4 This praxis approach to education is noted as being influenced by Paulo Freire's 'circle of praxis' (Sobrino, 2005, p. xxi).

5 Clodovis Boff, 1987, *Theology and Praxis: Epistemological Foundations*, New York: Orbis Books.

6 For further information, refer to Boff, 1970; Gutiérrez, 1973; Freire, 1996; Mesters, 1992.

7 Refer to Groome, 1991; Wijsen, Henriot and Mejia, 2005.

8 For further information, refer to Boff, 1970; Gutiérrez, 1973; Mesters, 1992; Freire, 1996; Turpin, 2014.

9 These were offered by Essex University's Social Work and Social Justice Division as well as Essex Police.

10 For further information, refer to Segundo, 1976; Boff, 1997; Green, 2009.

11 Refer to Boff, 1980, 1989.

12 Including Croydon Community Against Trafficking, http://theccat.com, and the Human Trafficking Foundation, www.humantraffickingfoundation.org.

13 With thanks to Kerry Brighouse and the STN Trust for sharing this model of survivor care that they developed in Norwich, Norfolk.

14 Name has been changed. With thanks to the Revd David Mayne, and Shoeburyness and Thorpe Bay Baptist Church for sharing this story.

15 Eastern Baptist Association, www.easternbaptist.org.uk.

16 Refer to www.togetherfree.org.uk.

17 'Modern Slavery and Safeguarding Guide', available from www.togetherfree.org.uk/resources.

8

Restoring What? A Critical and Restorative Justice Response to the 'Modern Slavery' Agenda

MYRA BLYTH AND JOSHUA FINDLAY

In section 1 of this chapter, we seek to problematize the modern slavery and human trafficking (MSHT) lenses through which we are encouraged to understand stories like Amna's, Stella's and Richard's. Their accounts are utterly tragic and should be troubling to us all. But, as we shall show, the MSHT construction predetermines how such stories are told and what conclusions we are supposed to reach. Not only is such a construction unhelpful but, as we shall describe, it amounts to an agenda that is actively harmful to the very people it claims to want to serve. In section 2 we consider one dimension of the problem faced by 'victims of MSHT' and explore through a restorative lens how the criminal justice system, if defined and practised in restorative terms, could enable those caught in exploitation – including those described as 'victims of MSHT' – to engage with the system without fear of being criminalized and re-victimized. In section 3 we consider actions appropriate to the churches' response to the MSHT agenda and the place of restorative principles and practices within these actions.

1 Problematizing modern slavery and human trafficking

The MSHT lens encourages the 'victim', in relaying their experiences, and us the readers in interpreting them, to emphasize or de-emphasize certain details of the story based upon what is highlighted in the publicity materials of anti-trafficking campaigns and the approved framework of state identification mechanisms. As a result, complex real-world problems, largely shaped by state-backed structural factors, are understood in a framework of extreme binaries. Instead of a gradation of power, freedom and opportunity, we are encouraged to understand slavery and freedom as oppositional categories (O'Connell Davidson, 2015). Similarly, rather than people who are put into situations in which only difficult choices are available, both 'victim' and 'trafficker' are robbed of key aspects of their humanity: the 'victim', by being robbed of any agency, conceptually unable to take ownership over any of their decisions for fear of giving up their 'victim' status; and the 'trafficker', whose unexplored profile is dismissed as evil, terrifying, unnecessary and irredeemable. All this takes place with structural factors as a vague and unexplored backdrop. This draws attention away from crucial details that easily go unexamined.

Consider Richard first. He writes:

> I have to ask myself, why did I stay with them so long? One reason is I am a vulnerable person. I wasn't very good at school. Job opportunities weren't very good. I was always thinking at the back of my mind: 'If I go back to England, I'll be on the dole and on benefits.' So I thought, this is better than being on the dole. At least there's a chance of getting some money and doing some work.

It is crucial that we consider the significance of what Richard reveals here. The harrowing story he is relaying should be contextualized within the framework that these words provide. While a minority of cases do involve literal incarceration, in the majority of instances described as MSHT, people evaluate their options and, rather than choosing something ideal, they are often left to choose the most preferable of several deeply unpleasant options. However horrendous this story of MSHT is, it should be understood that Richard considered returning to the UK and living on benefits – where he had previously been abandoned to homelessness – as a less preferable option. Within the binary of MSHT, Richard chose to stay in the realm of 'slavery' rather than return to the 'freedom' of homelessness or living on benefits. This is in no way undermining the hardship or injustice of Richard's circumstances, but rather highlighting that his hardship cannot be understood by focusing solely on the exploitation specifically perpetrated by the 'trafficker'. To what extent can we endorse a moralizing polarization between the 'evil/barbaric trafficker', and the 'good/civilized' British nation, when its victims consider the former preferable to the latter? Given this evaluation, to what extent is our concern over MSHT related to the suffering or the need of those we call its victims? In his narrative, Richard spends little time discussing his homelessness. But this is not what he is being asked to reflect on; he is not being asked to reflect on his suffering per se, but only that which can be specifically related to the practices of the 'trafficker'. In MSHT constructions the fundamental need that lies behind all of this is left as a vague backdrop, only minimally related to what is foregrounded throughout – the villainy of the 'trafficker'.

Consider Stella's story as well. She concludes by talking about running a 10 km race with a T-shirt brandishing the words 'Stop Human Trafficking', but human trafficking definitions do not cover everything included in her narrative. Her time in an immigration detention from August until November should not be perceived as a failing of the state to observe that she was a victim of MSHT. It should be understood as an abusive and exploitative experience equivalent to those perpetrated by non-state individuals. Immigration detention takes people, many of whom have committed no crime, and incarcerates them in repurposed prisons for indefinite periods of time, usually to be released again rather than deported (Phelps, 2010). Studies of the experience of detention show a repeated picture of significant trauma (Robjant, Hassan and Katona, 2009). Detention is found to cause anxiety, PTSD and depression in the majority of people, and the longer the detention the more severe these symptoms become (Keller et al. 2003), with long-term detention causing persistent psychological injury (Sultan and O'Sullivan, 2001). The running of all but one UK detention centre is outsourced to the private companies G4S, Serco, the GEO Group, and Mitie, the last of which won a contract in 2018 valued at over £500m (McIntyre, 2018). These private companies are permitted to pay wages of £1 an hour to those detained, under the dubious rationale that the work is 'voluntary' and is meant to help 'alleviate boredom' (Taylor, 2019, para. 3).

As a number of scholars have noted (O'Connell Davidson, 2016; Gadd and Broad, 2018), all of this is akin to 'modern slavery' when perpetrated without state support. But through the MSHT lens and its focus on the villainy of specific 'traffickers', this is not what Stella is being asked to reflect on. And as it is the state and big business who have the funds to publicize and thereby frame the problem and its solutions, these abusive and exploitative state-capitalist oppressions are unexplored. This is in spite of the fact that such structural oppressions are not just equivalent to circumstances described as MSHT, but underlie the power imbalances that explain how and why instances called MSHT are enabled in the first place. This is evidenced in Stella's story, as with so many 'trafficking' narratives, by the fact that the 'traffickers' prevented her escape by taking away her passport. This action only holds the power that it does in a context where the consequences of not being able to prove one's 'legality' are as dreadful as they are for people like Stella and Amna.

Despite this distracting fixation, the 'trafficker' is not someone we are actually concerned to hear from. While some insightful studies have carried out interview research with people involved in 'trafficking' activities (Mai, 2010; Broad, 2015), the voice of the 'trafficker' is silenced in all mainstream discourse and agendas on MSHT, including in the testimony framing of this book. Even in academic research critical of the dominant discourse, information on 'traffickers' has largely been sought through 'victim' testimonies, but these present a very limited perspective on motivations and operations, particularly if there is little contact between the 'trafficker' and the 'victim' (Broad, 2018). Given the lack of 'trafficker' testimonies to include in our contemplation (and not wishing to present imagined counter-narratives to those provided by Amna, Richard and Stella), we shall instead illustrate from existing knowledge why the blanket demonization of the 'trafficker' may be ill-judged.

The presentation of the 'trafficker' in popular discourse has been well recorded. Through emotive narratives 'traffickers' are portrayed as 'evil' (Aradau, 2004, p. 261) and, furthermore, a 'foreign evil' (Chacón, 2010, p. 1631). Traffickers are presented as social and spatial outsiders to the community (Molland, 2010). The threat that 'their' ways, morals and behaviours are not like 'ours' is intrinsic to the concept of the 'trafficker'. Slavery is seen as the mark of a pre-capitalist barbarism, brought into society by foreign, uncivilized men (Anderson, 2013). 'Traffickers' are subjected to a 'double narrative' (Molland, 2012, p. 57). On the one hand, there is a strong emphasis on 'traffickers' adapting to changing markets and anti-trafficking measures (Molland, 2012), connected with state-backed insistence that 'trafficking' is conducted by organized crime groups (see Home Office, 2014). On the other hand, the 'trafficker' is often depicted as interacting at a very informal level (Molland, 2012), even involving the abuse of familial trust (Gregoriou and Ras, 2018). In this way, the 'trafficker' can morph into whatever is most terrifying – an idea that is freely endorsed by culture and media. In 2019, the BBC showed two crime drama series concurrently, *Shetland* (Anderson and Sieb, 2019) and *Baptiste* (Sigþórsson, 2019), which both had 'human trafficking' storylines in which the 'traffickers' targeted the families of the detectives who were investigating their crimes. The picture given is one of immense power, invasive knowledge, and insidious integration of the criminal world into 'civilized' society. Such narratives help to nurture the idea that the threat to the 'trafficking victim' is a threat to us all.

But research with those involved in trafficking activity presents a different picture. When the power of the state has been wielded to construct scarcity, vulnerability and fear among any given population, the power play among the subjugated people will inevitably be unstable. But this does not mean that positions are fixed in such environments. Prior victimizations can provide pathways into roles that the criminal justice system prosecutes as 'trafficking' (Broad, 2015). Indeed, it is often the less powerful people in hierarchical enterprises who are 'successfully' prosecuted because of the amount of time they spend with 'victims' (Kangaspunta, 2015). Those who are seen as aiding and abetting 'traffickers' in one context may be regarded as personally coerced in another (Viuhko and Jokinen, 2009). In the UK, data sources on those convicted of 'trafficking' offences show a lack of previous convictions, especially for activity associated with organized crime (Broad, 2018). Instead, the same study found that social restrictions and exclusions – such as immigration controls, a lack of access to services, problems accessing employment or 'legitimate' income sources, and homelessness – were important factors for understanding their engagement in 'trafficking' activity (Broad, 2018). These are essentially the same factors as leave victims of so-called MSHT in such exploitative circumstances. This is important, among many other reasons, for showing the commonality across 'victims' and 'traffickers' in MSHT situations.

The shared subjugation that 'victim' and 'trafficker' can experience within wider structural systems does not just precede their shared encounter, but continues to run parallel throughout the response of the MSHT agenda. Initial anti-trafficking interventions are often feared and resisted by those later presented as 'victims' (Soderlund, 2005; Mai, 2013), and police raids subject all parties to state intervention. While those identified as 'traffickers' can experience prosecution, incarceration and deportation, those marked as 'victims' often tread a similar journey despite government claims about protecting and supporting them.

One can easily see why many people refuse referral into the National Referral Mechanism (NRM), the government framework for supposedly identifying and supporting MSHT victims, because of well-founded fears of what interacting with government will bring about, and many others enter because of misinformation about what the NRM is really like, and what its consequences could be. The NRM is not simply subordinate to the government's prioritized anti-migrant agenda, as many have claimed (ATMG, 2013; Roberts, 2019); it is part of the government's anti-migrant agenda, serving all of the same purposes. More generally, the role that anti-trafficking agendas serve in anti-migrant politics has been well established (Chapkis, 2003; Agustín, 2007; Nieuwenhuys and Pécoud, 2007; Anderson, Sharma and Wright, 2009; O'Connell Davidson, 2010; Lewis and Waite, 2015). Through MSHT interventions, 'traffickers' and 'victims' can both be subject to greater interaction with the state, further vulnerabilization, incarceration and deportation, all of which should be understood by anyone who contemplates facilitating the government's efforts in 'defeating modern slavery' (May, 2016, para. 1).

To understand the burgeoning of MSHT agendas, we must understand the neoliberal era. Our current age is defined by state apparatuses being wielded to the benefit of corporate capitalism, not least in the ever-changing regulations on immigration control, which are constructed for the primary purpose of minimizing the freedoms of migrants. Those who enter the country and fill the multiplicity of jobs at the bottom end of the economy are not embraced as citizens, with the rights, protections and acknowledgement of their humanity that this would entail. Instead, they are included under substantial restrictions over things like where they can work, what sector they can work in, who they can work for, what hours they can work, what support and services they are entitled to, whether they can get married, and how long they can stay. Such restrictions are constructed in order to decrease freedom, which increases vulnerability. This vulnerability is intentionally created in order to form a sub-class of society that can then be exploited in the fractured supply chains of corporate capitalism.

Enter the 'modern slavery' agenda, which mostly focuses on situations that fall outside the mainstream economy: sexual exploitation, domestic servitude, nail bars, stories of tarmacking enterprises – like the one Richard was working for – or the entirely overblown fixation on car washes. Why should these industries in particular be the focus of MSHT campaigns? Is there less exploitation in the supply chains that manufacture the products in our high street stores? Less abuse? Less suffering? No. But in those situations, the money is rising to the top of the economy, to the wealthiest and most powerful. And this is the crux of why MSHT campaigns are given so much attention and championed by governments and businesses alike. Those who run car washes tend to belong to the same socio-economic class as the people who work in them. Many 'bosses' will be subject to all of the same kind of restrictions as their workers, and for them to be profiting from the work of someone who has been vulnerabilized by state practices goes against every objective of neoliberal economics, which is about the upward movement of all money and power. Those people were made to be vulnerable so that big business could profit from them, not so that the poor and subjugated could profit from them instead.

Most of the conversations about the government's treatment of 'victims of MSHT' are therefore framed in a totally mis-guided way. Reifying MSHT, as if it denotes a specific kind of suffering, exploitation, trauma or need, depends on a privileged ignorance of the difficult decisions that subjugated people have to make in conditions imposed by state structures. Understand-ing this is important for understanding why anti-trafficking and anti-slavery measures are not just insufficient, but are them-selves deeply harmful.

This is not to disparage the sometimes remarkable work of certain organizations, and particularly of the people within them, who work hard to support the abused and champion them against further subjugation. But such workers are pushed into adopting MSHT language and constructions in order to interact and advocate for their clients within a system that will not listen to them if they do not. Services that work to meet people's needs and to advocate on their behalf in an adversarial system are important. But this should not be misconstrued as validating or legitimizing the language or actions made permis-sible through the MSHT construction.

All of this is lost in the wealth of state-capitalist campaigns.

And so without sufficient criticality, it is understandable that some parts of the Church have absorbed the MSHT construction wholesale, and put themselves at the service of the state. Just like many frontline services, posters and classes are now prevalent in UK churches encouraging parishioners to 'spot the signs' of 'modern slavery'. But what effect do such campaigns have?

Despite the best intentions, the Clewer Initiative's deeply problematic 'Car Wash' app[1] encourages people to look at small businesses run by poor migrants, and to ask questions like: 'Do workers have access to suitable clothing?' and 'Is there evidence of workers living on site?' These questions presuppose that poverty is of itself suspicious, and such observations of poverty become potential signs of 'modern slavery'. What else can we call this but stark discrimination against poor communities in our country who are trying to survive based on the same business principles as the wealthy, because nothing more inclusive is available to them? One can easily imagine how such scrutiny from the community comes across to new arrivals: 'We arrived in the country two weeks ago and have not yet made enough money for hazmat suits, so the locals think my dad's a slave driver and I'm a slave!' We have to understand that these locations are not just sites of potential exploitation; they are also the places in which people exercise what little freedom they have. Working at the local car wash is, for many, the preferred option. Ignoring this, the solution from the Office of the Independent Anti-Slavery Commissioner is to call for stricter enforcement of environmental regulations for car washes (Jardine, Trautrims and Kenway, 2018). This effort to throw the book at small businesses (as if car washes, not transnational corporations, are destroying the earth), forcibly shutting them down under the weight of rules and regulations, takes away a valuable choice for many marginalized people. Do businesses that profit the rich receive such scrutiny? No, on the contrary, corporate capitalism experiences pitiful regulation. But for the small-scale car wash, boss and worker alike will have little choice but to join other subjugated migrants who are being funnelled into the precarious world of fractured supply chains (except when being detained or deported in the process of their 'rescue'/prosecution). Through such measures it is the 'anti-slavery' campaigns that are not only reducing people's options but also serving the interests of corporate capitalism in the process.

It is very common for those working in car washes who are identified by frontline workers as 'potential victims of modern slavery' to insist they are not victims, that they want to be there, and that this is where they can make the most money. This gets reframed by government, the police and charities in the most infantilizing ways: 'It is difficult to spot [signs of modern slavery] because often victims don't even know they are being exploited.'[2] This is weak representation. They are rejecting the framework that ignores their circumstances and robs them of agency. They are often aware, whether frontline staff are or not, of what state intervention could really mean for them.

By trying to construct an agenda addressing 'exploitation' that excludes the basic tenets of state capitalism from the picture, MSHT campaigners guarantee that their understanding of the problem will not properly fit on to the experiences of many of those they try to 'save', and their 'solutions' will often result in unwelcome short- and long-term consequences. What is often couched as 're-trafficking' or returning to the 'trafficker', and is attributed to coercive control or Stockholm syndrome, is often an extension of this rejection of the 'trafficking' construction, as people evaluate their options and act accordingly (see Mai, 2010). What is more, no one can have their humanity truly recognized, neither the 'victim' nor the 'trafficker', if the circumstances that inform their decisions are dismissed out of hand. Only by understanding both the interests that the MSHT agenda serves, and the ultimate effects of the campaigns on the vulnerabilized people they interact with, can we see why it is such an unhelpful construction. From there we can allow ourselves to see all parties involved in these real-world situations for the human beings they really are.

2 Justice for victims of MSHT

Having problematized the 'modern slavery' and 'human traffick-ing' lenses, the question becomes: what can be done – and by whom – to bring justice to victims of exploitation, some of whom are currently called 'victims of MSHT'? How do we change the way society sees and responds to victims of exploit-ation, and their often also victimized exploiters? The root causes of social and economic exploitation highlighted in this chapter's analysis of the MSHT agenda point to the need for deep structural changes in our social and political infrastruc-ture. These will not happen without fresh political will and vision, and for that to happen it needs academics, practitioners and grassroots activists working together to change hearts and minds on a whole range of social justice issues. One battle-front among many in this multi-faceted struggle for social and struc-tural transformation concerns the criminal justice system. The current criminal justice system is in crisis and many people who work within it, or whose work intersects with it, are calling for alternative models of justice, such as procedural, restorative and transitional, to replace – or at least complement – the cur-rent retributive system. Over the last five decades in and around the edges of the criminal justice system, the restorative justice movement (comprising lawyers, academics and restorative practitioners) has been advocating a vision of justice that is relational rather than adversarial and restorative rather than retributive, and for a restructuring of the legal system in order to respond to crime according to restorative justice principles and practices. The call for a more restorative approach comes also from the victims of crime, including 'victims of MSHT'. Research shows that those identified as 'victims' are looking for a very different response from the justice system to cases of MSHT, including a more compassionate approach by jus-tice stakeholders, an end to the criminalization of survivors, greater diversity in recruitment by law-enforcement agencies, and improving training for system actors (Hussemann et al., 2018).

The churches have a long track record as advocates for penal reform, and Christians have been at the forefront of the restorative justice movement. So in a book that seeks to map the response of the churches to MSHT, this part of the chapter explores how reforming the justice system in a restorative direction is one change, among many, needed if society's response to 'victims of MSHT' is going to meet their basic needs and rights.

To be clear on what a restorative response to victims of exploitation might entail, a brief overview of the origins and inspiration for restorative justice is necessary, including consideration of its core principles and conceptual roots. The beginnings of the modern restorative justice debate are often credited to articles by Christie (1977), Barnett (1977) and Eglash (1977). Christie argues that the conflict between citizens has been stolen by the state. His point is that, by restricting criminal procedures and laws to the narrow legal definitions of professionals and specialists, society has been robbed of the opportunity to establish its own norms and procedures for dealing with conflict. The strength and appeal of restorative justice are that it seeks to reclaim the space necessary for victims and the wider community to participate in norm setting. In doing so it calls for a re-examination of the assumptions underlying the present system and proposes a new paradigm for justice based not on punishment but on restitution. Barnett (1977, p. 280) describes the criminal justice system as being in 'the death throes of an old and cumbersome paradigm, one that has dominated Western thought for more than 900 years'. Frustrated by the normal court system, Barnett started to experiment with new ways of dealing with crime, and in the process realized that the needs of victims, offenders and the community were not separate, but instead interdependent issues that the justice agencies needed to address together. The first comprehensive account of restorative justice as an alternative paradigm to the traditional justice system is widely attributed to Zehr, whose seminal 1990 book *Changing Lenses* suggests that justice needs to be viewed through a restorative lens rather than a retributive one. The retributive lens views justice as abstract and impersonal while the restorative lens views justice as relational. In stark terms he compares the two perspectives, as shown in Table 1 (Zehr, 2005, pp. 184–5)[3]:

Table 1 Restorative and retributive justice compared

Retributive lens	Restorative lens
Crime defined by violation of rules (i.e. broken rules)	Crime defined by harm to people and relationships (i.e. broken relationships)
Harms defined abstractly	Harms defined concretely
Crime seen as categorically different from other harms	Crime recognized as related to other harms and conflicts
State as victim	People and relationships as victims
State and offender seen as primary parties	Victim and offender seen as primary parties
Victim's needs and rights ignored	Victim's needs and rights central
Interpersonal dimensions irrelevant	Interpersonal dimensions central
Wounds of offender peripheral	Wounds of offender important
Offence defined in technical, legal terms	Offence understood in full context: moral, social, economic, political

In the light of this alternative vision of justice, Zehr called for a different way of addressing and approaching the problem of crime and punishment. From his vision of justice, three core principles can be extrapolated that will be foundational to this discussion on a renewed approach in criminal justice to cases currently characterized as MSHT. The first principle (radical participation) reflects how in restorative justice the offender, victim and community are participants, not spectators, in the judicial process. The second principle (righting wrong in a morally serious way) puts the focus less on punishing wrongdoing and more on establishing and maintaining right relationships; it seeks to establish what happened, to name the harm done, and to agree on what is needed for the hurt to be repaired and for victim, offender and community to be restored. The third principle (reintegration) underlines that restorative justice is forward-looking and transformative, looking to reintegrate the lives of those affected by crime and wrongdoing back into mainstream society, in ways by which they can live unhindered by the past.

If now we take these principles and apply them to Amna's, Stella's and Richard's stories, what will we discover?

Radical participation

Stella's repeated cry was for justice. She looked to the justice system for answers but was frustrated because her perception of justice, as with the majority of 'victims of MSHT', was not just about punishing her 'trafficker', it is about being able to move on, free from the 'trafficker', and being empowered by the process to recover dignity and agency. Restorative justice advocates the radical participation of key stakeholders ('harmers' and 'harmed') because it is through real and empowering participation, not passive or partial participation, in the processes of justice that freedom and agency are realized. Stella, like most victims, wants more than anything to be able to move on, free from the threat of the 'trafficker' and able to regain a normal life. She wants Rodrigo punished and future victims protected, but justice involves much more than this. She wants to have a voice in the legal procedure where her 'trafficker' is sentenced. She wants to be able to influence the outcomes so that she can restore her agency, enjoy freedom and find healing. Research shows that what 'victims of MSHT' want is to be treated as subjects not objects; not bystanders in a system that measures success solely in terms of the prosecution of 'traffickers' (Hussemann et al., 2018, pp. 12–13).

Victims of MSHT do not trust the system because experience tells them that in its current form it cannot meet their needs. Many support-agency professionals also share this view. Professional legal actors do not disagree with this, but they argue that the system cannot – and should not – meet these justice demands because it is not designed for such. It exists to prosecute and sentence offenders and its success is measured on these terms. However, given that even on its own terms the system is failing, the call from victims for alternative models deserves to be heard. Survivors of both sex and labour 'trafficking' do not all endorse traditional forms of retributive justice (such as incarceration) for their 'traffickers'. Some maintain instead that justice could be better achieved through alternative routes such as restorative justice (Hussemann et al., 2018, pp. 18–20). This response suggests that victims sometimes see how the 'trafficker' who has harmed them is also somehow caught in a cycle of fear and violence and sees no way out. In the court system, unlike a restorative justice process, the relationship between victim and 'trafficker' is not explored through dialogue, and thus the realization of complex and multiple harms within both the harmed and the harmer is left unaddressed, conveniently put aside by a binary judicial system. This brings us to the second principle.

Moral seriousness: righting wrong in a morally serious way

It is often argued in the legal world that complex and serious crimes are not suitable for alternative models of justice. This has been the reason given for barring cases of sexual abuse from being processed through restorative justice channels. But this is contested in recent research (Zinstagg and Keenan, 2017, pp. 4–5). The danger of re-victimization or of causing more harm is a real concern and certainly means that some cases will not be suitable, but the reality is that some victims want the opportunity to tell their harmer directly the damage they have done, and believe that this will be the only way that they can find closure. It is also the case that when this happens the impact on the harmer can prove to be transformative. By itself it may not be enough to change lifestyle patterns, but as part of a comprehensive approach to meeting needs (housing, employment and mental health provision) the chances of recidivism are reduced and further harm prevented.

Moral seriousness in the restorative justice process is about giving space for people to tell their story, in their own words and without filtering or framing them into a preconceived narrative. The restorative justice conference operates on a very simple conversation script, facilitated not by the legal profession and not in a courtroom scenario, but by a trained practitioner and in the company of a group of people from the community who represent the main actors' wider friends and sphere of influence. In the conference both harmed and harmer tell their story: they recall what happened, what impact this had at the time, and how it has felt since. The conversation moves into the future by asking what needs to be done in order for wrong to be righted, harm to be healed, and closure to be found. The unexpected often happens: tears, empathy, regret, remorse often flow from this honest, costly dialogue. Hardly imaginable given the binary framework of the MSHT narrative, but very conceivable where the process focuses on human relational needs and harms. In this context, the state's word 'trafficker' can lose its value entirely.

Critics of restorative justice call it soft on crime but this is a misconception and/or a gross caricature. Nothing is harder for a harmer than to meet their victim and to account for their actions. Victims often find that not only is their initial expectation met, of letting the harmer know the true impact of their crime, but beyond their expectations in that they learn about aspects of the harmer's story that puts their behaviour into a new context and causes a measure of empathy in the victim that they never expected to feel. There is nothing weak about this process and the outcome does not ignore the element of punishment. The difference is that punishment is framed in restorative terms and the victim has their say in what that outcome needs to include.

By contrast, the integrity and moral seriousness of the current judicial system in cases of 'trafficking' is questioned, in different ways, by victims, legal officials, law-enforcement officials and support-agency providers alike. Interviews with survivors of MSHT, like Amna, Stella and Richard, speak of facing many obstacles in their engagement with law-enforcement officials: past experience with the law can work against their being believed, so they are not seen and acknowledged as victims, or are arrested for activities related to their experiences of exploitation. Service providers offering support to victims criticize the current system for being too convoluted and lengthy to facilitate survivor recovery, which often leads to re-traumatization.

Reintegration

A major flaw in the justice system, also mirrored in part within restorative justice processes, is a lack of rituals of reintegration. Harmed and harmers need help to return into mainstream society. It takes more than just good intention to move on and start again. There needs to be a plausibility structure or community of support that enables good habits and practices to be restored. This includes social structures that enable survivors to find a safe place to live and work to sustain a viable lifestyle. Advocates and practitioners of restorative justice, unlike the legal profession, maintain that this is part of the responsibility of the legal system together with civil society. Leaving prison and leaving the 'trafficker's' snare need to be marked by rituals of restoration and reintegration in order for a new alternative future to become a reality. Braithwaite among others has argued that rituals of reintegration are vital to help harmers to transition back into society (1989, p. 6). Based on the findings of research with harmers and harmed (Blyth, Mills and Taylor, 2020, chapter 1), the restorative justice conference script functions as a ritual of restoration and reintegration for both harmer and harmed.

In spite of the huge progress that has been made in developing restorative justice practice and building the evidence for its effectiveness, many in the legal world remain sceptical about it and try to keep it marginal to the vision and core objectives of the justice system. That struggle will continue for the restorative justice movement and for churches and faith-based organizations like Prison Fellowship. Partnership and participation between statutory and voluntary bodies – including the churches – is not without its problems, as illustrated in section 1, but with care can be nurtured to good effect. A vision of civil society working in this way with the justice system is key in the long term to transforming it. Working to reform the criminal justice system in a restorative direction is, however, but one piece in the larger struggle for social transformation that marginalized and exploited people face, including those termed 'victims of MSHT'. Besides pushing away at incremental change to the criminal justice system, the churches need a broader overall response to the MSHT agenda, as seen in the next section, where we explore a range of actions for the churches together with the place of restorative justice principles and practices within those actions.

3 Proposed action for churches

This final section proposes four areas of action where churches can respond in solidarity with the vulnerabilized and exploited, including those caught up in the MSHT agenda.

Education: *unlearning and learning afresh*

Churches and faith-based actors should educate themselves, their congregations and anyone else who will listen about the politico-economic roots of the problem affecting both 'trafficker' and 'victim'. In particular, they should avoid buying in to the current state narrative described and analysed in this chapter. Only by busting the myth of the MSHT narrative can the agenda be re-set according to the needs of those trapped in exploitation because of systemic injustices that made them vulnerable.

The MSHT agenda should stand as a warning to the Church about the consequences of looking to the most oppressive institutions of our day to define injustice for us. The degree of collaboration between churches and third-sector organizations with government is unsettling. It results in a situation in which even the most compassionate people become servants to the most brutal policies, simply because of a lack of criticality when listening to the claims of our governing institutions. The first mistake is assuming that the government is genuine in its concern, and that the effect of its encounters with vulnerable people will be positive for these people in the long run. The Catholic Church, the Church of England and the Salvation Army have all sought to throw their weight of support behind state-led enterprises, citing inappropriate parallels to Wilberforce and the transatlantic slave trade, and the Church's role in its abolition. While acknowledging the compassion, hard work and personal support provided by individuals within these organizations, we observe that where once the Salvation Army collided with opposing authorities,[4] it is now the gentle face placed in front of the most oppressive immigration controls in the history of the British nation state, where criticism of policy might risk loss of substantial government funding.[5]

After his long and appalling ordeal, Richard graciously writes: 'The most helpful thing in recovering is the help I've received from the church and other people within the community. They tried to make it as easy as possible.' This is who the Church can be: a church that is concerned to meet the needs of the needy, rather than the needs of the exploited, can be a church that helps prevent exploitation and abuse in the first place, or bring restoration where harm has been done. Leafleting homeless people with information about 'modern slavery' will not alter the decision they later face between a winter on the streets and the offer of work from a passer-by. Only the provision of accommodation can do that. The question we have to ask ourselves is this: what do we really care about?

Systemic change: where we cannot reform the whole system, we must work for incremental change

The work of churches and faith-based organizations must keep substantial social transformation as a goal, and when reforming a whole system is not possible – for example, when seeking to reform the criminal justice system – then a patient, persistent incremental-change approach is needed. The key danger for faith-based organizations, including those working to promote anti-slavery campaigns, is not maintaining sufficient independence when in a funding partnership with the state, thereby muting their critical voice. At what point does cooperating with and working within the system damage the Church's potential for being a critical voice, or for protecting victims who are afraid to engage with the system?

We must tread with care. 'Victims' of MSHT, so identified by the government, are not entitled to any rights beyond a few weeks after their 'conclusive' identification as a 'genuine victim'. This means that they, like their 'trafficker', are liable for state-enforced deportation, detention or destitution, further preventing the possibility of restoration. For this reason, until such a time as the criminal justice system is substantially transformed, communities and churches are much more likely sites for 'victims of MSHT' to find restorative engagement, where the needy, the exploited and the abusive can come and have their needs met, engage in dialogue, heal harm and reform character, all free from the threatening involvement of the state. Churches could serve this important purpose – if only, that is, we can start looking for the needy and the desperate, and stop looking for 'signs of modern slavery'.

Churches have historically offered sanctuary to those who are vulnerable and on the margins of society and legality. Listening to the voices of victims and exploiters/abusers is key to re-setting the justice agenda according to the experience and needs of those trapped in exploitation. By drawing upon restorative principles and practices and working with trained restorative justice facilitators, the faith sector can provide spaces where the stories of victims can be heard without fear of being demonized or criminalized. For this to be developed, not for the victims but *with* them, careful collaborative work is necessary to build trust between the stakeholders: victims, exploiters, churches, faith-based agencies and restorative justice practitioners. The principle of radical participation applies here on several levels: first, by giving priority to the voices of the marginalized; second, by opening up opportunities for third-sector actors (in this case, churches and restorative justice practitioners) to offer a restorative approach to cases of trafficking; and third, by prioritizing a community-based, restorative approach to righting wrong rather than a crime-based punitive approach.

Solidarity: stand alongside and advocate with exploited people to prevent structures and systems doing more harm

Solidarity involves advocating for rights and protections that people can build their lives upon. Victim rights are transient, and as such we would point to faith-based organizations and churches that champion more fundamental rights: status to be in the country, access to public services, housing, workers' rights and human rights, as well as drawing on the time, monetary and land resources of church members. This means opening up homes and church premises, providing administrative, educational or legal support, and direct financial giving, as well as advocating for people within the asylum system and similar bureaucratic processes. A good example can be found at Cemetery Road Baptist Church in Sheffield,[6] where diversity is embraced in worship, in leadership and in active support of asylum seekers in their community.

Champion restorative practices: nurture restorative culture by practising and embedding restorative values within institutions

While remaining absolutely clear that working and campaigning for real change is essential, without which the rest is something of a betrayal, the churches should consider how they can be communities of 'restoration'. We offer two suggestions here: 1) modelling restorative practices when division and tension arise in their congregations, and 2) identifying where in the community restorative justice principles can be applied to bring people together to cooperate on shared problems rather than perpetuating division and discord.

The initiative of New Road Baptist Church in Oxford is an interesting example of a local congregation looking to embed restorative justice practices into its life and mission[7]. The church is located at the heart of the city, which provides it with amazing opportunities to offer hospitality and welcome to thousands of shoppers, tourists and retailers as well as to a vibrant international student population. The church has a long history and a strong tradition as a radical non-conformist congregation. Its founding members were true pioneers, denominating themselves as a 'Protestant Catholic Church of Christ' and welcoming into membership those who held different views on baptism (Chadwick, 2003, p. 401). Today the church aspires to continue in that same generous and courageous spirit by embedding restorative principles and practices into its life and mission. Church meetings and leadership meetings use restorative practices as a means to ensure that every voice is heard, and that decisions result from collective discernment processes. For example, restorative practices and techniques – ranging from circle time techniques to global café-style events – enabled a collective vision-setting exercise over 24 months that re-imagined the ministry of the church and informed the appointment of a new minister. This intentional way of attending to how decisions are reached has injected new energy and meaning into Baptist convictions about congregational governance and every-member ministry. Likewise, by using restorative principles and practices such as those advocated in the groundbreaking resource 'Creating Sanctuary',[8] the church has moved gently and consensually over the last five years towards receiving into the fellowship, and into the leadership team, members of the LGBTQ community.

Looking outwards into the city, the church has adopted the same strategy and has founded the Oxford Centre for Restorative Practice,[9] which brings together people of all faiths and none to promote and facilitate restorative practice in the city. The Centre has brokered many conversations and partnerships across the city, and has advocated the case for restorative practices through networking events, and provided training and support of employers and employees who seek to change the culture of their working environments from discord and division to collaboration and trust. Through the work of the

Centre the church has found a place at the table of policy decision-makers in the city and the county, and has won their trust through delivering valuable training and support services. The church is demonstrating in small but significant ways how practical action and policy development are both being re-imagined by restorative principles and practices.

In all of the above we have sought to re-ground our understanding of exploitation and harm in a realistic evaluation of the politics of our day, and to humanize the representations of, and responses to, all those who bear the heaviest cost of structural harm. Re-examining the MSHT agenda illustrates that, when it comes to loving our neighbour, we need a critical posture towards authorities and a restorative and compassionate response to those most ostracized by dominant agendas.

Bibliography

Agustín, L. M., 2007, *Sex at the Margins*, London: Zed Books.

Anderson, B., 2013, *Us and Them? The Dangerous Politics of Immigration Control*, Oxford: Oxford University Press.

Anderson, B., Sharma, N. and Wright, C., 2009, 'Editorial: why no borders?', *Refuge* 26(2), pp. 5–18.

Anderson, G. and Sieb, I., 2019, *Shetland*, London: BBC.

Aradau, C., 2004, 'The perverse politics of four-letter words: risk and pity in the securitisation of human trafficking', *Journal of International Studies* 33(2), pp. 251–77.

ATMG, 2013, *Hidden in Plain Sight – Three Years On: Updated Analysis of UK Measures to Protect Trafficked Persons*, London: ATMG.

Barnett, R. E., 1977, 'Restitution: a new paradigm of criminal justice', *Ethics* 87(4), pp. 279–301.

Blyth, M., Mills, M. and Taylor, M., 2020, 'Restoring lives', manuscript submitted for publication.

Braithwaite, J., 1989, *Crime, Shame and Reintegration*, Cambridge: Cambridge University Press.

Broad, R., 2015, '"A vile and violent thing": female traffickers and the criminal justice response', *British Journal of Criminology* 55(6), pp. 1058–75.

Broad, R., 2018, 'Assessing convicted traffickers: negotiating migration, employment and opportunity through restricted networks', *Howard Journal of Crime and Justice* 57(1), pp. 37–56.

Chacón, J. M., 2010, 'Tensions and trade-offs: protecting trafficking victims in the era of immigration enforcement', *University of Pennsylvania Law Review* 158(6), pp. 1609–53.

Chadwick, R. (ed.), 2003, *A Protestant Catholic Church of Christ*, Oxford: New Road Baptist Church.

Chapkis, W., 2003, 'Trafficking, migration, and the law: protecting innocents, punishing immigrants', *Gender and Society* 17(6), pp. 923–37.

Christie, N., 1977, 'Conflicts as property', *British Journal of Criminology* 17(1), pp. 1–15.

Eglash, A., 1977, 'Beyond restitution: creative restitution', in J. Hudson and B. Galaway (eds), *Restitution in Criminal Justice: A Critical Assessment of Sanctions*, Lexington, KY: Lexington Books.

Gadd, D. and Broad, R., 2018, 'Troubling recognitions in British responses to modern slavery', *British Journal of Criminology* 58(6), pp. 1440–61.

Gregoriou, C. and Ras, I. A., 2018, '"Call for purge on the people traffickers": an investigation into British newspapers' representation of transnational human trafficking, 2000–2016', in C. Gregoriou (ed.), *Representations of Transnational Human Trafficking: Present-day News Media, True Crime, and Fiction*, eBook: Palgrave Macmillan, pp. 25–60.

Home Office, 2014, *Modern Slavery: How the UK is Leading the Fight*, London: Home Office.

Hussemann, J. et al., 2018, *Bending Towards Justice: Perceptions of Justice among Human Trafficking Survivors*, Washington DC: Urban Institute.

Jardine, A., Trautrims, A. and Kenway, E., 2018, 'Labour exploitation in hand car washes', available at www.antislaverycommissioner.co.uk/media/1238/labour-exploitation-in-hand-car-washes.pdf, accessed 20.11.20.

Kangaspunta, K., 2015, 'Was trafficking in persons really criminalised?', *Anti-Trafficking Review* no. 4.

Keller, A. S. et al., 2003, 'Mental health of detained asylum seekers', *Lancet* 362(9397), pp. 1721–3.

Lewis, H. and Waite, L., 2015, 'Asylum, immigration restrictions and exploitation: hyper-precarity as a lens for understanding and tackling forced labour', *Anti-Trafficking Review* no. 5, pp. 49–67.

Mai, N., 2010, 'The psycho-social trajectories of Albanian and Romanian "traffickers"', *ISET* no. 17, London.

Mai, N., 2013, 'Embodied cosmopolitanisms: the subjective mobility of migrants working in the global sex industry', *Gender, Place and Culture* 20(1), pp. 107–24.

May, T., 2016, 'My government will lead the way in defeating modern slavery', *The Daily Telegraph*, available www.gov.uk/government/

speeches/defeating-modern-slavery-theresa-may-article, accessed 20.11.20.

McCoy, E. et al., 2018, *Delivering Justice for Human Trafficking Survivors*, Washington DC: Urban Institute.

McIntyre, N., 2018, 'Private contractors paid millions to run UK detention centres', *The Guardian*, available at www.theguardian.com/uk-news/2018/oct/10/private-contractors-paid-millions-uk-detention-centres-some-firms-making-30-percent-profit, accessed 20.11.20.

Molland, S., 2010, '"the perfect business": human trafficking and Lao-Thai cross-border migration', *Development and Change* 41(5), pp. 831–55.

Molland, S., 2012, 'The inexorable quest for trafficking hotspots along the Thai-Lao border', in W. van Schendel, L. Lyons and M. Ford (eds), *Labour Migration and Human Trafficking in Southeast Asia: Critical Perspectives*, Abingdon: Taylor & Francis, pp. 57–74.

Nieuwenhuys, C. and Pécoud, A., 2007, 'Human trafficking, information campaigns, and strategies of migration control', *American Behavioral Scientist* 50(12), pp. 1674–95.

O'Connell Davidson, J., 2010, 'New slavery, old binaries: human trafficking and the borders of "Freedom"', *Global Networks* 10(2), pp. 244–61.

O'Connell Davidson, J., 2015, *Modern Slavery: The Margins of Freedom*, London: Palgrave Macmillan.

O'Connell Davidson, J., 2016, 'De-canting "trafficking in human beings", re-centring the state', *International Spectator* 51(1), pp. 58–73.

O'Nolan, C., Keenan M. and Zinsstag, E., 2018, 'Researching "under the radar" practices: exploring restorative practices in sexual violence cases', *Temida* (Journal of Victimology Society of Serbia) 21(1), pp. 107–29.

Phelps, J., 2010, *No Return, No Release, No Reason: Challenging Indefinite Detention*, London: London Detainee Support Group.

Roberts, K., 2019, 'Human trafficking: addressing the symptom, not the cause', in G. Craig et al. (eds), *The Modern Slavery Agenda: Policy, Politics and Practice in the UK*, Bristol: Polity Press, pp. 145–66.

Robjant, K., Hassan, R. and Katona, C., 2009, 'Mental health implications of detaining asylum seekers: systematic review', *British Journal of Psychiatry* 194(4), pp. 306–12.

Sigþórsson, B., 2019, *Baptiste*, London: BBC.

Soderlund, G., 2005, 'Running from the rescuers: New U. S. crusades against sex trafficking and the rhetoric of abolition', *NWSA Journal* 17(3), pp. 64–87.

Sultan, A. and O'Sullivan, K., 2001, 'Psychological disturbances in asylum seekers held in long term detention: a participant-observer account', *Medical Journal of Australia* 175(11–12), pp. 593–6.

Taylor, D., 2019, 'Judge rules £1/hr wages for immigration detainees are lawful', *The Guardian*, available at www.theguardian.com/uk-news/2019/mar/27/judge-rules-1hr-wages-lawful-for-immigration-centre-detainees, accessed 20.11.20.

Viuhko, M. and Jokinen, A., 2009, *Human Trafficking and Organised Crime: Trafficking for Sexual Exploitation and Organised Procuring in Finland*, Helsinki: European Institute for Crime Prevention and Control.

Zehr, H., 2005, *Changing Lenses: Restorative Justice for Our Times*, 3rd edn, Scottdale, PA: Herald Press.

Zinstagg, E. and Keenan, M. (eds), 2017, *Restorative Responses to Sexual Violence: Legal, Social and Therapeutic Dimensions*, London: Routledge, pp. 4–5.

Notes

1 www.theclewerinitiative.org/safecarwash, accessed 20.11.20.

2 www.hopeforjustice.org/news/2017/08/modern-slavery-in-uk-even-more-widespread-than-previously-thought, accessed 20.11.20.

3 From *Changing Lenses: Restorative Justice for Our Times* by Howard Zehr, © 2015 Herald Press. All rights reserved; used with permission.

4 www.salvationarmy.org.uk/about-us/international-heritage-centre/international-heritage-centre-blog/opposition, accessed 20.11.20; https://www.salvationarmy.org.uk/news/salvation-army-awarded-new-government-modern-slavery-contract, accessed 20.11.20.

5 The total value of the Home Office tender is stated as £281 million: https://ted.europa.eu/udl?uri=TED:NOTICE:353051-2020:TEXT:EN:HTML, accessed 20.11.20.

6 www.crbchurch.org.uk, accessed 20.11.20.

7 www.newroad.org.uk/mission-statement, accessed 20.11.20.

8 www.creatingsanctuary.org.uk, accessed 20.11.20.

9 The Mint House, Oxford's Centre for Restorative Practice (www.minthouseoxford.co.uk, accessed 20.11.20), was founded and is supported by New Road Baptist Church, and through its minister and members is working with restorative justice practitioners across the city to promote restorative justice practices in a number of contexts and institutions, most notably training NHS staff.

9

Suffering, Slavery and Participating in the Triune God

PAUL S. FIDDES

In the doctrine of the Holy Trinity, early Christian thinkers were finding a concept to express and communicate an experience. They were living in a community where they believed that they were experiencing the presence of the Christ who had been crucified but was now risen from death, and that this happened especially when they shared a meal together. They had inherited stories and sayings of the Christ from some who had experienced his presence as Jesus of Nazareth, and hearing these stories and sayings increased their sense of encountering the risen Lord. They were experiencing an energy and had received gifts for living which was like a new breath in their bodies – 'Spirit' – in circumstances where many were still enslaved persons, and yet where all felt they had been liberated from pressures upon them from outside and within that had been spoiling life.

In this situation it was no longer possible just to say the word 'God', even if they had come to call this God by the intimate word 'Father' at the express bidding of the Christ. Their experience of the richness and depth of relationships in which they were living, among themselves and with God, compelled them to confess that God was 'Father, Son and Holy Spirit'. They found themselves journeying in strange spiritual territory in which they had to find new words, and where they had to experiment with old words (like spirit, wisdom, word, *Logos*) in new ways. The technical concepts theologians developed later – that God was one holy and unique reality and yet also three distinct realities (one *ousia*, three *hypostases*) – were only a kind of grammar for a language they were already speaking out of their experience. They were actually *sharing* in the life of this triune God. Further, as they reflected on their experience and their words, they came to realize that in some way this vision of God must be relevant not only for their own small community, often meeting secretly for fear of persecution from a larger society, but for all humanity and even for the whole cosmos (see Colossians 1.15–20).

Since the doctrine of a triune God gradually emerged like this in a community of people who were experiencing suffering and slavery, and if we today accept their conviction that this God embraces all people, it ought to be possible to place the experience of modern slavery in this context too, and for this to be a meaningful thing to do. But we come immediately to a problem. People who are the victims of modern slavery have been exploited and manipulated, and it would increase the wrong for theologians to use their experience for the benefit of theologizing. Theology too can be a means of exploitation. Might it then be better to follow those who urge that we should simply listen respectfully to the stories of those who are, and have been enslaved – such as the stories in Part 2 of this book – and be silent? (cf. Surin, 1980, p. 162). I am, nevertheless, going to take the risk of theological reflection, with the hope that it might assist in trying to 'see' the enslaved, and to motivate us to overcome a terrible wrong inflicted on fellow human beings. Reflection on the stories of Amna, Stella and Richard will also be to receive from them the gift of talking about God ('theology' as God-talk), and deepening our understanding of God's own painful experience of the world. I aim not to impose on the enslaved an experience that is not genuinely theirs, and at the outset I ask forgiveness from them for any element of exploitation that might remain.

A context of invisibility

In all three stories we can see that there was a hidden enslavement, an intolerable cruelty happening while the mass of the world continued with its daily life unseeing and unregarding (*We See You*, n.d., pp. 8–9; cf. Quirk and O'Connell Davidson, 2015, pp. 112–15). At times this was a literal imprisonment, as Stella was locked in a house all day until she was taken out at night to work on the street under a watchful eye, or Richard was confined in a freezing truck until he was called out to a tarring job, or Amna was shut up in the house where she was working in England under threat of being notified to the immigration authorities. At other times those enslaved were 'hidden in plain sight', their plight unknown – or not properly known – to those who came into contact with them. Amna recalls that while she was in India people were scared of interacting with her, and her husband behaved well to her when other people were around; people met Stella on the streets or abused her there, and others must have seen her travelling from place to place as the prostitution racket moved addresses; customers and suppliers certainly met Richard on his back-breaking tarmac jobs, as did the Austrian police whom, he notes, 'never asked if I was OK' and 'weren't bothered about me'. Similar stories could surely be told of people coming into contact in the course of travel or work with fruit-pickers enslaved in a work-gang, or children running 'county lines' with drugs, or young women working under constraint in nail bars, or those offering hand washes for cars, or those taking young children out for walks who seem strangely subdued and who avoid contact with others. It seems an irony of modern slavery that, unlike lines of enslaved persons labouring out in the open in the cotton or sugar fields of the American South or British Jamaica, modern victims are unseen and unheard, trafficked across borders in a hidden slave trade.

The reflection offered by Alastair Redfern of the Clewer Initiative on Anti-Slavery Day 2019 is absolutely appropriate for this context of invisibility and inaudibility. Commenting on Jesus' parable of the unjust judge and the poor widow (Luke

18.1–8), he notes that the two characters appear to be trapped in separate environments that 'prevent any proper understanding of justice', and he suggests that the two worlds can 'only be opened up to each other through prayer'. The widow cries out continually in a prayer for justice, and her hidden voice eventually touches the judge. God, affirms Redfern, grants justice to all who call out, and does this by 'empowering the oppressed to call out, and by touching the hearts of the powerful to hear and respond'. The parable urges us to 'teach ourselves to hear the Hidden Voices of the exploited and excluded of our own time' (Redfern, 2019), and to amplify the voices by becoming advocates for them to the 'judges', or the powers of the state. Redfern implies that cries for justice, heard by God, are effectively prayers, whether they are intended to be or not. Similarly, David Ford develops a theology of the cries of the disadvantaged (Ford, 2007, pp. 14–45, 261–2, 350, 357–60, 375–6). There is indeed a poignancy in the final words of Stella, addressed ambiguously to God: 'My aim is to jail those people. I swear to God.'

Now, I want to suggest that placing these 'prayers' in the context of the triune God may well help us to become more sensitive to them, and give us the courage to become advocates. When early Christian thinkers looked for concepts to express their experience of God and lighted on the notion of three 'persons', they were not thinking of three divine 'beings' or a kind of heavenly society; they were articulating their sense of being immersed into a flow of love and justice that they could only say was *like* a relation between persons as they knew it in daily life, but deeper, limitless and inexhaustible. The philosophical word *hypostasis* does not mean a psychological centre of consciousness but a 'distinct reality' that is more full of being than anything that we know, and the early theologians insisted that this was a reality that was totally relational. Augustine declared, rather playfully, that 'the names, Father and Son, do not refer to the substance but to the relation, and the relation is no accident' (Augustine, *De Trinitate* 5.6). Thomas Aquinas echoed him later on, stating that '"divine person" signifies relation as something subsisting' (Aquinas, *Summa Theologiae*

1a.29.4). Though they were both working within the philosophical boundaries of their time, they were evoking the nature
of God as being rich in relationships, and indicating that the
language of Trinity is not a matter of observation ('that's what
God looks like') but participation ('this is what it's like to share
in God'). Talk of 'Trinity' makes sense as a witness to being
engaged in movements of love and justice that we experience as
being *like* a relation between a son and a father, a relation that
is all the time being deepened and opened to the future by what
feels like an energetic wind or breath.

In Christian tradition it has sometimes been asserted that
the triune God is self-sufficient in God's inner relations of love
(Augustine, *De Trinitate* 6.9; see Burnaby, 1938, pp. 160–2).
Mystics such as the Anglican Thomas Traherne have known
differently, asserting that God 'is from eternity full of want, or
else He would not be full of treasure ... For had there been no
need He would not have created the world, nor made us, nor
manifested His wisdom, nor exercised His power.' Traherne
concludes that for God, 'infinite wants satisfied produce infinite
joys' (Traherne, 1966, *Centuries* 1.42–3). If the love of God is
to have any analogy with the love that we know, God knows the
'need' of receiving the love of others outside God. This need not
mean any deficiency in God, or contradict God's self-existence
(Ward, 1982, p. 86), if the need springs from God's own will and
desire (Fiddes, 1988, pp. 66–8; Brümmer, 1992, p. 237). From
eternity, we may say, God desires to be a Creator, freely opening God's own life of loving relations to make room for created
beings and their relations with one another. Thus, we can only
know God's relations of love when we meet them through the
relations of human persons, and in the relations between other
living beings too, though God's love always exceeds any human
love; with God there is always excess, always something 'more'
(Marion, 2002, pp. 196–9). This is why the Trinity can and
must be gendered variously, and it is just as appropriate to talk
about relations of love in God as being like those of a mother
or a daughter as it is to say that they are like a father and a son.
Early Christian thinkers knew this when they pictured God's
self-expression as being as much like sending out a female Wis-

dom, or *Sophia*, into the world, as speaking out a male Word, or *Logos* (Theophilus of Antioch, *To Autolycus* 2.15; Irenaeus, *Demonstration* 9–10; cf. Johnson, 1992, pp. 103, 123, 191–3).

If God has made room in God's self for all created persons to dwell, then the being of God is a vast network of relationships of which the World-Wide Web is only a very pale imitation. This is the limitless space of interrelations and interconnections that we enter in prayer (Fiddes, 2000, pp. 115–51). Making words for their experience, the earliest Christians witnessed that they prayed 'to the Father, through the Son and in the Holy Spirit'. Redfern in his reflection urges that the poor widow and the uncaring judge meet one another in the act of prayer, and I suggest that the image of Trinity tells us why this is so. The enslaved and the free meet each other in the interweaving relations of love and justice that are the triune God. When the enslaved cry out to God for justice, we hear this cry in God, who embraces both the enslaved and the free. If the triune God is the medium of communication between us, this has a number of practical consequences. Redfern suggests that God brings justice by a kind of persuasion within the human consciousness, urging the enslaved to cry out and prompting the powerful in society to hear them and act. From a trinitarian perspective we may say that our prayer for those enslaved augments the persuasive love of God with our own love and care; God takes our love and makes it part of God's own pressure of love and justice. It is not that our prayer adds to the love of God in any kind of mathematical way, but it seems that God has willed, by creating free beings in the first place, to work in cooperation with them to achieve a flourishing of life. God desires a blending of uncreated and created love. Such prayer on our part will thus be most effective if it is informed, instructed by making ourselves familiar with the facts of modern slavery, enabling us to enter with imagination into the situation.

Engaging with the triune God who holds the enslaved within God's own relations of love will also make us sensitive to seeing the enslaved where they are invisible and to hear them when they are inaudible, and both will prompt and enable us to act as their advocates with the powerful. Further, it puts us in their debt; it is not all a question of the giving of those who are free and the receiving of those who are unfree. If we encounter God in and through human relationships, then this happens through the relation that the enslaved, as created beings, have with their Creator, whether or not they are conscious of it. Our lives are intertwined with their relation to God, and as we enter more deeply into their situation our own sense of the presence of God is deepened, and conceptually we understand more of what it means for God to be a liberator. And yet there is something more dark, mysterious and awful as well. The enslaved live in relationships with others that are often distorted, broken and destructive. These relations too are held within God, and God feels the pain of them; there is a never-ending cross in the heart of God, and we encounter the triune God at that cross and in that desolation. This brings us to a second theme of the stories we have been given.

A context of vulnerability

In all three stories, the vulnerability of the tellers becomes clear. It is perhaps most evident in Richard's story, as he appears to have come to a strong self-awareness of this aspect of his personality. Asking himself 'why did I stay with them so long?' he gives his own answer: 'I am a vulnerable person.' He describes being easily persuaded by specious offers ('conned', he says), having a fragile mental health, being 'scared of trying to get a normal job', and being unable to make decisions for himself; looking back, he thinks he was 'brainwashed', and just 'accepted' the situation. A picture of dependence on his abusers emerges, starting from a situation where he was homeless after having lost his family home after an argument with his father. He remains at the end of his account reliant on universal credit and deprived of any expectation of a pension, but he shows a determination to challenge his vulnerability by telling his story with the hope that it 'might stop others ending up as victims and being abused'.

Another kind of vulnerability appears in Amna's story, where the culture of her society put her in an exposed position of not being 'allowed to make my own decisions and choose my own life'; taken out of school, she was vulnerable to the extreme stresses of household over-work, early pregnancy and forced abortion. A doctor informed her that 'my body was weak', and finally she was unable to have more children. In the household slavery she experienced in the UK, she was vulnerable as a result of being an illegal immigrant, through susceptibility to the 'mind-games' played by her employer, and through exploitation of her own love for the children she was caring for. A constant vulnerability was separation from her own children, and being told by her husband that she would have to earn the money herself for a flight to be reunited with them. She has a strong self-awareness of being manipulated by others, though her strength of character enabled her to resist being forced into prostitution.

Stella comes across as a strong and determined person, who finally achieved her own escape from sexual enslavement, and insists now that she has 'the will to live'. But her story begins in vulnerability when cancer destroyed her financial position, resulting in her being forced to leave university – and finally losing her job. Like Amna and Richard, she lost the support of her family at a critical time – in her case, because of sexual abuse by her father. She sums up that 'There was no one to help me ... I had no support'. Once trafficked as a sex-worker, her vulnerability was intensified by being deprived of her passport and any means of external communication, and by (as is typical of those trafficked) having a debt imposed on her for accommodation and cost of travel. Once escaped and back in Colombia, the police gave no support, and she was homeless again. Like Amna and Richard, she was exposed to being wounded – the literal meaning of vulnerability – by suffering violence and threats of violence.

In the image of God as Trinity, there is room in God's relations of love and justice for this vulnerability. As Hans Urs von Balthasar puts it, in the 'self-destitution' and 'self-gift' of the Persons within the triune God there is a 'gulf' of absolute Love (Balthasar, 1990, pp. viii–ix; cf. Balthasar, 1994, pp. 323–5).

To those who object that God must be absolutely unconditioned by anything outside of God's self, and so cannot be vulnerable either to injuries inflicted on God in the history of salvation, or to the pain that issues from divine empathy with the injuries that human beings inflict on one another, Karl Barth rightly asserts that:

> According to the biblical testimony, God has the prerogative to be free without being limited by His freedom from external conditioning, free also with regard to His freedom ... God must not only be unconditioned but, in the absoluteness in which He sets up this fellowship [i.e. with humankind], He can and will also be conditioned. (Barth, 1936–77, II/1, p. 303)

God is free to choose to be vulnerable, as God is free to choose to be in need. As Moltmann perceives, the event of the cross of Jesus is a disclosure of God as Trinity: 'the doctrine of the Trinity is no longer an exorbitant and impractical speculation about God, but is nothing other than a shorter version of the passion narrative of Christ.' We can say that 'the form of the crucified Christ is the Trinity', since it shows us the forsakenness of the Son, the grief of the Father, and the hope of the Spirit that opens up the future towards Easter morning. Further, Moltmann declares, all the suffering of human history is 'taken up into the history of God' in the cross – that is, into the Trinity (Moltmann, 1974, pp. 246–7). We may add that among the early Christians, language of Trinity actually developed as a way of talking about their experience of identification with the crucified Christ. They believed they were taking up the cross in the path of their Master, and could only express what this was like by speaking of God as Father, Son and Holy Spirit: as Paul puts it in Romans 8, they found that no persecution could separate them from the God 'who did not withhold his own Son', that no suffering could part them from 'the love of God in Christ Jesus our Lord', and that they were sharing in the 'groaning' of the Spirit who was leading all creation to redemption (Rom. 8.23–39). They found themselves participating in a movement of love that was like a father grieving for a lost son, or a mother for a daughter, and were yet sustained by what felt like a breath of hope. Vulnerability in God does not therefore mean that God is the victim of a cruel universe; God knows that suffering love is the only power that will finally overcome evil and turn sorrow into joy, but faith has to take a risk on this, without any other security.

Recognizing that there is vulnerability, an openness to being wounded, within the relations of the triune God, should make an impact on the way we approach the vulnerability of others, especially the enslaved. For all the positive benefits of the modern practice of 'safeguarding', it does tend to identify a particular group of people as the 'vulnerable', and therefore different from others who are supposedly *not* vulnerable. The result may be a failure to recognize our own vulnerability, or to try to evade becoming vulnerable by exercising power over others, or to avoid those who are obviously vulnerable in case we become uncomfortable by being reminded of our invulnerability. Typecasting a group as the 'vulnerable' may also give them an identity that they will struggle to escape. If the uncreated God is vulnerable, then it is clear that all created beings are vulnerable, and we need to face this reality. The feminist philosopher Judith Butler, surveying groups who seem to be especially vulnerable – women, the poor, 'slave labour' – stresses that vulnerability is a universal condition, and she is sensitive to the violence that results from trying to avoid this truth. However, she refuses to accept that vulnerability is a matter of the being or essence ('ontology') of humanity. What is a matter of 'being' is dependence on our relations with others; vulnerability is the way that dependent relations work out in actual circumstances of life and history. Vulnerability is thus embedded in complex networks of relationship, especially loving relationship, in which the human being is mysteriously enmeshed from the earliest days of development as a child, even before the formation of 'I', myself (Butler, 2006, pp. 22, 27–8, 46). Our dependence on these relations means being vulnerable, or as she puts it strikingly: 'Let's face it. We're undone by each other. And if we're not, we're missing something.' We are 'dispossessed in being for another' (Butler, 2006, pp. 23–4). The body is the site of this common human vulnerability, tied as it is to others; associated with it is the experience of grieving or mourning loss. She points out that it is unjust for society to count some lives as being 'grievable', and others as not (Butler, 2006, pp. 28, 32, 34).

Yet to make vulnerability a matter of 'being' human, will, she thinks, result in assigning the special vulnerability suffered by some in our world to their very being and so make it impossible for them to escape it. Thinking of the poor, women and enslaved, she writes, 'vulnerability and invulnerability are not essential features of men or women' (Butler, 2015, pp. 145, 147). By its very being the body is held in an interdependent network of relations, but the vulnerability that *arises* from this interdependence in particular situations is not ontological. Vulnerability always occurs in a specific historic situation, with its politics and economics. This is what makes some groups of people especially vulnerable (Butler, 2015, p. 148). She emphasizes that in the instance of 'slave-labour', the evil is in 'forced dependency', or the 'tactical exploitation of dependency', not dependency in itself (Butler, 2015, p. 147). Butler is not interested in belief in God, but I would like to suggest that her distinction between 'being' and 'historical' particularity is true of the triune God. In very being, God exists in interdependent *relations* by God's own desire, both internally and externally; God then becomes *vulnerable* in the situations into which God freely and willingly enters in the history of the redemption of creation, which is a process that begins at its very source. It is by embracing all relations of created beings that God knows vulnerability in the network of relations in which God lives.

In approach to those who are enslaved, we surely need to keep a balance between recognizing their special vulnerability, and so being vigorous in working for their freedom, impassioned by finding them in the history of God's own passion, while at the same time not fixing them into a class of the 'vulnerable'. Nurturing the ability of the enslaved to liberate themselves, at least psychologically and socially once physical restraint has been removed, is essential (Mathewes, 2017, pp. 165–84). We read

Amna's testimony that 'I now feel free', but also need to listen to her admission that 'I find it hard to trust anyone anymore.' We read Stella's bracing assertion that 'When I run, it feels like I'm free', but we also need to give attention to her complaint that 'Inside I feel bitter. It burns inside of me.' We rejoice with Richard that, once homeless, he can now organize himself in his own flat, but we also need to hear his saying that 'I don't know what to do with my days.' Each of the three shows aspects of their personality beyond vulnerability in the way they tell their stories, and we need to be sensitive to ways these qualities can be helped to flourish.

There are aspects of dependence that are healthy, but only in the context of interdependency. It is, I believe, by sharing in the vulnerable life of the triune God that we learn true interdependency. Theologians of the Trinity have laboured over the years to articulate the way that the Persons of the Trinity depend on one another – for example, that the Father is only Father because the Son is begotten, or that the Son is Son only because there is a Father. But I have been arguing that we should consider the 'Persons' not as beings or agents who *have* relations, but as movements of relation in themselves, which cannot be unwoven from the relations of created beings that they contain. Dwelling in the vulnerable Trinity we thus learn how indebted we are to others, that we are – as Butler puts it vividly – 'undone' by one another.

A context of injustice

Each of the stories we have been given contains a strong thread of injustice suffered by the storyteller. This is most obvious in Stella's account, who became a law student, motivated by the horrific experience of being raped by her father, and yet had to give up her studies through lack of an adequate health service. She subsequently suffered continual injustice, not only from her abusers but – as she felt – from the authorities of the state: French authorities deported her from France; French and Colombian authorities released her abusers Rodrigo and Luca early in their sentences; immigration authorities in Switzerland would not admit her; and UK authorities incarcerated her in a detention centre. Her cry rings through her account: 'Can anyone explain to me where is the law? It is unjust', and it is not surprising that she is now strongly motivated to continue her law studies to put her in a position 'to jail those people'. Richard suffered injustice from the business that exploited his vulnerability, and again also – he felt – from state authorities: he carried the blame for the illegal activities of his abusers, and served sentences in Dutch, English and Danish prisons, despite the fact that he asserts: 'The police know all about what I went through. I talked with them about it.' Amna's position in India was made worse because her father-in-law was a lawyer, 'a well-known and respected man' who had reason to suppress the facts of her ill-treatment. After reading the stories of Richard and Stella, it comes as a slight relief to hear that when the immigration authorities finally caught up with Amna in the UK, she was not arrested but entered into the National Referral Mechanism (NRM) and taken to a safe house.

The injustice inflicted on these three by those who enslaved them is obvious, while it is hard to assess the accusations of injustice by the structures of the state without further details (see Haynes, 2016, pp. 33–56; Kotiswaran, 2015, pp. 72–5). We can say that our storytellers *felt* they had, for the most part, suffered structural injustice and their experience must be taken seriously. Not to do so would be to continue abuse. At the very least there seems to have been a reluctance and impatience by the authorities to listen to them, which underlines the need for advocates on behalf of the enslaved to mediate with the powers of the state. At the basis of this injustice there is a neglect of human rights (see Weatherburn, 2016, pp. 184–94), as defined by the Universal Declaration of Human Rights of the UN; most immediately, clauses 3 and 4 state that: 'Everyone has the right to life, liberty and security of person. No one shall be held in slavery or servitude; slavery and the slave trade shall be prohibited in all their forms', but the even larger issue is that of 'human dignity' that underlies the whole Declaration. Those enslaved are given no dignity, typified by Amna's recollection that at times she did not eat in the house of her 'employer' since she was told she could not touch the food – presumably being treated as unclean. Richard recalls that 'They used to say, "I own you", like a piece of furniture', and speaks of being treated like a 'spare wheel' or a 'robot'.

We should notice that writing a list of human rights does not make observation of them a straightforward affair. A sense of injustice can often arise when one human right appears to clash with another, or one person's rights appear to conflict with another's, and such ambivalent situations can only be resolved by decisions of the law courts. This exactly calls for the kind of advocacy that is sensitive to the situation of the enslaved, especially where enslavement and abuse is present but not obvious, as in much domestic servitude in the UK.

Theologians have been divided about whether there is a basis for human rights in the Hebrew and Christian Scriptures. Some have been concerned that a stress on *human* rights undermines the righteous action of *God* in bringing about 'just order' in society, and others have claimed that this is a human-centred approach stemming from what are claimed to be selfish property rights (Hauerwas, 1993, pp. 55–73; O'Donovan, 1997, p. 145). I suggest that an appeal to human rights is a kind of 'fuzzy' language, setting out an area within which human dignity is to be respected and injustice rectified. While 'human rights' may not be a strictly *theological* concept in itself, the idea is essential in practice to denote a sphere of discourse in which basic aspects of humanity are being defended. It is a kind of legal tool of theology, helping to establish an ethos that is consistent with Christian Scripture, or it is a 'boundary discourse' that marks out an area of respect for all human beings (Regan, 2010, pp. 13–14, 178–9). Scripture stresses that God has 'rights' and 'worth' as Creator, and the affirmation that all human beings are made in the image of God transfers these rights to them (Wolterstorff, 2008, pp. 94–5, 352–60). Further, as Malcolm Evans has urged in a Lambeth Inter-Faith lecture, placing religious freedom in the context of the international movement for human rights will strengthen the motivation to argue for the freedom of religions other than one's own (Evans,

2012, pp. 5–14). There is a distinct tendency for Christians in the West to suppose that they are discriminated against, to become absorbed in this sense of injustice, and so to ignore the need to act for the rights of others.

A deliberate dwelling in God as the Holy Trinity will, I believe, help to cultivate sensitivity for the rights of others, and in particular for the enslaved. Karl Barth has argued that the creation of human beings in the 'image' of God is fulfilled through transformation into the 'image' of God carried by Jesus Christ, as Son of the heavenly Father. *He* is the true and archetypal image (Barth, 1936–77, III/2, pp. 218–23). Now, if we understand experience of God as Trinity to be a sense of being immersed into currents or flows of love and justice like relations between persons, then we can identify a movement like that between a father and a son (or a mother and a daughter). In the traditional language of Trinity, the Father 'begets' the Son eternally – that is, 'sends out' the Son into the created world on the mission (the 'sending') of the Father to transform all life. Early Christians experienced the call to participate in this movement of God's mission in the world, carrying the image of the Son in becoming children of God. From the Gospel accounts of the baptism of Christ, we can draw out the experience of early Christians as sharing in this divine 'sending' in their own baptism. Identified with Christ, they knew that – like Christ – the Holy Spirit rested on them, and that they too could hear the heavenly voice declaring: 'You are my son, my daughter, the beloved one' (Mark 1.11; Matt. 3.17; Luke 3.22). Baptism was thus another moment of experience that compelled early Christians to use language of Father, Son and Holy Spirit, as is evident from the command of the risen Christ in Matthew's Gospel that his followers were to 'Go therefore and make disciples of all nations, baptizing them in the name of the Father and of the Son and of the Holy Spirit' (Matt. 28.19).

As this commission indicates, disciples of Christ were to be 'sent', just as Christ was being 'sent' as Son by the Father. In John's Gospel this is made explicit as the risen Christ tells his disciples, 'As the Father has sent me, so I send you', and the threefold language is completed as the Evangelist continues, 'he breathed on them and said to them, "Receive the Holy Spirit"' (John 20.21–22). This movement of being sent out recalls the language of Psalm 2, which the Gospel writers employ in telling the story of the baptism of Jesus: 'You are my son; today I have begotten you' (Ps. 2.7). This commissioning, addressed to the Davidic king in Israel and to Jesus at his baptism, is repeated to all disciples in *their* baptism. They too are 'begotten', sent out from the life of God, bearing the image of the offspring of God, as daughters and sons. All this theology is, I suggest, simply a conceptualizing of experience: to participate in the flow of the Trinity is to experience a movement that is like that of 'being sent'.

The human rights of all people, including the enslaved, are based in being made in the image of God and sharing God's rights and worth. Through the taking of humanity by Christ, all people also bear – to some extent – the fulfilled image of the Son of God, and all participate in the life of the triune God. But those who know and live by the story of Christ can be drawn deeper still into the fellowship of God's life, and can deliberately seek to show his image in the world. Experiencing the movement of 'sending' in the flow of the Trinity, they can be sensitized to opportunities of being 'sent' to defend the rights of others, to recognize the face of Christ in unlikely places and to free the captives.

A context of fear

The dark undertone of fear suffuses all three narratives. Amna was 'scared' of her husband and his violence, was frightened of the immigration authorities in the UK, was 'controlled through fear' of her so-called employers, and is still afraid of a future where her immigration status is 'up in the air' (cf. Anitha, 2015, pp. 92–5). Stella, in the house of prostitution, was controlled by threats of violence, remembering that 'He was capable of doing anything', and when Luca and Rodrigo were released she was worried they were going to find her and kill her. Richard was forced from one job to another under threats to himself and his family, explaining 'I was scared'. Fear is clearly a powerful weapon of control. What emerges from the three stories is the nature of fear as being afraid of what might happen in an unknown future – to oneself, one's family or friends – either in the present or in the future. Amna continues to be afraid because she does not know whether she will be reunited with her children. In the narrative of an imprisoned Danish sailor, Kim Malthe-Bruun, enduring torture during the Second World War, we have a significant witness to this fear of what might have happened or what was going to happen. After an experience of suffering that left him unconscious he wrote in his diary: 'Immediately afterwards it dawned on me that I have now a new understanding of the figure of Jesus. The time of waiting, that is the ordeal . . . the waiting in the garden – that hour drips red with blood' (in Gollwitzer et al., 1956, p. 71).

That appeal to the experience of Jesus as recorded in the Gospel story of praying in Gethsemane, waiting for the next day and probable crucifixion, brings us a long way into answering the question as to whether God takes fear into God's-self in the life of the Trinity. Can God be fearful as well as vulnerable? The Gospel writers emphasize the stress that the Christ of Gethsemane undergoes, not knowing whether he would be required to drink the most bitter cup of the cross, and the writer of the Letter to the Hebrews underlines it, recalling how Jesus 'offered up prayers and supplications, with loud cries and tears, to the one who was able to save him from death' (Heb. 5.7). Unless we are to take the route of attributing such experiences only to a human nature of Jesus, we must conclude that in some way fear touched the experience of God in that moment, and the belief that God continually empathizes with all who are afraid in suffering leads us in the same direction. For God even to know what fear is *like*, there must be something unknown in the future for God and not only for created beings.

To affirm that there is a future for God does not mean that it would be exactly like our future. We must try to speak of something 'new' lying ahead for God, yet not exactly as it would for us, of a path that God treads towards a goal, yet not exactly as we would. To allow created beings a real freedom, and to make cooperation between God and human persons meaningful (such as adding our love to the love of God), God must limit God's knowledge of the future. One way of conceiving this would be to suppose that God knows all the general possibilities of the way things will work out, as we certainly do not, but that God does not know particular actualities, details as they will be brought about through an interaction of God with creation in co-creativity. God knows everything there is to be known, but some things are just unknowable within the limits of creation as God intends it to be (see Hartshorne, 1970, pp. 58–9, 65; Ward, 1982, pp. 154, 165; Fiddes, 1988, pp. 96–7). In this case, while God would not know fear in exactly the way that we do, God would experience uncertainties of the future sufficiently to be able to empathize with the fear of persons who are held within the relations of love and justice that are the being of God.

Thus God knows, we may say, an openness to the future and a hope for the future that overcomes fear. As we participate in the triune God we find that the movements that are like a father sending forth a son, and a son responding in love to a father, are interwoven by a third: they are continually being opened up to new depths of relationship and to new possibilities of the future by a movement that we can only call 'Spirit'. For this third movement the Scriptures give us a whole series of impressionistic images – a wind blowing, breath stirring, oil trickling, wings beating, water flowing and fire burning – evoking an activity that disturbs, opens, deepens, provokes and promises.

Such a vision of the Trinity not only assures us that the triune God truly embraces those who are afraid, but gives some clue as to how those who are not enslaved and who dwell in the Trinity can draw alongside those who are. Experiencing the fear of others as held within God, and overcome by the love of God, they can become advocates and mediators for the enslaved without being themselves overcome by fear. They need not be overwhelmed by the depths of sorrow and the vastness of the problem, but can learn a way of engaging that is always hopeful, infecting others with hope. There is an extraordinarily generous testimony by Richard to some who have helped in this way, both inside the Church and more widely in the community, when he says, 'They tried to make it as easy as possible.'

Bibliography

Anitha, S., 2015, 'Immigration status and domestic violence', in S. Okyere and P. Kotiswaran (eds), *Gender*, Beyond Trafficking and Slavery Short Course, vol. 8, openDemocracy, at www.opendemocracy.net/en/bts-short-course, accessed 20.11.20.

Aquinas, T., *Summa Theologiae*, 1963, Blackfriars Edition, vol. 6, London: Eyre & Spottiswoode.

Augustine of Hippo, 1963, *The Trinity*, trans. S. McKenna, *The Fathers of the Church*, Washington DC: Catholic University of America Press.

Balthasar, H. Urs von, 1990, *Mysterium Paschale* (trans. A. Nichols), Edinburgh: T & T Clark.

Balthasar, H. Urs von, 1994, *Theo-Drama: Theological Dramatic Theory*, vol. IV, *The Action*, trans. G. Harrison, San Francisco, CA: Ignatius Press.

Barth, K., 1936–77, *Church Dogmatics*, trans. and ed. G. W. Bromiley and T. F. Torrance, Edinburgh: T & T Clark.

Beyond Trafficking and Slavery Short Course, 8 vols, at www.opendemocracy.net/en/bts-short-course.

Brümmer, V., 1992, *The Model of Love*, Cambridge: Cambridge University Press.

Burnaby, J., 1938, *Amor Dei: A Study of the Religion of St. Augustine*, London: Hodder & Stoughton.

Butler, J., 2006, *Precarious Life*, London: Verso.

Butler, J., 2015, *Notes Towards a Performative Theory of Assembly*, Cambridge, MA: Harvard University Press.

Craig, G., Balch, A. and Lewis, H. (eds), 2019, *The Modern Slavery Agenda: Policy, Politics and Practice in the UK*, Bristol: Policy Press.

Evans, M., 2012, 'Advancing freedom of religion or belief: agendas for change', Annual Lambeth Inter-Faith Lecture 2011, *Oxford Journal of Law and Religion* 1(1), pp. 5–14.

Fiddes, P. S., 1988, *The Creative Suffering of God*, Oxford: Clarendon Press.

Fiddes, P. S., 2000, *Participating in God: A Pastoral Doctrine of the Trinity*, London: Darton, Longman & Todd.

Ford, D., 2007, *Christian Wisdom: Desiring God and Learning in Love*, Cambridge: Cambridge University Press.

Gollwitzer, H. et al. (eds), 1956, *Dying We Live: The Final Messages and Records of Some Germans Who Defied Hitler*, trans. R. C. Kuhn, London: Harvill Press.

Hartshorne, C., 1970, *Creative Synthesis and Philosophic Method*, London: SCM Press.

Hauerwas, S., 1993, *Fullness of Faith. The Public Significance of Theology*, Mahwah, NJ: Paulist Press.

Haynes, J., 2016, 'The Modern Slavery Act (2015): A Legislative Commentary', *Statute Law Review* 37(1), pp. 33–56.

Hulland, L., 2020, *Stolen Lives: Human Trafficking and Slavery in Britain Today*, Inverness: Sandstone Press.

Irenaeus, 1920, *The Demonstration of the Apostolic Preaching*, trans. J. Armitage Robinson, London: SPCK.

Johnson, E., 1992, *She Who Is: The Mystery of God in Feminist Theological Discourse*, New York: Crossroad.

Kotiswaran, P., 2015, 'Law's mediations: the shifting definitions of trafficking', in P. Kotiswaran and S. Okyere (eds), *State and the Law*, Beyond Trafficking and Slavery Short Course, vol. 8, openDemocracy, at www.opendemocracy.net/en/bts-short-course, accessed 20.11.20.

Marion, J., 2002, *Being Given: Towards a Phenomenology of Givenness*, trans. J. L. Kosky, Stanford: Stanford University Press.

Mathewes, C., 2017, 'Vulnerability and political theology', in H. Springhart and G. Thomas (eds), *Exploring Vulnerability*, Göttingen: Vandenhoeck & Ruprecht.

Merry, S. E., 2015, 'How big is the trafficking problem?', in J. Quirk and J. O'Connell Davidson (eds), *Popular and Political Representations*, Beyond Trafficking and Slavery Short Course, vol. 1, openDemocracy, at www.opendemocracy.net/en/bts-short-course, accessed 20.11.20.

Moltmann, J., 1974, *The Crucified God*, trans. R. A. Wilson and J. Bowden, London: SCM Press.

O'Connell Davidson, J., 2015, *Modern Slavery: The Margins of Freedom*, London: Palgrave Macmillan.

O'Donovan, J. L., 1997, 'The concept of rights in Christian moral discourse', in M. Cromartie (ed.), *A Preserving Grace: Protestants, Catholics and Natural Law*, Grand Rapids, MI: Eerdmans, 1997.

Quirk, J. and O'Connell Davidson, J. (eds), 2015, *Popular and Political Representations*, Beyond Trafficking and Slavery Short Course, vol. 1, openDemocracy, at www.opendemocracy.net/en/bts-short-course, accessed 20.11.20.

Redfern, A., 2019, *Reflection for Anti-Slavery Day*, based on the Gospel reading for Sunday 20 October: Luke 18.1–8, at www.theclewer initiative.org/news/2019/9/12/a-reflection-for-anti-slavery-day, accessed 20.11.20.

Regan, E., 2010, *Theology and the Boundary Discourse of Human Rights*, Washington DC: Georgetown University Press.

Surin, K., 1980, *Theology and the Problem of Evil*, Oxford: Blackwell.

Theophilus, 1975, *To Autolycus*, trans. A. Roberts and J. Donaldson, *The Ante-Nicene Fathers*, vol. II, Grand Rapids, MI: Eerdmans.

Traherne, T., 1966, *Poems, Centuries and Three Thanksgivings*, ed. A. Ridler, Oxford Standard Authors, London: Oxford University Press.

Ward, K., 1982, *Rational Theology and the Creativity of God*, Oxford: Blackwell.

We See You: A Theology of Modern Slavery, n. d., the Clewer Initiative, at www.theclewerinitiative.org, accessed 20.11.20.

Weatherburn, A., 2016, 'Using an integrated human rights-based approach to address modern slavery: the UK experience', *European Human Rights Law Review* 2, pp. 184–94.

Wolterstorff, N., 2008, *Justice: Rights and Wrongs*, Princeton, NJ: Princeton University Press.

PART 4

Wider Faith Responses to Modern Slavery

10

The Role of the Church in Responding to Modern Slavery and Exploitation

ALASTAIR REDFERN

Introduction

The key role of the Church in the fight against modern slavery can be focused on the gospel privileging the poor and oppressed; a commitment to go the extra mile for the sake of those in need (especially important given the limited resources of other agencies); a unique convening power reaching across many sectors; a real-time connectivity with grassroots communities, citizens and consumers; a message of hope in an age of anxiety; and a political emphasis upon freedom being used for service rather than for individual self-satisfaction.

This chapter will highlight how local churches are being catalysed to support victims and build community resilience against modern slavery. It will draw on the experience of the Clewer Initiative (the Church of England's response to modern slavery) and the work of the Global Sustainability Network, formed as a result of a declaration by religious leaders against modern slavery in December 2014.

The challenge

Modern slavery is growing, with increasingly sophisticated oppression and abuse, largely hidden from plain sight, which exploits both hope and the increasing desperation of vulnerable people. The drive is our personal satisfaction and constant demand for cheap goods and services, with no concern for the providers. This connects with the growing number of vulnerable people, and the ever more efficient operation of a highly sophisticated crime which targets and traps people in ways that deny any agency or personal fulfilment.

Foundational to a Christian response is the fact that the gospel of Jesus Christ privileges the excluded and the oppressed. The Lord's ministry begins in Luke 4 with the call to give priority to the needs of those whose suffering is hidden and whose existence is a sign of the damaging of the image of God in which they have been created, 'to bring good news to the poor. He has sent me to proclaim release to the captives and recovery of sight to the blind, to let the oppressed go free' (Luke 4.18).

Similarly, when Jesus summarizes his entire ministry in Matthew 25, the key marker and measure is the way respondents have noticed the unnoticed and brought freedom to the oppressed:

> Lord, when was it that we saw you hungry or thirsty or a stranger or naked or sick or in prison, and did not take care of you? Then he will answer them, 'Truly I tell you, just as you did not do it to one of the least of these, you did not do it to me.' (Matt. 25.44–45)

The point of human life on earth is to be embraced in the kingdom that unfolds into eternity, illustrated and measured against this simple criterion. The summary of the law for humanity, to love God and to love one's neighbour as oneself, calls for human aspiration and desire to be shaped according to the eternal purposes of the Creator, and the well-being of all creatures. The self becomes an agent of service to this primary agenda and finds its fulfilment and meaning in this pursuit of a common good for a common destiny. Because there are so many counter-markers to this kind of behaviour and these values, the Christian witness will sometimes be seen as a way of the cross. The fact that the Lord's Prayer points directly to the prevalence of evil, temptation and the need for forgiveness means that there has to be a discipline of teaching, practice, repentance and willingness to try again in pursuing the good news that the kingdom seeks to offer.

As a faith that puts the other first, and is willing to go the extra mile, Christian commitment can add vital resources to hard-pressed professional and statutory services. Victims need love, and systems need extra capacity. These are ingredients that need a commitment that goes further than carefully planned and measurable outcomes, including financial constraints, together with partnerships founded in a generous mutuality, rather than a precise delivery of particular aims and objectives. The key challenge is to enable Christians to translate this gospel, and the nourishment of public and private worship, into appropriate activities that will enable those who are being oppressed and abused to be noticed, cared for, and drawn into partnerships of restoration and new life. Lessons can be learned that might help the development of policies and practices in many aspects of public life, from law and order to social service provision and policy framework.

Response in the community

The Clewer Initiative has developed a range of resources that enable local churches to learn how to build community resilience in particular contexts, and use local resources in appropriate ways so that awareness is raised, care can be provided, and others encouraged to learn to see more clearly the sufferings and the vulnerabilities of people around, as well as to be better equipped to be citizens and consumers in the global marketplace where indifference so easily allows exploitation to thrive.

Of particular significance is the Hidden Voices programme, which brings together local people from within and beyond the Church to unite around a common concern. This concern is for the well-being of people in the community and for the witness that might be made to help others beyond those boundaries, but possibly exploited through unthinking behaviours and values. Each community contains assets in terms of people, buildings and other resources, and a web of contacts – besides the deep aspiration in almost every human heart for the well-being of those who are suffering and the crafting of effective rescue and response (Matt. 5.1–12).

This grassroots activity is crucial since the spread of vulnerability is ever-increasing and it is only in particular contexts that those around can learn to notice, protest, protect and respond appropriately. Churches have a huge range of gifts and experiences within local congregations, as well as good connections with a variety of agencies both voluntary and statutory. The deep moral aspirations of the Beatitudes in terms of concern for the poor, those who mourn, the meek, those who hunger and thirst for righteousness, alongside the value of qualities such as mercy, purity of heart and peace-making, express sentiments and aspirations around which human hearts can unite. The challenge is to find appropriate understandings, imagination, resources and partnerships in order to translate such spiritual awareness into ways of influencing individual lifestyles, community behaviours, and values that translate into modelling alternative ways of being a neighbour, sharing citizenship, and reaching out to those who so easily become hidden and trapped in a world of hopelessness.

Key to this activity is recognition of, and the careful handling of, the fact that in the public space the Church is credited generally to be on the side of goodness but with limited areas of particular expertise. This fact means that the Church can become an ideal convener to bring experience and passions into dialogue and hold the ring by creating a common commitment. This convening role can unite the aspirations of human hearts, real-time wisdom and systems development, and appropriate sensitivity to particular contexts, into schemes where those involved play complementary parts, learn with and from one another, and together develop a greater capacity and potential for making a difference than would be possible if approaches were limited to particular methods and agencies. Further, the experience of the Church at grassroots level can provide insights and data that others need in order to have a proper picture of the challenges and the possibilities of effective response.

The response of partners to the invitations of the Church at local and regional level, and nationally, shows how this spirit of collaboration and cooperation can add value to all those concerned, and create a real spirit of common endeavour and achievement. Christians would recognize this as part of the unfolding of God's power and purpose, while other participants would use different language about the common good and the responsible use of resources and required standards.

A good example would be the Farm Work Welfare app, launched by the Clewer Initiative in the summer of 2020 to enable casual workers, and employers, to have a resource that indicates the marks of good practice, legal rights and responsibilities on both sides, and the real possibility of identifying corrupt and oppressive practice, to enable business to flourish properly and fairly. The app was supported by the National Crime Agency, the National Farmers Union, the Church Commissioners of the Church of England and the Gang Masters Licensing and Abuse Authority. Such a coalition indicates how responsible specialist organizations can only benefit from being drawn into a wider working relationship that goes beyond the bounds of basic professional commitments. This would enable the enlarging of vision, the creation of synergies, and much more effective ways of involving a wide coalition of resources in dealing with the exploitation of some of the most vulnerable people both within the UK and from overseas.

This kind of initiative highlights the fact that modern law enforcement requires public participation as eyes and ears in order to notice exploitation, and to better inform established agencies about the commitment of crime, the abuse of people and the development of a common culture of care and pushback.

Vision and values

In a similar way, Christian values are widely disseminated across contemporary society, and thus there is common ground to examine the immediate selfishness and desire that drives so many of us to respond to the culture of advertising by seeking the cheapest goods and services and asking no questions about how they are provided.

Consumers need to be challenged about the dissidence between this kind of behaviour, which creates oppression and modern slavery, and the values of the Beatitudes in human hearts, which respond generously to human suffering and wish to be part of the solution. This is a key area where the Church has a role both to preach a gospel about values but also to offer opportunities for their enactment whatever people's self-perceived views might be concerning how to behave and on what terms.

Demand and desire need to be socialized against the dictates of the market economy, so that there is deeper concern for the way in which goods and services are created and provided, and an expectation of higher standards in terms of the human element of production and provision. Thus there is an urgent task for the churches to lead a public debate, and provide credible models of alternatives, around the handling of sexual desire, consumer demand and the provision of services such as cheap car washes, cheap labour and corrupting systems of drug supply.

Work undertaken by the Clewer Initiative about victim care and support provides another example of how, in practice, this agenda can begin to be tackled in a way that crosses boundaries of formal faith understandings, religious behaviour or political allegiances. In practice, people from all walks of life and ranges of experience can be gathered through the invitation of the churches to cooperate in the crafting of local responses both in terms of awareness-raising and the provision of suitable and effective ways of identifying and working with victims. This kind of collaboration naturally extends to the enhancement of connections with other providers of care and opportunities for recovery.

However, our current political world is dominated by an atmosphere of crisis, fear and the need for survival. This reinforces the inducements of the market economy for individuals to look after themselves as a priority and not notice the needs or sufferings of others. The Church can bring to this context the banner of faith in the future and the confidence to work with others to create better possibilities. The deep desire for a common good that manifests itself when there are particular crises of suffering needs to be nourished and given ways for more concerted and committed expression in order to create new models of operation and aspiration as part of everyday values and living.

A good example would be the work of the Clewer Initiative with the homeless. Many churches and other agencies work with homeless people, and in recent years there has been an increasing recognition that food banks, night shelters and other resources for people in such dire straits provide easy recruiting grounds for those seeking to exploit vulnerability and entrap people in modern slavery.

A poignant example is Charlie's story, available through Clewer's media channels.[1] As a result, the Clewer Initiative has been able to work with others to provide resources and then reinforce them each autumn and Christmas when there is a particular awareness of homelessness and its devastating effect on needy people. Thus, what is universally recognized as a season of goodwill can be translated into a common spirit of grace towards generally unseen neighbours, a proactive looking-out to notice and respond, and resourcing by working with other partners in terms of care and the development of systems to provide protection and better opportunities in the future.

As our plural liberal society thrives on the rhetoric of individual freedom and autonomy, there is an urgent need for the enabling of more community-centred models of relationship and operation. The strapline of the Clewer Initiative is 'we see you', a commitment to notice and respond with care, collaboration and a spirit of working together for a common good.

These kinds of endeavour are ways of inviting citizens and consumers to assume a new identity – one in which the needs of others become a priority, and discipline is developed whereby there is a willingness to go the extra mile in order to try to notice need, alert those who might be able to make an informed judgement about it, and participate in creating appropriate care and new possibilities. None the less, such is the legacy of a welfare-state mentality that many people who do notice signs of possible exploitation are reluctant to report, feeling that this is the job of the police and the statutory authorities.

The partnerships that the Clewer Initiative has enabled clearly illustrate that public agencies increasingly require the proactive cooperation of those who can reach into spaces generally unobserved by public systems unless there is a particular crisis or call for help. This was the rationale behind the Car Wash app that was developed in 2017 in partnership with the Association of Car Wash Operators. Good business is undermined by corrupt and illegal business. People were rushing to have their cars cleaned at very low prices, often undercutting the deals offered by reputable operators, without asking who might be providing the service, on what kind of terms, and the conditions in which people were being asked to live and work. Initially there was a reluctance to report suspicions even when the Car Wash app was being used, and was indicating high elements of risk. Understandably there is a slow culture change and churches need to be in the forefront of challenging citizens to put common values into practice and be proactive in noticing and reporting suspicious activities and practices. A statutory agency that is properly qualified will willingly investigate and make a judgement, but this extra hinterland of intelligence is vital in a world where our concern for survival, and anxiety, means that many are indifferent to what goes on around them and who is providing goods and services.

Children and young people

Of particular importance in the last two years has been work the Clewer Initiative has pioneered about the phenomenon of county lines. This is a growing business of drug distribution and supply around the country from groups operating in the big cities, which have undermined and dismantled more local systems of drug selling, through the intervention of highly professional and aggressive gangs. Much of the distribution is undertaken by children and young people, many of whom are very vulnerable, not least in their attraction to membership of a gang and an apparently grown-up culture. County lines material, available through the Clewer Initiative, enables local communities to begin to identify how best to work with young people in particular contexts. This both provides resilience against the temptations and invitations of drug operators, and begins to open people's eyes to help them be a better community working towards an appropriate policing of these kinds of activities. Often the response requires people to notice what is going on in the flat next door and be willing to raise a question.

The county lines phenomenon is part of an alarming growth in the exploitation of children, and indicates that what was once a moral stop in terms of a person being young has now been abolished. Hence the rise of the county lines operation in terms of recruiting young people for drug distribution, and also the increasing exploitation of children for sexual gratification.

Drivers here are personal satisfaction and pleasure, not concern for the well-being of others. In such contexts the Church has an important resource in the gospel understanding of sin, repentance, forgiveness and the possibility of new life, for both the perpetrators and the victims. For many people in our society this language and these practices are almost wholly alien, with an alarming growth, fuelled through the social media engine, of self-righteousness about narrow concerns and perspectives. There is an important role for the churches to witness to our own sinfulness and failings, and the way a loving God can offer healing and hope.

This needs to be modelled, shared and offered as an invitation to those who might not want to use our language or rituals, but who again would in their hearts recognize how necessary such grace and restoration continue to be in a world of shrill criticism and narrow identity protection. There is a richer and more realistic register than the agenda of individual rights and carefully protected experiences.

International roles

The Church also has an important international vision. Every creature is made in the image of God. Modern slavery is a global industry, often exploiting people by crossing national boundaries and therefore trapping victims in an unfamiliar culture, lacking language skills and often proper documentation. Thus the exploited person is totally dependent upon those who abuse them. The familiar pattern to reinforce this reality operates through the confiscation of passports, and the provision of carefully controlled translation services for any necessary interchange with local people – for instance, for medical needs, banking or shopping.

It is important for us to learn to look for the signs of stress and entrapment among those who can too easily be dismissed as 'foreign'. A particular example would be the recent profusion of street beggars, many of whom are controlled by gangs, and who provide a rich source of income for their controllers because of the generous Christian spirit in so many hearts of those who pass by. To drop a coin in the receptacle salves the conscience and compounds the problem from the point of view of the exploited person by witnessing to the profitability of the crime. This provides a testing example for Christians about the need to challenge what might appear to be simple charity, by raising awareness of deeper issues and a context beyond the one that presents to the public at face value.

An interesting indicator of the sophistication of this crime is the fact that, in recent times, those begging in our large cities have placed before them a cup of coffee and a half-eaten sandwich. This gives a clear message that they want money and not help in kind. This is to maximize the profits of the exploiters and shows the sophistication of the business model and its ability to adapt and maximize profitability.

On the international scene the Global Sustainability Network provides a similar example of church-led initiatives. The network arose from initiatives led by the Roman Catholic Church through the Pontifical Academy of Sciences, the Church of England and Muslim and Hindu partners.

It operates by bringing together people from the world of business, government, faith, media, academia, sport and NGOs. The interchange of these different perspectives is crucial in becoming better equipped to fight the sophisticated nature of the crime of modern slavery – not just to raise awareness but to share wisdom and develop effective and innovative practices. Examples would be the coordination of media activity in different countries, work around brick kilns in India, job creation in Pakistan and schemes to tackle sexual exploitation in Latin America. In these and many other areas, churches provide local networks of contact and community resourcing, high-level contacts among policy-makers and leaders of business and research, together with the provision of a forum whereby community and charity organizations can both inform these other sectors and also benefit from the contacts they provide. Thus policy-making can be enhanced in its awareness and precision, and business practice can be challenged to develop appropriately, as can messaging and the urgent task of exploring values and best practice in many different contexts.

Similarly, the Clewer Initiative works with the Anglican Alliance, a body that connects Anglican churches in 162 countries around the globe, and with the World Council of Churches, to look at ways in which the material developed in the UK can be shared more widely, and at learning from good practice from different partners in order to provide inspiration and modelling for others. This international Christian work is finding a particular focus around concern for children, their protection, and the adjustment of systems of care to take seriously their particular needs and vulnerabilities.

The calling and the commitment

In conclusion it is important to stress the particular contribution that Christians can make both through individual witness and the witness of church organizations.

Fundamental is the urgent need in the modern world for more public debate about values – the instinct in the human heart to honour the spirit of the Beatitudes – that so easily becomes obscured and overridden by a market-driven ideology of self-preservation and self-development.

Second, there is the challenge to provide a currency of common life that can be shown to enhance the welfare of the most vulnerable, and also bring satisfaction to citizens and consumers. There is an urgent need for new models of mutuality, generosity and grace-sharing. These models need to be developed locally, regionally, nationally and internationally. The Church is a unique institution in being able to play a key part in such an agenda.

Third, the increasing exploitation of children for sexual purposes, cheap labour and drug distribution is a scandal that must be arrested – not just through trying to challenge its practice but rather by highlighting the ways young people can so easily be abandoned into such a destructive and death-dealing kind of existence. Again, concern with children touches human hearts deeply, and the Church needs to find ways of making this call and offering paths of appropriate response. Our current concern in our own society with safeguarding illustrates something of the challenge, and of the opportunity that a carefully considered response might craft.

Fourth, there is a strange silence about sexuality and relationships in terms of commitment, responsibility and structures for the kind of safety and mutuality that enables human flourishing in its fullest sense. Rather, the discourse is wildly aimed at freedom, self-expression and the fulfilment of personal desire understood as pleasure. This shallow and often crippling approach to one of the deepest aspects of human being requires much more imaginative investigation, challenge and the offering of attractive models of seeking fulfilment through the frameworks of family and committed relationship upon which the Church is founded.

Fifth, the call to develop the convening capacity of churches at every level presents a real opportunity, from enabling local awareness and action, to facilitating and supporting regional, national and international partnerships.

Sixth, ways need to be found to enable the agenda, trapped

in Christian language and practice about sin, repentance, forgiveness, healing and new life, to become more universally available as a resource to those beset by anxiety and the apparently personal struggle to survive. What can public repentance and renewal look like?

Seventh, the credibility of the Christian gospel in our times depends upon our witness to a coming kingdom that is inclusive, healing and hopeful. This presents a task for Christian preaching, teaching and apologetics, measured by the practical outcomes that can be counted in terms of the liberation of the oppressed and the embracing of those in need in new forms of fellowship and community.

Eighth, Christian mission would thereby be invited to shift from an inward-looking obsession with our own structures and organization towards a form of outreach that collaborates with the victims of exploitation in a common creation of safer and mutually supporting local networks. The Christian ecclesia would become a laboratory for new forms of healing households and committed mutual relationships.

Ninth, the potential of the political influence of committed Christians can be much better developed and expressed around these kinds of tangible, practical issues. These issues would unite rather than divide people, if handled well in public discourse and discernible examples. People's hearts are attracted to the outworking of compassion and the joining together in common goodness. This would provide an important agenda for those who make policy and design ways of ensuring good practice.

Tenth, the churches have an opportunity to nurture a public spirituality that can focus upon the well-being of the vulnerable, the improvement of systems and standards for work and welfare, the shaping of common values around sacrificing the self for the well-being of others, and high standards of mutual responsibility and care.

Note

1 Available from www.theclewerinitiative.org/resources, accessed 12.01.21.

II

Christianity with Its Sleeves Rolled Up: The Salvation Army and Responses to Exploitation

KATHY BETTERIDGE AND

HEATHER GRINSTED

Introduction

The Salvation Army was formed on the streets of east London in 1865. William and Catherine Booth left Methodism and more traditional ideas of church at the time in order to practise a practical Christianity of 'soup, soap and salvation – to encourage both social and spiritual transformation among society's most vulnerable and marginalized people' (The Salvation Army, *Our History*). Focus was given to setting up homeless shelters, soup kitchens and rescue homes for women fleeing domestic abuse and prostitution. The Booths also set up the world's first free labour exchange and campaigned to improve working conditions.

This movement, known as the Christian Mission, with William Booth as its general-superintendent, grew beyond London. The name changed to The Salvation Army (TSA) in 1878 and the organization adopted military-style uniform and a military organizational structure. TSA movement spread across the UK and subsequently around the world, including Europe, North America and South Africa:

The challenges people were facing in the late 19th Century – homelessness, addiction, loneliness and unemployment – are much the same as today. The Salvation Army has continued its founders' work, tackling issues and working at the heart of communities to offer practical help, unconditional assistance and support to transform lives. Today, The Salvation Army is a church and charity that is active in virtually every corner of the world and serves in more than 130 countries offering God's hope and love to all those in need without discrimination. (The Salvation Army, *Our History*)

This chapter will first highlight how TSA's historic responses to exploitation and serving the vulnerable have influenced our present responses. Two historic case studies relating to labour and sexual exploitation will be presented. Second, TSA's recent responses to modern slavery and human trafficking (MSHT) will be explored. This will include an overview of how TSA delivers the government contract to provide specialist support under the National Referral Mechanism (NRM) for victims of modern slavery. This will be followed by three survivor case studies. TSA's CONNECT programme will be highlighted, including how church and faith communities are involved. The chapter will conclude with exploring how responses to modern slavery can develop.

TSA's historic responses to exploitation

Labour exploitation and 'phossy jaw'

In the 1880s, TSA responded to societal injustices of its time through developing work among vulnerable groups of people. TSA focused its attention on the homeless, ex-prisoners and factory workers, including women and children. A particular focus was given to labour exploitation, or what was known as '"sweating", a labour practice characterized by high workload, long hours and low pay' (Flore, 2019).

The Matchwomen's Strike of 1888, led by Annie Besant, at the Bryant and May Match Factory in Bow, east London, highlighted appalling working conditions. Striking factory women raised awareness of the long working hours and fines imposed by their employers. These strikes drew attention to the medical condition known as 'phossy jaw'. This condition was the result of the production process of making matchsticks with toxic yellow phosphorus, contaminating workers' hands and food. This contamination caused jawbones to decay, with potentially fatal results.

TSA, led by its director of social work, commissioner Elijah Cadman, responded to Annie Besant and the sweated match-makers by opening its own match factory in 1891. Following approved trade-union conditions and using no chemicals, matchsticks were produced. These matchsticks in turn became the focus of a Salvation Army consumer activist campaign. The campaign encouraged consumers to make ethical purchases through awareness of the exploitation of sweating resulting in phossy jaw, in order to buy ethically produced matches. There was slow uptake, however, due to the ethical matchsticks being more expensive than the cheaper variety. Such a challenge remains today, with consumers often choosing cheaper products over ethically produced ones (Flore, 2019).

The Maiden Tribute of Modern Babylon and Eliza Armstrong

In the 1880s, TSA developed its political engagement and supported the Criminal Law Amendment Bill, which included raising the age of female sexual consent from 13 to 16. The Bill was introduced to Parliament in 1883, but by 1885 it had still not been passed and was on the verge of being abandoned. In response to the widespread exploitation of teenage girls, TSA joined forces with those known as 'social purity campaigners', such as Josephine Butler, and initiated mass meetings to raise awareness. Within several weeks a petition to protect young girls had gathered 250,000 signatures. Catherine Booth wrote several letters to Queen Victoria to highlight these concerns.

The most controversial act in fighting against the exploitation of young girls came through TSA's collaboration with William Stead. He was editor of *The Pall Mall Gazette*, which ran a series of articles, known as the 'Maiden Tribute of Modern Babylon'. These articles highlighted child prostitution in London. Some of the narrative came from the experiences of residents in TSA's refuge for women. Rebecca Jarrett, a reformed former brothel owner, gave one such narrative. Jarrett had received assistance in TSA's rescue home in 1884. TSA's chief of staff and son of William and Catherine Booth, Bramwell Booth, requested that Jarrett stage the procurement of a girl of 13 who was being sold in prostitution. TSA's International Heritage Centre notes:

> Without actually being physically harmed or violated, the girl was put through the motions of what a child sold into prostitution would experience in order to demonstrate how easily this could be achieved. After steps such as ascertaining her virginity had been completed, the child was placed in the care of The Salvation Army in France while the 'Maiden Tribute' revelations were published. (The Salvation Army International Heritage Centre)

These facts, highlighting the ease of buying a 13-year-old girl, were published in the Maiden Tribute articles. Stead, Jarrett and Bramwell Booth were identified as culprits and put on trial for the abduction of Eliza Armstrong. Booth was acquitted of all charges; however, Stead and Jarrett were convicted and served a six-month and three-month prison sentence respectively.

Although Victorian society was scandalized, the Maiden Tribute of Modern Babylon exposé became 'the catalyst for significant legislative change for women and girls in the form of the Criminal Law Amendment Act of 1885. The Act raised the age of consent for girls from 13 to 16 and strengthened legislation condemning prostitution and brothel keeping' (Chloe, 2017). These events in turn stimulated more response from TSA in its social justice work among women and the protection of young girls in British society.

TSA's recent responses to modern slavery and human trafficking

For many presently serving in TSA, it is this history of fighting against the ill-treatment of individuals that has captured their passion and imagination, resulting in a sense of God's calling and vocation to work towards justice.

This historic passion lives on in TSA's ministry of being a voice for the marginalized. The strong response to justice comes from an understanding of God and humankind. God is viewed as the Creator, having created human beings in his image, as equal, as precious and as sacred. God's intention of creation is for the created to flourish, to have freedom of living and to enjoy God's creation. In contrast, especially relating to crimes of slavery, humankind in its selfish, sinful nature takes advantage of that sacredness and misuses and abuses. TSA's work and ministry is rooted in pursuing justice in order to serve suffering humanity.

Within the UK today, TSA is a church made up of 650 corps (parishes or church units), with 54,000 members. The overall vision of TSA is to save souls, serve suffering humanity and grow saints. TSA is a Christian Church whose main focus, existence and being is about helping and supporting somebody to understand God's love and then for them to choose to make their own response. Our vision as disciples of Jesus Christ is to be a Spirit-filled, radical, growing movement, with a burning desire to lead people into a saving knowledge of Jesus Christ, actively serve the community, and fight for social justice.

In England, TSA's long history of working with the exploited, and particularly vulnerable women and women in prostitution, also continued. For example, Salvation Army officers have walked for many years around King's Cross station, meeting individuals who were already in the sex industry, as well as those newly arriving into London for that purpose. Contact was made with these sometimes vulnerable individuals, and relationships developed.

Both authors, before heading up TSA's Anti-Trafficking and Modern Slavery Unit, served exploited women in the Gulf and

Scotland respectively. In the Gulf, foreign domestic workers, mostly women from Asia and Africa, play an essential role in nearly every household in the Gulf countries. While some employers develop a considerate relationship with the women who care for their children, cook their meals and clean their homes, others take advantage of weak legal protections and an isolated home environment that shields human rights abuses from outside scrutiny.

Many migrant people are tricked into coming to the Gulf by fraudulent schemes, and find that the promised work does not exist, or conditions are completely different. Although they were recruited in their home countries with promises of work in hospitality and retail, they can end up in domestic servitude or a forced labour situation. Their documents are often taken away and they too may be held to pay off a debt, which accumulates from the inflated costs of travel and housing.

Part of TSA's social programme in the Gulf was to offer a safe place for domestic workers in distress, many of whom had been caught up in the global problem of human trafficking. The women were cared for while their legal cases were being resolved through negotiation with agents, employers, government and embassy officials, and eventually they were repatriated. The women's essential needs were met and a schedule of programmes was created – with the support of volunteers – to equip and enhance basic skills, including classes in language, domestic skills, nutrition, aerobics and handicrafts.

In Edinburgh, Kathy's work involved working with women in prostitution. Through working as a prison chaplain, she encountered women who would share openly with her about their vulnerabilities. These women had been rejected or abused by their families and society and turned to prostitution to get money to feed their drug habit. They would talk to her about their feelings of worthlessness. It annoyed Kathy to hear how people took advantage of these vulnerable women. It also impassioned her to believe TSA could do more. She was able to work with the women in prostitution through TSA Edinburgh Street Project, using a mobile van to provide a safe place for the women to receive support, refreshments and the opportunity to keep warm during their working night. There was also the opportunity to become the voice for TSA on the governmental cross-party groups in Scotland; this enabled Kathy to continue highlighting the experiences of these exploited women and the injustices they suffer.

TSA's historic reputation has resulted in government and key parliamentary figures listening to what we have to say. With the help of TSA Public Affairs Unit, clear and sound evidence was provided, demonstrating the impact that policy decisions will have on the most vulnerable and marginalized in our society. This relates not only to anti-trafficking and modern slavery but also to those who are homeless, unemployed and victims of debt, food poverty and substance misuse. It also relates to the elderly.

Such ministry is viewed as 'Christianity with its sleeves rolled up'. In order to help someone understand God's love we need to serve them as well. It is this Christianity that encouraged TSA to set up their Anti-Trafficking and Modern Slavery Unit in 2008. The Unit is viewed as a practical expression of God's love, in serving humanity with the aim of seeing modern slavery abolished. In pursuing that, compassionate care is also exhibited. From 2008 to 2020, the Unit grew rapidly, resulting in 100 staff working within the Unit and 300 volunteers supporting the work.

Securing the government's contract to provide specialist support

The development of TSA's Anti-Trafficking and Modern Slavery Unit has been most notably achieved through successfully securing in 2011 the government contract to provide specialist support services for adult victims of modern slavery in England and Wales.

This support service provides services to meet victim entitlements under the Council of Europe Convention on Action Against Trafficking in Human Beings (ECAT, 2012). Article 12 states: 'Each Party shall adopt such legislative or other measures as may be necessary to assist victims in their physical, psychological and social recovery' (2012, p. 10). This includes providing accommodation, psychological and material assistance, access to medical treatment, translation and interpretation services, counselling, legal assistance and access to education for children.

In 2011, the £2 million contract enabled TSA to develop a specialist support programme. In order to access this support, potential victims of modern slavery enter the National Referral Mechanism (NRM), which is the process by which an individual is identified as a victim of modern slavery. Referrals to the NRM are made by authorized agencies known as First Responders. These authorized agencies include the police, social services, Home Office and some non-governmental organizations, including TSA. The government's NRM team have five working days from receipt of a referral to decide whether there are reasonable grounds to believe a person is a potential victim of modern slavery. If it is decided the person is a potential victim, they will then be offered safe accommodation and be able to access specialist support. During this time, further information is collected about their case and a conclusive-grounds decision will be made to confirm the person is indeed a victim of modern slavery.[1]

TSA manages this specialist support service, which provides accommodation, protects and cares for victims and provides them with access to confidential client-based, tailored support services, including safe houses run by our partners and contracted service providers (across England and Wales), legal advice, counselling, health care, education and training, and outreach support for those individuals who do not require accommodation. If a survivor is pregnant or has dependants, special provision is also made for them, such as access to school education. TSA has successfully held the contract since 2011 until the present.

It has been essential to explore in our present work the relationship between TSA being a church with an Anti-Trafficking and Modern Slavery Unit, while also delivering the government contract. In delivering the contract we can't be explicitly evangelical, as that's not permitted. We do it, however, with a God-focused intention, knowing that we have the opportunity to deliver the contract in a godly way. If people want to know more about faith, they can ask questions. We don't force it on them in any way. But through our love and actions we believe that God comes into those situations. We can deliver the contract in a way that enables us to share that love and understanding. For example, when our volunteer drivers pick up a victim of modern slavery to take them to a place of safety, the feedback that we get from clients is that it was the first time someone smiled at them, or it was the first time someone showed them some tenderness.

In 2011, TSA supported 378 individuals from 43 different countries (The Salvation Army, 2012, p. 4). In subsequent years, the quantity of individuals supported has increased. During 2019, TSA and partner organizations supported 5,880 individuals from 99 countries. This was a 15 per cent increase on the number (4,512) who received support in the previous year. For the seventh year running the highest number of women who entered the service were from Albania. For the third year running the highest number of men who entered the service were from Vietnam. In 2019, 243 victims referred to TSA were British nationals, a 79 per cent increase on the previous year. Between 2011 and 2020, TSA supported 12,568 recovering victims of modern slavery (The Salvation Army, 2020, pp. 5–9).

These statistics highlight the extent of the problem of modern slavery in the UK. Each of these numbers represents a valuable person who is often traumatized through their experience of exploitation. The following narratives highlight three individuals who TSA has served.

Survivors' narratives

County lines and homelessness

J,[2] a 34-year-old British man, had battled substance abuse for many years but with little success. Keen to live a productive life, he often rushed back into employment before he was ready, which led to him relapsing and becoming reliant on drugs again. More recently his drug problems had increased in severity and things began to spiral downwards, leading to him becoming homeless. During this extremely vulnerable stage of his life, J was targeted by drug dealers who forced him to sell drugs on their behalf around the country, without pay.

J's relationship with the dealers quickly changed from false promises of money to threats and coercion, making it impossible for him to escape his situation. This nightmare ended when police became involved and recognized that J was a victim, and not a perpetrator of these crimes. He was referred to TSA for support and moved to another part of the country, far from where his traffickers were operating. He was supported in a Salvation Army safe house for victims of modern slavery.

Specialist support workers worked with J to link him to local services, helping him with his substance-abuse problems. It was also arranged for J to access a programme at a local gym, which gave him a meaningful activity each day and improved his health. In the meantime, they worked alongside J to help him decide what he wanted to do with his new-found freedom.

Salvation Army support workers also helped J to access the benefits he was entitled to and address his debt issues to give him a fresh start. J recently received a positive conclusive-grounds decision, which is when the authorities conclude that there is definitive evidence that someone is a victim of modern slavery.

J was helped to find, and move into, independent accommodation in the same area as the safe house so he is able to keep in touch with staff as he progresses along the road to full recovery. TSA's victim care fund and other charitable support helped J secure a deposit and basic furniture to start his new life in his own flat. He is connected to a range of ongoing support networks and continues to address his addiction. J's self-esteem is growing and he hopes eventually to become totally free of these problems and be able to support himself through work.

J states: 'I was in a very difficult part of my life and being taken advantage of. After discovering the NRM, The Salvation Army has given me all the support I needed to start again and I am very optimistic for my future.'

Trafficked and sexually exploited across Europe

D is 41, and lived in Albania with her husband and daughter. Her husband was abusive and would beat her up. One night, D went to a party where she met a man who was kind to her. They became close and D told him about her life at home. The man took her to his flat and promised he would look after her. D wasn't able to leave as the man kept her intoxicated with alcohol and drugs. He then began to bring men to sleep with her. When D became sober she told the man, who she had previously thought of as her boyfriend, that she didn't want to do this. D was told if she did not have sex with the men, then they would kill her daughter. D said that some nights she would have to sleep with up to five men. She felt this had brought shame on her and was terrified in case her family found out, being sure they would disown her.

With the help of a friend, she managed to escape to Italy. When she arrived there, she was moved to the UK and told that she would be found a good job there. When D arrived in the UK she was immediately taken to a house where other women lived. Once again, men would come to this property to have sex with the women. D was very distressed as it seemed as if her ordeal had started again. At first she refused to sleep with the men, but she was then beaten for days and not fed. The housekeeper burnt her with a cigarette, as she didn't do as she was told. Eventually D gave in to their demands.

Four months later she managed to escape by taking the key (the house was always locked) from the housekeeper when she was asleep. When D realized she had actually managed to escape, she just kept running. She described running through fields, over bridges, catching bus after bus to get as far from the house as possible. Eventually someone saw her in distress and took her to the Home Office. From there she was referred to TSA for specialist support and taken to a safe house.

D was given emotional, financial and legal support and, with the help of her support worker, she made an asylum claim and went to the police to tell them about her traffickers. The police are still investigating her case. During the support from TSA's service, D has received psychological counselling, which she says helps her mentally to deal with what happened, giving her a safe place to share her feelings. She goes to English classes at a local church to improve her English, thereby allowing her more independence. She was supported in getting clothes from a local charity and help in registering with a local GP and dentist, to ensure she receives the medical support she needs.

D says she now feels at ease as she is getting support and knows where to go and what to do should something happen to her. When D was referred to our service she was very scared, quiet and emotionally closed off. Initially she didn't trust her support worker or any new people she met. When the support worker explained to her what support she was entitled to, D felt it was too good to be true that someone genuinely wanted to help her. After a couple of months, when reminded of this, D said that she now believes that there are genuine organizations that help people regain their lives. She now sees some light at the end of the tunnel, even though at times she is still scared about her future. D says she wants to go into nursing after improving her English at college, and make something out of her life.

Coffee shops and labour exploitation

M[3] is 30. She comes from Mumbai, where her parents saved up for years to give her the opportunity to come to the UK to study. She arrived about three years ago, just before the college term started. Adapting to a new country, M tried to find friends among people from Mumbai who were living in London.

Among the connections she made was a woman who ran a coffee shop in a London underground station. Initially this woman was friendly, kind and warm, so when she offered M some work as a cashier in her coffee shop, M didn't hesitate to accept. Over time they became closer and M accepted the offer of accommodation with her new friend. Just before M was due to start the new term at her college, the woman (M calls her 'the bad lady') asked her for a favour. She explained that she had to go abroad for a serious heart operation and wondered if M could work extra hours at the coffee shop, to help her during this time. M accepted, even though this meant she wouldn't be able to start studying for a couple of weeks. During this time, she discovered from 'the bad lady's' son that there had been no operation, just a holiday, so M confronted her on her return.

From this point on the relationship soured. 'The bad lady' then started to bamboozle M with threats about her status in the UK, explaining that as she had failed to attend college for the first weeks of term, her visa to study was now invalid and she was remaining illegally in the UK. M had limited English and no knowledge of UK law, so wasn't able to tell whether this was true or not. By making her fearful in this way, 'the bad lady' forced M to continue to work at the coffee shop for long hours, seven days a week, and for very little pay.

M soon discovered that most of the staff at the coffee shop were illegal immigrants and being forced to work in similar conditions. The woman, their trafficker, controlled everyone through threats and by making their working conditions difficult, including limited toilet breaks. There was closed-circuit television (CCTV) in the coffee shop. If M was seen to engage in more than a transactional conversation with a customer, her trafficker would ring up instantly, having been watching on CCTV, asking why she had spoken to that person and commanding her not to do so again.

M lived like this for two years, until one day she was spotted quietly crying at her till because she had hurt her leg but was not allowed to stop working or go to the doctor. Two members of the British transport police and London underground staff, who also worked at the station, had become concerned about M. They used this as an opportunity to see if they could help. They were able to engage briefly in conversation and one person surreptitiously handed over her business card with a number for M to call at any time.

In addition, M, who had to walk home alone at 1 a.m. every day from the coffee shop, was followed home one night by a man. This terrified her, so she dialled the British transport police number at 2 a.m. and asked for help, thinking that, should her trafficker discover what she had done, M could fool her into thinking that she was simply reporting the potential stalker. M was then rescued and referred to TSA, who transferred her to a safe house in London run by its subcontractor, Hestia.

M has now been at the safe house for several months and is flourishing in the supportive environment and through the specialist counselling, legal and medical help she is receiving. She is also helping the police with enquiries regarding her trafficker, and is passionate about making more people aware of the possibility of falling prey to someone like this. When asked if she would be happy to talk to a journalist M replied: 'If by telling my story I can prevent the same happening to someone else, then yes, I want to speak out.'

Continued support and the CONNECT programme

The narratives above highlight the vulnerability of individuals who have been exploited. They also refer to the services that TSA offers to these individuals, having been identified as victims of modern slavery. In delivering the contract, it is an opportunity to continue TSA's work and ministry of serving suffering humanity. Through recent experiences of working with survivors, one of the biggest challenges they face is when they have been living in a safe house and have to move on to live in the community. Moving away from specialist support to a community where they are more vulnerable can be challenging. Gaining confidence is important and can be developed through specialist support, to lessen vulnerability. In order to respond to this, TSA have been piloting the CONNECT programme.

The CONNECT programme is an initiative developed by TSA with Juliana Semione, research associate at the University of Nottingham's Rights Lab. For victims of modern slavery who receive help through the NRM, the programme supports them on their journey from victim to survivor. The word 'connect' is what we do – we connect people with community. People who have come out of an exploitative situation are potentially still quite vulnerable. It is important for them to integrate in society and in their community. The CONNECT programme is currently based in six Salvation Army centres, where staff and volunteers offer a variety of services. Managed from our Anti-Trafficking and Modern Slavery Unit, we work alongside a local church, which recruits a team of volunteers, including those from other faiths, who support the programme. In turn, these volunteers are supported by a programme co-ordinator who gives guidance and training.

There are three parts to the programme. First, there is a drop-in service for those who are referred. Each referred individual will have a two-hour window in the week to a drop-in service where there will be people to welcome them, build relationship, and give support and signposting to other services within the community. Emphasis is put on connecting those individuals to others within the community. Crèche services are included.

Second, a mentoring service connects the referred person with two mentors. Having two mentors models healthy relationships as well as being appropriate for safeguarding. This lasts for an initial 12 months with the possibility for extension.

Third, the programme encourages community social engagement for those referred. Volunteers meet with a group of survivors and accompany them to places of interest within the community, such as parks and leisure centres. For survivors who have experienced exploitation, this will encourage confidence to grow in going out and interacting in the community.

This programme works best when there is ownership from the local church and it is integrated into the overall vision of the church and their mission. Volunteers coming from Salvation Army churches, as well as from other faiths, gain a greater understanding of one another through their mutual interaction.

Local church involvement

The relationship between the Anti-Trafficking and Modern Slavery Unit and local Salvation Army churches is an essential one. On a practical level, the large number and network of volunteers from Salvation Army churches has helped in the support of potential victims and survivors. Volunteers are able to become involved in several ways.

TSA is a first responder organization, and the Unit offers training to volunteers to help deliver the responder role. This involves interviewing a newly identified potential victim of modern slavery, and often these volunteers are the first people a victim meets following their rescue. The first responder volunteer will support a potential victim to understand the process of being referred into the NRM, what their entitlements are and whether they want to come into this specialist support service, and will also help to identify needs. The final decision as to whether this person is a confirmed victim is made by the Competent Authority within the Home Office.

Moving a potential victim from their place of rescue or referral to a place of safety is also the role of our trained volunteers. Volunteers from local churches, the wider community and TSA have been trained to deliver this service. Drivers and chaperones understand the requirements of this role and we have a system and process that enables this nationwide network of volunteers to respond.

In addition, we offer raising-awareness information and training sessions for groups within faith communities and the wider community. This enables people to learn about the issues of modern slavery and to understand them, to be able to identify potentially exploited people, and to safeguard. TSA has particular annual days that focus on modern slavery. These include our international anti-trafficking day of prayer. Resources are produced such as sermon outlines, stories, dramas and prayers. These help people engage with the issues and how the Bible can help teach and understand how God views this situation, and how we should respond. TSA also participates in the UK's anti-slavery day held in October. Every year we have a campaign that enables people to get involved and highlight the issues associated with this criminal activity.[4]

Just as during TSA's nineteenth-century campaigns of buying ethical matchsticks, when TSA educated people to be aware of the issues involved, we also highlight ongoing issues occurring today. We encourage people to ask questions about what they are purchasing, such as clothing and everyday products, and how to challenge the supply chains involved to ensure there is no exploitation within those chains.

We support and encourage the involvement of individuals, communities and churches to fund-raise so that additional resources are available for survivors of modern slavery. Within our Salvation Army churches, modern slavery has proved to be a unifying issue, connecting the generations. All can see that exploitation is wrong and all can engage and work together on this common issue.

For our volunteers, they have indicated that being involved in this work has transformed their lives and opened them to a greater understanding. For some, they can identify and relate to the survivors of modern slavery, as they too have experienced similar situations (albeit different in the detail) in their own lives. Hearing and sharing stories has helped bring healing and greater understanding as a result. For others, it has been a waking-up to the reality of this happening around them and they feel the need to respond and take action. Volunteering in this area enables people to truly serve humanity and make a difference to individual lives.

Moving forward

In moving forward there is still a lot to do! Awareness-raising is important so that people can learn to recognize the signs of modern slavery and can then report suspicions. Modern slavery does not mean that someone is locked away. It is possible to have control over someone by threatening their family or saying that they owe money. There is a need to support the building of resilient communities that will also take responsibility for stopping modern slavery. One way that this may be practically demonstrated is through enabling survivors to have volunteering, learning and employment opportunities. TSA's Employment Plus, and Co-Operative's Bright Future Initiative,[5] are good examples of this. These initiatives give the opportunity of a paid work placement and job for those who have been rescued from modern slavery.

Support to survivors is required as people move on in the recovery of their lives, whether they have chosen to enter our specialist support service or not. Some of these people will want to return to their home country, but others are unable to do so. For survivors, settling into their local community can be a challenge, so a sense of belonging is therefore vital. A development of trust is essential to enable a survivor to feel safe and secure even if they were to experience a relapse or were re-traumatized in some way. There is a need therefore to equip communities and help them to understand and enable a survivor to be who they are and not have to fit into any particular mould. This is true not only for survivors of modern slavery but also for survivors of domestic violence, ex-offenders, the homeless and so on. It is about giving and showing unconditional love.

Finally, a big challenge for TSA and other faith communities is the activity of perpetrators and traffickers themselves. William Booth said 'We go straight for the souls, and we go for the worst.' We should therefore be as concerned for the traffickers as we are for the survivors, and try to comprehend their situation. This would require careful consideration and understanding.

TSA's long history in responding to societal injustices, and its theological values, have shaped and informed our responses – and continue to do so. Through the work we do in this area of anti-trafficking and modern slavery, we seek to demonstrate a practical Christianity, with its sleeves rolled up. There is still much to be done but we will continue to give the care and support to the many victims of slavery because we believe God loves, knows and cares for each one and longs for them to flourish and enjoy freedom.

Bibliography

Chloe, 2017, 'Josephine Butler, Florence Booth and "The Maiden Tribute of Modern Babylon"', The Salvation Army International Heritage Centre, available from www.salvationarmy.org.uk/about-us/

international-heritage-centre/international-heritage-centre-blog/
josephine-butler-florence, accessed 16.11.20.

ECAT (Council of Europe Convention on Action Against Trafficking in Human Beings), 2012, Treaty Series 37, available from https://assets.publishing.service.gov.uk/government/uploads/system/uploads/attachment_data/file/236093/8414.pdf, accessed 16.10.20.

Flore, 2019, 'Matches and Morals', The Salvation Army International Heritage Centre, available from www.salvationarmy.org.uk/about-us/international-heritage-centre/international-heritage-centre-blog/matches-and-morals, accessed 16.11.20.

The Salvation Army, 2012, *Supporting Adult Victims of Human Trafficking*, available from www.salvationarmy.org.uk/modern-slavery/modern-slavery-latest-reports, accessed 16.11.20.

The Salvation Army, 2020, *Supporting Victims of Modern Slavery, Year nine report on The Salvation Army's Victim and Care and Co-ordination Contract*, available from www.salvationarmy.org.uk/sites/default/files/resources/2020-10/SA%20Modern%20slavery%20report%202020%20FINAL%20%281%29.pdf, accessed 16.11.20.

The Salvation Army, *Our History*, available from www.salvationarmy.org.uk/about-us/our-history, accessed 25.09.20.

The Salvation Army, *Supporting Survivors*, available from www.salvationarmy.org.uk/modern-slavery/supporting-adult-victims, accessed 25.09.20.

The Salvation Army International Heritage Centre, *The Criminal Law Amendment Act, 1885*, pp. 1–2, available from www.salvationarmy.org.uk/sites/default/files/resources/2019-09/4._criminal_law_amendment_act.pdf, accessed 16.11.20.

Notes

1 For further information, refer to The Salvation Army, *Supporting Survivors*, available from www.salvationarmy.org.uk/modern-slavery/supporting-adult-victims, accessed 25.09.20.

2 The case studies are shared with the survivors' permission, and initials are used to protect their identities.

3 As M's trafficker is still at large and she is involved in a police investigation, her identity and any personal details, including locations where events took place, could not be published.

4 For further information, refer to www.salvationarmy.org.uk/news/record-numbers-uk-nationals-need-help-break-free-slavery, accessed 25.09.20.

5 For further information, refer to www.co-operative.coop/ethics/bright-future, accessed 16.11.20.

'Thank God for Not Making Me a Slave'

GABRIEL KANTER-WEBBER AND MIA HASENSON-GROSS

The Jewish narrative on slavery

Slavery is fundamental to the narrative of the Jewish people. The Jewish festival of *Pesach* (Passover) recalls the story of Exodus, in which the Israelites were liberated from the shackles of slavery, and we acknowledge our freedom in prayer:

בָּרוּךְ אַתָּה יְיָ אֱלֹהֵינוּ מֶלֶךְ הָעוֹלָם, שֶׁלֹּא עָשַׂנִי עֶבֶד

Blessed are you, Adonai, our God, ruler of the universe, who did not make me a slave. (Magonet, 2008, p. 33)

Yet at the same time, slave ownership was sanctioned – the Torah presupposes and allows the possession and purchase of slaves. Despite this tension, however, the Jewish community has always been guided by fundamental principles of *Tikkun Olam* and those of justice and fairness – principles that continue to be at the centre of the 'Jewish response' to slavery in modern times. In the words of the UK's Chief Rabbi, Ephraim Mirvis:

The foundations of Jewish belief stand on the principle that all people are created in the image of God and every single person deserves to be treated with respect. Speaking out against the flagrant violations of human dignity implicit in modern slavery should be in our DNA. (Mirvis, 2017)

In the first five books of the Hebrew Bible, God reminds the Israelites no fewer than 36 times that they were slaves in Egypt (Waskow, 1991, p. 78). The legacy of having been an enslaved people is a defining characteristic – perhaps *the* defining characteristic – of what it is to be Jewish. Every spring, a whole week is devoted to the festival of *Pesach*, celebrating our liberation. It is indeed our liberation, not just our ancestors' liberation; as Rabban Gamliel, a leading first-century rabbi, writes: 'In each and every generation, a person is obligated to view themselves as if they [personally] came out of Egypt' (*Mishnah, Pesachim* 10.5).[1] Furthermore, every single morning, observant Jews will read a blessing thanking God 'who did not make me a slave' (Magonet, 2008, p. 33). We were all slaves. We are all thankful for our lives of freedom.

Yet Jews could own slaves! Despite possessing a deep religious, cultural, historical and personal understanding of slavery's misery – of the bitterness and humiliation of what it is to be a slave – Jews were allowed to have slaves. The Torah, in fact, contains a detailed set of laws regarding the acquisition, ownership, transfer and manumission of slaves. These laws were developed in later Jewish sources up to, and including, the *Shulchan Aruch* in the late sixteenth century (Faber, 1998, pp. 15–16).

The first part of this chapter will explore Jewish attitudes towards slavery, identifying three strata: (1) an approach that is tolerant of slavery, or even in favour of it, provided that Israelites/Jews are not the enslaved; (2) an approach that disapproves of slavery on the basis of it being bad for the slave owners; and, more recently, (3) an approach that universally condemns slavery and endorses modern global efforts to outlaw it. The chapter will then explore the relevance of Jewish principles of justice and human dignity. This part will then conclude by arguing that the journey through these strata is closely linked to wider developments in the way Jewish people have connected with events in the world around them.

The second part of the chapter will explain how, in practice, through the work of René Cassin, the Jewish community builds on Jewish principles of justice to bring a distinctive and unique contribution to the fight against modern slavery.

'Who, then, will wait upon me?'

This section will examine the first stratum identified above – namely, that which is sympathetic to, or in favour of, widespread slave ownership. Biblical restrictions on the acquisition and treatment of slaves were, traditionally, defended as a worthwhile system of regulation. For example, the Babylonian Talmud (approximately fifth century) defends Deuteronomy 21.10–14, which allows the sexual exploitation of female prisoners of war, by asserting: 'The Torah only spoke in response to the evil inclination' (Babylonian Talmud, *Kiddushin* 21b). The suggestion is that people have an evil inclination and are going to exploit female captives come what may; better that they do so in a regulated manner with at least some biblically mandated limits.

The same argument has been applied to laws regulating slavery. For instance, Katz (1925, pp. 30–1) describes how early rabbis went to great lengths 'in their efforts to protect this submerged class of beings', yet does not reflect on the obvious question of why the early rabbis did not abolish the status of 'slave' altogether.

Arguments such as Katz's are, of course, apologetic at best. Jewish law actively endorses the prospect of slave ownership where it need not have done so. One particularly glaring illustration of this is the fact that immediately after the biblical prohibition on ill-treating Israelite indentured labourers comes a series of verses (Lev. 25.44–46) permitting the enslavement of foreigners. Given that the former contains an explicit commandment in the earlier verse not to treat Israelite workers ruthlessly, the only possible implication from its absence in the latter is that it is permissible to treat these foreign slaves ruthlessly.

Some historical Jewish voices have displayed the same sense of pure entitlement to own slaves as must have motivated those who enslaved our ancestors in generations past.

In fact, some voices went even further than the Torah in supporting slavery. For instance, Deuteronomy 23.16 commands: 'You must not hand a slave over to their master if they seek sanctuary with you from their master.' Later generations of rabbis substantially scaled back this protection. First, they limited it to slaves who left a master outside the land of Israel and fled to somewhere within the land of Israel. Second, they required the slave to compensate the ex-master out of their (that is, the slave's) future earnings (Shulchan Aruch, *Yoreh Deah*, 267.85).

A particularly egregious example of a pro-slavery attitude is in the commentary of Rashi – Rabbi Shlomo Yitzchaki, an eleventh-century French biblical commentator – on these very verses: 'Lest you say, "If it is the case [that I cannot oppress Israelite servants], who, then, will wait upon me?", [the Torah answers: people] from other nations, they will be your slaves' (Rashi, Lev. 25.44).

Rashi's starting point treats biblical laws against the ill-treatment of Israelite servants as unwelcome restrictions. The verse in question left him with a follow-up question: 'If I cannot enslave and ill-treat Israelites, who *can* I enslave and ill-treat?' Seemingly it never occurred to Rashi that the answer to his conundrum was *do not enslave anybody*.

This coincidence of attitude between Rashi and the Egyptian slave-drivers might not, in fact, be pure coincidence. There is much precedent for the early Israelites naively and innocently adopting practices they learned in Egypt. Perhaps the most obvious is idolatry; the construction of the Golden Calf (Exod. 32.1–6) was an Israelite attempt to copy the polytheism that they had had an opportunity to observe while enslaved (Exodus Rabbah 43.7). The Israelites are recorded as having been anxious to copy other nations' government structures (1 Sam. 8.5). It is very possible that the custom of socialized slave ownership, a society built around an understanding that people own slaves, and with social structures designed to accommodate this, was also learned from the Egyptians.

Buy a slave, obtain a master

This section will examine the narrative that slavery is to be deprecated because of its negative effect on the slave owner. The Babylonian Talmud records the opinion that 'any [Israelite] who buys an Israelite slave is viewed as if they bought themselves a master' (Babylonian Talmud, *Kiddushin* 20a). This refers to what the Talmud views as particularly onerous burdens on a slave owner. The master's duty to feed, clothe and house are characterized as inverting the slave–master relationship. The implication is that it would be altogether simpler (and perhaps cheaper) for the potential slave owner instead to recruit an ordinary employee.

An older passage, from the book of Ben Sira, states that the main reason not to mistreat a slave is the risk of their deciding to flee, 'and then how will you find them?' (Ecclus. 33.33). The outcome being urged – that slaves should not be ill-treated – is of course perfectly laudable. But the framing and the reasoning is completely alien to more recent Jewish understandings of justice.

These are just two examples of many Jewish teachings that, while militating against the keeping of slaves, are not intrinsically anti-slavery but rather take the position that slaves are more trouble than they are worth. The lack of ethical or theological reasoning is striking.

It is true that, historically, slavery has been bad for economies. An economy reliant on 'traditional' slavery – widespread ownership of slaves by individuals – eventually withers because of that reliance. Anyone in the ancient world who was interested in doing well economically would have been well advised to steer clear of slaves (Wright, 2017, p. 1).

This can potentially work well as a tactical argument to deter evil and immoral people from getting involved in the slave game. However, as an ethical-theological argument, it is rather lacking. The most obvious and compelling ethical-theological argument against slavery is not that slavery injures the trader but that slavery injures the slave. We oppose slavery because it is (morally) wrong, not because it is unprofitable.

Some are enslaved, none are free

The final stratum is that in which Judaism came to recognize a moral dimension to arguments against slavery, rather than confining itself to the practical points discussed above. Rabbi Ya'akov Yehoshua Falk, an eighteenth-century Talmudist known by his pen name of P'nei Yehoshua, had a particular attachment to the idea that society, as a whole, is enslaved so long as anyone within it is enslaved. Commenting on the verse, '[In] the fiftieth year, you shall proclaim freedom over the land and all its inhabitants' (Lev. 25.10), he taught:

> It is not said, [proclaim freedom over] all its slaves; rather, over all its inhabitants. For in a state in which there is no freedom, even where this affects only a minority of its inhabitants, everyone who lives there is enslaved. We feel freedom only when there is no slavery at all in the state. Slavery is an affliction, and slave and master are afflicted by it together ... By manumitting its slaves, all the inhabitants of the state become children of freedom. (Greenberg, 1995, p. 143)

Of course, to a modern reader, this argument feels to some extent self-centred. While the P'nei Yehoshua was obviously right to state that slavery has a deleterious effect on everybody in society, he chooses to emphasize the disadvantages it has for those who are not enslaved. This seems misplaced and appears to put the cart before the horse. Yes, slavery is spiritually corrosive, but it is spiritually corrosive because of the horrific tangible impact it has on its victims. Good people should, in the first instance, strive to avoid spiritually corrosive activity not as a way of obtaining moral absolution but as a way of sparing its victims. What happened to the narrative of 'because we were slaves'?

Slavery: a global challenge

> There is a hint ... in Deut. 24:7 of the slave trade ... which is
> known to bring slaves from the land of Kush (Ethiopia) in the
> continent of Africa: its cruel leaders lead [the slaves] a very
> long way, [feeding them] poor food, clothing them badly and
> keeping them under guard until eventually they are infected
> by extremely virulent diseases.

So wrote Meir Loeb ben-Jehiel Michael Weisser, a nineteenth-
century Torah commentator known as the Malbim, on Deuteronomy 24.7. This was not a passage written in the 'because
we were slaves' mould. On the contrary, it was clearly the
then-contemporary transatlantic slave trade whose human
ramifications so deeply discomfited the Malbim. Faced with a
Torah, which explicitly permitted slavery, even with the limits
and 'safeguards' discussed above, his conscience moved him to
issue an extraordinary pronouncement:

> Know that, where we say one is permitted [to treat another
> as a slave], this only means that they will not be punished by
> the *beit din* (rabbinic court). However, is it not certain that
> they will be severely punished – in every generation – accord-
> ing to the law of the land? (Malbim, 1990, on Deut. 24.7)

Of course, Judaism has long recognized the authority of the
civil law. The principle of *dina d'malchuta dina* (the law of
the land is the law) places Jews under a religious obligation
to comply with secular legislation (Licari, 2019, pp. 143–51).
However, this principle is in great tension with a traditional
distrust of secular authorities and a desire that Jews should,
in general, not come into contact with the secular legal system
(Berman, 2016, pp. 1–2).

The Malbim's decision not just to accept the yoke of an
external legal system but actively to embrace it, and to embrace
it as helping to resolve a contradiction within the moral fabric
of the Torah, was remarkable. What can explain it? It is clear
that his position was underpinned by personal revulsion at the

treatment he had witnessed being meted out to (non-Jewish) slaves.

This marks a significant theological transition from particularism to universalism. Originally, Jewish attitudes to slavery were founded solely on our own experience; we were slaves, and we did not like it. Sometimes this attitude took a selfless approach: 'We did not like it so should not treat Israelites/ Hebrews/ Jews in such a way.' But it all flowed from the central narrative of Jewish peoplehood as being based within our own experience of slavery.

However, the Malbim's decision to define his position on slavery not by reference to his ancestors' experiences in the distant past but by reference to the experiences of other ethnic groups in his present, shows an increasing awareness and acceptance of Jews' role as members of society. It was no longer enough to isolate ourselves and stick to our own laws as much as possible, in part because those laws were clearly insufficient to tackle what was a global problem. The fact that he refers both to Africa (a contemporary place name) and to Kush (a biblical place name: Esth. 1.1) shows that he wrote with one foot firmly rooted in his Jewish heritage and another equally firmly rooted in the modern world. Slavery is a biblical phenomenon that continues to exist in the present day, across the globe, and its defeat requires a synthesis of these two approaches. Crucially, the two approaches need not be in tension. Slavery finds support in Jewish texts, but so does a quest for justice.

The king is enslaved

The Malbim would certainly not have used language referring to a 'contradiction within the moral fabric of the Torah'. As an Orthodox rabbi living in an age of growing biblical criticism, one of the factors motivating him to publish his commentary was to rebut any such suggestion (Silverberg, n.d., p. 2).

Nevertheless, through the fog of detailed laws authorizing and regulating slavery, it is possible to see a set of broader fundamental Jewish principles that deprecate any form of enslavement and uphold the innate dignity of every human being.

First and foremost, among these is the notion of *b'tzelem Elohim* (in the image of God) (Gen. 1.27). This is given extraordinarily wide application in the Jewish tradition. The Babylonian Talmud records a parable:

> To what can we compare this matter [the public display of corpses of executed criminals]? To two twin brothers [living] in one city. One of them was the king, and the other went out [to work as] a highwayman. The king commanded [that action be taken against his brother], and they hanged him. All who saw [his body] said, 'The king has been hanged!' The king commanded that they take [his body] down. (Babylonian Talmud, Sanhedrin, 46b)

As with many rabbinic parables, the king is a stand-in for God (Hasan-Rokem, 2000, pp. 114, 145). Even a highwayman, a real scourge of society, is a twin of the king. Because of their resemblance to the king, there are some minimal standards of treatment, which are non-negotiable. The levying of any humiliation, however one might try to justify it, could be mistaken for the levying of that humiliation on God. If a criminal is entitled to basic standards of dignity, *kal v'chomer* (all the more so) a slave, who has done nothing wrong. And if a corpse is entitled to basic standards of dignity, *kal v'chomer* a living person. *B'tzelem Elohim* is universal, applying to every human being, regardless of race (Shultziner, 2006, p. 668).

The phrase taken from an early verse of Genesis is just one of several maxims of human dignity, which are central to the Jewish understanding of the world and of God's place in it. In a judgment (in a secular matter) in the 1980s, Justice Menachem Elon of the Israeli Supreme Court referred to a dispute between two second-century rabbis, treating their words as inherently relevant to any issue of justice:

> According to Rabbi Akiva the supreme value in human relations is love of one's fellow man; and according to Ben Azai,

the supreme and preferred value is the equality of man, since every man was created in the image of God. And these two values – equality and love of one's fellow – came together as one at the hands of the Jewish nation, together forming a cornerstone of Judaism throughout its generations and history. (Barak, 2015, p. 21)

The principle of *b'tzelem Elohim*, and both other adages cited by Justice Elon, naturally have great application to the concept of slavery. They provide all Jewish people with a theological imperative to work towards a world where all are treated as emanations of the Divine image. Whenever we see anybody being oppressed or victimized, anyone enslaved, we too should cry out, 'The king has been enslaved!' and seek to remedy the situation.

What else can we do?

The endorsement of slavery by the Hebrew Bible, both Talmuds and later codes of Jewish law, has long formed the basis of anti-Semitic attacks (Zakim, 2000, pp. 38–40). In fact, there is extremely little evidence that the corpus of Jewish law on slavery was ever put to significant practical use. It was discussed, debated and refined through the generations because that is what Jews do. We argue about the meaning of our texts and we record the conclusions of those arguments.

It is no surprise that readers today are more comfortable with the timbre of more recent arguments than with earlier ones. Yet, in fact, an early source may provide a theological platform for Jewish anti-slavery activism.

The Jerusalem Talmud, compiled around a century before its Babylonian counterpart, engages in a discussion of which commandments apply to slaves and which do not. It concludes that slaves should not pray, because prayer is only for those whose immediate master is God – whereas a slave has 'another master' (Jerusalem Talmud, Berachot 3.3, 6b), an intermediate master: a human master. In one sense, this is a terrifying image, all the more so because of its piercing accuracy. A slave's master is as a god to them.

Today, we know that no person should ever hold so much power over another that they assume godlike dominion over that other's life. We know that slave traders assumed godlike powers over their 'cargo'. The idea of being in this position should strike fear into the heart of any Jewish person who has a relationship with God. What has gone so wrong with the slave's status as *b'tzelem Elohim* if they have an intermediate, human god, whom they do not resemble?

As well as striking fear, however, the Talmud's 'other god' description of the slave–master relationship can also be one of empowerment. Power can be used for evil but, critically, it can be used for good. The more absolute the power, the more good can be achieved. If a master is like a god to a slave, the master no longer has the luxury of holding up their hands, shrugging their shoulders and demanding rhetorically: 'What else can I do but keep slaves? Who, then, will wait upon me?' There is something faintly ridiculous about a godlike figure using their own alleged powerlessness as a defence. If a master is like a god to a slave, there is always another option. There is always something else a god can do to restore a fellow human's innate Divine dignity.

The Jerusalem Talmud's imagery, then, is somewhat degrading in its depiction of slaves, but its accuracy is a lesson in human power: the power to do good and the power to be oppressive. Faced with a dilemma, where one choice brings personal discomfort but the other makes us complicit in the oppression of another human being, we can, like Rashi, ask the question: 'What else can I do?' But we must ask it not rhetorically but sincerely. What else can we do? How can we work to end contemporary slavery and proclaim freedom over the world and all its inhabitants?

The right organization, at the right time

Writing in 2016, the UK's first Anti-Slavery Commissioner, Kevin Hyland, reported that he was 'pleased to see faith groups taking admirable action against this gross injustice [modern slavery]. The organization René Cassin, the Jewish voice for human rights, is in a unique position to bring change where change is needed most' (René Cassin, 2017, p. 2). This unique position brings with it a responsibility to act, to work, as concluded above, to end modern slavery.

René Cassin mobilizes the UK's Jewish community to tackle the reality of modern slavery by building on Jewish principles of justice and engaging both today's leaders and tomorrow's leaders to bring a distinctive and unique contribution to the fight against modern slavery. We work to promote and protect universal rights, drawing on Jewish values and Jewish experience. We believe that, as survivors of intolerance, slavery and persecution, and as 'speakers by experience' who understand the need for empathy and solidarity, the Jewish community has a uniquely authoritative voice in speaking out against slavery and speaking up for its victims. Thus, Jewish history and Jewish principles of justice and fairness can bring a distinctive and powerful contribution to the fight against modern slavery.

The lessons of our tradition to be thankful for our lives of freedom and for the human power to do good, the recognition and acceptance of Jews' role as members of society, and global history together should be enough to teach us that slavery is one of the great evils to eliminate from our world. Unfortunately, lessons are one thing; acting on them can be quite another. The uncomfortable truth is that today we are still direct beneficiaries of slavery in the modern world. As members of the Jewish community, we share a powerful story that compels us to take action to end slavery.

'No one shall be held in slavery'

The right to be free from enslavement in its many forms is one of the most fundamental human rights. Articles forbidding slavery are carefully articulated in the Universal Declaration of Human Rights (1948); the European Convention on Human Rights (1950); and in the UK's Modern Slavery Act (2015). The Universal Declaration of Human Rights states: 'No one shall be held in slavery or servitude; slavery and the slave trade shall be prohibited in all their forms' (United Nations, 1948, Article 4).

With a host of international, regional and domestic laws in place to prohibit it, the expectation is that slavery should be a thing of the past. However, there are tens of millions of men, women and children suffering different forms of slavery and exploitation all around the world.

The Minderoo Foundation's Global Slavery Index estimates that 40.3 million people are enslaved, including 24.9 million in forced labour and 15.4 million in forced marriage; over two-thirds of all victims were female (Minderoo Foundation, 2018). When we buy our clothing, technology or certain types of food, we may well be profiting from slave labour used in the supply chains of these products.

Although slavery is illegal everywhere, it can happen anywhere, including in the UK. The same Global Slavery Index estimates that there are 136,000 victims of modern slavery in the UK, trapped in forced marriage and/or sexual exploitation, or forced to work in the drugs trade or sectors like food packaging, car washes, nail bars, driveway and block paving, construction, agriculture and food processing. Particularly shocking is the fact that almost half of cases coming to the attention of the UK's official National Referral Mechanism (NRM) involved children under the age of 18 (Minderoo Foundation, 2018).

This is despite the existence since 2015 of the Modern Slavery Act, which includes provisions to increase the maximum sentences for human traffickers; assured protection for victims; higher requirements of accountability in supply chains; and the establishment of the UK's first Independent Anti-Slavery Commissioner.

A strong voice ... in the community

Grounded in a moral imperative backed by legally binding principles and a real sense of urgency, René Cassin acts as a strong voice in the Jewish community, galvanizing support from the community and beyond. By linking a Jewish narrative with a contemporary human rights narrative of modern slavery and identifying opportunities where the interplay between these two narratives can best be used, we have created a unique role as a faith-based organization campaigning for change. We believe that to achieve long-term change we must mobilize Jewish social activists and build networks of partnerships and communities, empowering them to become advocates for human rights. The challenge is in identifying the right approaches and opportunities.

The combination of religious and secular narratives enables effective partnerships across the divide. René Cassin's introduction, in 2017, of a Jewish spiritual leader, the UK's Chief Rabbi, Ephraim Mirvis, to a civil society leader, the UK's Independent Anti-Slavery Commissioner, Kevin Hyland, led to a powerful joint call to action. The meeting underlined the urgency of the Jewish community's response to the reality of modern slavery and added a significant Jewish spiritual voice of authority in support of efforts to end it.

Timing is another consideration. The use of 'hooks' in the form of significant Jewish and/or human rights dates can provide unique platforms for a combined Jewish and human rights message. For example, in December 2017 René Cassin's 'Human Rights Shabbat' (designed to help the Jewish community mark International Human Rights Day on 10 December) was dedicated to the topic of modern slavery. This was an opportunity to provoke community-wide reflections and discussions on slavery-specific statistics and personal case studies, and to look at how Judaism engages with the topic of slavery. Using the opportunity created by the 'natural' (weekly) gathering on Shabbat allowed for a tailored and effective means for awareness raising and sharing calls for action.

The success of this work and the continuity of the community's response depends very much on how effectively we can influence the influencers. At the core of René Cassin's work is the belief that the legacy of human rights can only truly survive through the engagement and empowerment of the community's leadership – current and future (something that can equally be said about the continuity of the community itself). For the community's response to truly be effective and long-lasting, it is important to involve its young people and provide them with meaningful and stimulating ways of engaging, such as offering a platform to explore the issue of modern slavery through the values that underpin their Jewish identity.

For some, this led to them writing about their reflections and motivations through a series of informative blogs on key issues at the heart of the debate including, for example, the difficulty victims experience in getting Legal Aid (Cartwright, 2018); how we should respond to the National Crime Agency statistics showing an increase in slavery victims (Bordell, 2019); and how interfaith action can help to combat the problem (Steinberg, 2018).

For others, it meant seeking opportunities for social action. For example, René Cassin has trained Jewish volunteers working in soup kitchens, homeless shelters and asylum drop-in centres on the growing link between modern slavery and homelessness. Led by external trainers, these sessions alert frontline volunteers to the dangers of modern slavery and give them the tools to spot the signs and respond appropriately. An intervention like this builds on the strong foundation of 'social action' and volunteering within the Jewish community alongside growing community-based initiatives to tackle homelessness, and adds another dimension to driving values of 'equality and love of one's fellow', as quoted above.

Working across the Jewish community's youth movements and Jewish student societies we often build on their ideological and ethical principle of *Tikkun Olam* (repairing the world), a useful framework for Jewish social justice by which, as Jews, we have a foundational responsibility, a moral obligation, to act not only for ourselves, our families and our people, but also for the global community and to empower them to draw on their Jewish identities and values for the purpose of social justice. A good example of this is the project to raise funds for the Snowdrop Project, a charity based in Sheffield that provides long-term community support to empower survivors of human trafficking:

> RSY-Netzer [Reform Judaism's Youth Movement] is so proud of the £350 raised to support survivors of human trafficking. Crucial to our movement's ideology is the importance of Tikkun Olam – repairing the world. Improving the lives of victims of human trafficking in the UK allows us to start locally and extend ourselves beyond. (René Cassin, 2018b, p. 31)

... and in Parliament

A successful campaign is measured by its ability to affect decision-making. Success is most often achieved through a mix of voices, including those from faith communities. Given the strong resonance of the story of Exodus and the Jewish journey from slavery to freedom, the ability to mobilize the Jewish community to use its voice and channels of influence on the UK's response to slavery is of particular significance.

As a Jewish human rights organization, therefore, it is important that we contribute a Jewish perspective to the decision-making and legislative process relating to the UK's response to modern slavery. When the draft Modern Slavery Bill was introduced to the House of Commons in June 2014, René Cassin played an active role in the legislative process, providing written evidence to the Bill's parliamentary committee. Our intervention was designed to help the resulting law be more effective and achieve its objectives in both preventing modern slavery and protecting victims and survivors. Prominent among our recommendations was our view that it was vital that victims of modern slavery should receive appropriate compensation, in one of two ways:

- a statutory victim compensation fund, which is funded by confiscation orders through which a victim can be compensated, *or*
- a statutory scheme in the Bill through which a court can directly order the defendant to compensate the victim for the crime.

Financial compensation is essential to any effort to let victims of slavery get their lives back on track, not only economically but psychologically and emotionally too. Any response to slavery should take recovery and rehabilitation seriously, and therefore the Modern Slavery Act should be driven by victims and their freedom rather than overly focus on the perpetrators and their punishments. An approach that treats compensation as the starting point on a journey towards autonomy and dignity will make justice about the people who are innocent as much as those who are guilty.

The introduction of the Modern Slavery Act was a welcome step and a measure of the success of the anti-slavery campaign to that point in time. But the Act is far from perfect, and the problem of slavery, and the suffering of its victims, persist. So it is important that we have continued to work on the issue, informing the debate within the Jewish community and pressing parliamentarians from across the political spectrum to build on the momentum the Act created, mitigate some of its shortcomings and voice their concerns about the importance of the protection of victims. Parliament, and other powerful coalitions formed and strengthened with like-minded organizations, are important platforms through which we bring the Jewish perspective and support for changes in legislation.

Linking modern slavery with other contemporary human rights issues in the UK, such as the indefinite immigration detention policy of asylum seekers and migrants, is another way in which René Cassin uses multiple approaches of policy and advocacy work to raise concerns on modern slavery. In September 2018, René Cassin submitted evidence to the Home Affairs Select Committee Inquiry (René Cassin, 2018a), looking at what progress has been made in the three years since the

Modern Slavery Act came into force and what more remains to be done. In the submission, we examined the 'guidance' statutes of the Act, which is less influential than the 2016 Immigration Act when it comes to the treatment of victims of slavery who do not have leave to remain in the UK. For victims of modern slavery and human trafficking, the detrimental impact of their immigration status is most notable when this results in their detention in an Immigration Removal Centre, and undermines the protection for victims who are apprehended in criminal exploitation settings.

Conclusion

This chapter describes the Malbim's embracing of an external, non-Jewish legal system as a significant 'transition from particularism to universalism'. René Cassin, the Jewish voice for human rights, takes its name from Monsieur René Cassin, the French-Jewish co-author of the Universal Declaration of Human Rights, the foundation stone of international human rights law. Monsieur Cassin was a proud Jew but helped ensure that universalism was written into the very core of the Declaration. Its second article proclaims: 'Everyone is entitled to all the rights and freedoms set forth in this Declaration, without distinction of any kind, such as race, colour, sex, language, religion, political or other opinion, national or social origin, property, birth or other status' (United Nations, 1948).

We share Cassin's pride in Jewish roots and his commitment to universalism. At the core of our vision statement, we aspire to a world where:

- everyone fully enjoys all their human rights as enshrined in the Universal Declaration of Human Rights, *and*
- members of the Jewish community are actively engaged in promoting and protecting these rights.

Everything in our work stems from those aspirations, and our success demonstrates the value of tapping into both the spiritual and secular elements of identity. And, of course, in that same spirit of universalism we acknowledge that the potential of such an approach is not unique to Judaism. It applies equally to all religions and is one of the reasons René Cassin has always sought to foster and partake in multi-faith initiatives on slavery and other human rights issues.

Every year, at the Jewish Passover meal, we still taste the bitterness of slavery by eating bitter herbs, and the tears of its victims by partaking salt water. But we remind ourselves that the journey from slavery ended in freedom. And in choosing freedom, we are commanded to ensure the same for others and to embrace a moral society, based on fairness and justice.

Bibliography

Babylonian Talmud, Vilna edition (1870–90).

Barak, A., 2015, *Human Dignity: The Constitutional Value and the Constitutional Right*, trans. D. Kyros, Cambridge: Cambridge University Press.

Berman, S. J., 2016, *Boundaries of Loyalty: Testimony against Fellow Jews in non-Jewish Courts*, Cambridge: Cambridge University Press.

Bordell, W., 2019, 'As modern slavery starts to emerge from the shadows are we ready for it?', available from, www.renecassin.org/as-modern-slavery-starts-to-emerge-from-the-shadows-are-we-ready-for-it/, accessed 1.10.20.

Cartwright, B., 2018, 'Modern slavery victims and legal aid', available from www.renecassin.org/modern-slavery-victims-and-legal-aid/, accessed 1.10.20.

Exodus Rabbah [Hebrew], Vilna edition (1878).

Faber, E., 1998, *Jews, Slaves and the Slave Trade: Setting the Record Straight*, New York: New York University Press.

Greenberg, A., 1995, *Itturei Torah*, vol. 4: 'Vayikra' [Hebrew], Jerusalem: Yavneh.

Hasan-Rokem, G., 2000, *Web of Life: Folklore and Midrash in Rabbinic Literature*, trans. B. Stein, Stanford, CA: Stanford University Press.

Jerusalem Talmud [Hebrew], Venice edition (1522–4).

Katz, M., 1925, *Protection of the Weak in the Talmud*, New York: Columbia University Press.

Licari, F., 2019, *An Introduction to Jewish Law*, Cambridge: Cambridge University Press.

Magonet, J. (ed.), 2008, 'Forms of prayer', in vol. 1, *Daily, Sabbath and*

Occasional Prayers [partly Hebrew], 8th edn, London: Movement for Reform Judaism.

Malbim, Meir Loeb ben-Jehiel Michael Weisser, 1990, *Ha-Torah v'ha-Mitzvah* [Hebrew], commentary to Deuteronomy 24.7. Mishor edition (B'nei Brak).

Minderoo Foundation, 2018, 'More than 136,000 people are living in modern slavery in the United Kingdom', *Walk Free Global Slavery Index*, available from www.globalslaveryindex.org/news/more-than-136000-people-are-living-in-modern-slavery-in-the-united-kingdom/, accessed 1.10.20.

Mirvis, E., 2017, 'We must all fight slavery', *Jewish Chronicle*, available from www.thejc.com/comment/opinion/chief-rabbi-ephraim-mirvis-we-must-all-fight-slavery-1.449795, accessed 1.10.20.

Mishnah, The [Hebrew], Albeck edition (Jerusalem, 1952–9).

Rashi, Commentary to Leviticus 25.44, quoted in *Mikra'ot G'dolot* [Hebrew]. Netter edition (Vilnius, 1859).

René Cassin, 2017, *Human Rights Shabbat 5778 Resource Pack: Modern Slavery and Human Trafficking*.

René Cassin, 2018a, *René Cassin Submission to the Home Affairs Select Committee Inquiry: Modern Slavery Act 2015*, available from www.renecassin.org/wp-content/uploads/2018/09/Ren%C3%A9-Cassin-submission-to-the-HASC-inquiry-MSA-2015.pdf, accessed 1.10.20.

René Cassin, 2018b, *Making the Jewish Case for Human Rights in the UK*.

Shulchan, A., *Yoreh Deah*, 267.8.

Shultziner, D., 2006, 'A Jewish conception of human dignity: philosophy and its ethical implications for Israeli Supreme Court decisions', *Journal of Religious Ethics* 34(4), pp. 663–83.

Silverberg, D., n. d., 'Torah Min ha-Shamayim: the Divine Origin of the Torah', Maimonides Heritage Center, available from www.mhcny.org/pdf/Holidays/Shavuoth/9.pdf, accessed 1.10.20.

Steinberg, E., 2018, *Faiths to Freedom: Interfaith Action on Modern Slavery*, available from www.renecassin.org/faiths-to-freedom-interfaith-action-on-modern-slavery/, accessed 1.10.20.

Modern Slavery Act, 2015, available from www.legislation.gov.uk/ukpga/2015/30/contents/enacted, accessed 1.10.20.

United Nations, 1948, 'Universal Declaration of Human Rights', available from www.un.org/en/universal-declaration-human-rights/, accessed 1.10.20.

Waskow, A., 1991, 'God's joke: the land twice promised', in O. Maduro (ed.), *Judaism, Christianity and Liberation: An Agenda for Dialogue*, Eugene, OR: Wipf & Stock, pp. 73–82.

Wright, R. E., 2017, *The Poverty of Slavery: How Unfree Labour Pollutes the Economy*, Cham, Switzerland: Palgrave Macmillan.

Zakim, L. P., 2000, *Confronting Anti-Semitism: A Practical Guide*, Hoboken, NJ: KTAV Publishing House.

Note

1 All Hebrew-language sources were accessed via the Bar Ilan Responsa Project (www.responsa.co.il), and translations are the author's own.

13

Awakening Our Slumber: A Missiological Response to Global Modern Slavery

KANG-SAN TAN

Globalization has created both good and evil. Together with transnational opportunities for trade, globalization has also resulted in syndicated modern slavery of over 46 million people. Too often, the onus of eliminating modern slavery is placed only on the countries where the crime is perpetrated. An atrocity as large and pervasive as modern slavery requires a united and global response. This chapter seeks to contribute towards a Christian understanding of modern slavery in Britain from a missiological perspective, arising from issues and challenges of lower-income countries. Therefore, Christian responsibilities in combating the problem of modern slavery and human trafficking involve both local responses as well as addressing some of the root issues arising from global contexts.

Christians today can be encouraged to work together to speak against modern slavery. The fact that modern slavery is so prevalent in our societies is a scandal in terms not only of the lack of morality in our society but also of the limited vision and mission of the Church.

The chapter will offer brief outlines of the sociological causes of modern slavery in the developing countries, indicating the crucial roles for local churches in addressing issues of injustice and social development in those global contexts. We will then reflect on the concept of the mission of God (or *missio Dei*) as the basis for a Christian response to the problem of modern slavery. Finally, the chapter will offer some practical recommendations for Christians everywhere to join in seeking God's kingdom through our advocacy and to fight against modern slavery and human trafficking. We will also outline BMS World Mission's new strategy towards 'People on the move', as a case illustration of a contemporary mission response to the issue of refugees coming to Europe.

In 2019, over 40 million people exist in a state of modern slavery. For instance, the UK alone imports over $18 billion of goods every year that are very likely to have incorporated slave labour in their production (Minderoo Foundation, 2018). Research conducted with leading UK retail brands found that 77 per cent of companies, when interviewed anonymously, thought it likely that modern slavery occurred in their supply chains (Lake et al., 2016, p. 8). Evidence collected by charities and academics would suggest that this is in fact likely to be far more widespread, and poses a significant challenge to the reputations of the businesses in whom we invest.

Modern slavery is the process of holding a person in forced service. The UK's 2015 Modern Slavery Act[1] identifies this as being comprised of four related areas: slavery, servitude, forced compulsory labour, and human trafficking.

While slavery is outlawed today, contemporary trade practices have created a modern equivalent of debt bondage. We remember the story of Amna in Chapter 4, who was brought to the UK by her husband and forced to work for various families, without proper work contracts, as she overstayed her tourist visas. There is no protection for workers such as Amna who are then subjected to abuses even though she was able to move from one family to another to work. In 2007, I met David, a young Malaysian Chinese who came to the UK to work as a cook in a Chinese restaurant. His travel fares were paid by the restaurant owner, who was introduced to him through a friend. David's low wages meant that he needed to work for a few years in order to be released from his work contract. His employer kept his passport, but did not renew his work permit. David overstayed and continued to work in different restaurants for another few years as an undocumented worker. He has limited freedom to move as he is now an illegal worker in the UK.

David shared with me how employers abused him, did not pay his wages and how he was moved to various towns in England with the constant fear of being arrested by the police.

Stories such as David's are quite common, but go unnoticed in society as the average citizen seldom takes the extra step of finding out about their stories and their hidden struggles. We may meet individuals as we frequent Chinese restaurants, but we do not normally know their names or work conditions. Therefore, modern slavery is a scourge in the UK that is often hidden from view. Debt bondage arises when workers are exploited and subject to extremely poor labour conditions because they must repay a debt. Human traffickers capitalize on desires of those in poor communities who seek a better future in countries such as the UK through migration. It is important to distinguish people-smuggling from human trafficking; the former is often accompanied with consent to be smuggled, while the latter involves victims of crimes without consent.[2] While people-smuggling involves illegal border crossings, human trafficking can be across or within national boundaries. However, whether people's movements occur with consent (people-smuggling) or without consent (trafficking), once there are elements of debt bondage and exploitation, those people who are moved eventually emerge as victims of trafficking.

Sociological causes of human trafficking in the developing countries[3]

Life is so confusing. Even now that I am safe from my husband and the families who exploited me, my circumstances are still uncertain. My immigration status is up in the air. I spend so much time thinking about all I've been through and worrying about the future. I do not know what it feels like to be happy. (Amna)

The story of Amna illustrates the need for us to understand complex sociological factors in developing nations that are behind modern slavery in the UK.

Definition of trafficking

The US Trafficking Victims Protection Act defines 'severe forms of trafficking in persons' as:

> (a) sex trafficking in which a commercial sex act is induced by force, fraud, or coercion, or in which the person induced to perform such an act has not attained 18 years of age; or (b) the recruitment, harboring, transportation, provision, or obtaining of a person for labor or services, through the use of force, fraud, or coercion for the purpose of subjection to involuntary servitude, peonage, debt bondage or slavery. (US Department of State, 2007, p. 18)

The causes of human trafficking in developing countries are complex and often reinforce one another. The *supply* of victims is encouraged by many factors ('push' factors):

- Poverty;
- Economic instability;
- Political instability;
- Public and private corruption;
- Organized crime;
- Violence against women and children;
- Armed conflict;
- Natural or man-made crisis forcing migration and vulnerability (may involve the loss of parents etc.);
- Lack of education (resulting in people being less informed and less qualified to get jobs);
- Lack of employment opportunities;
- Discrimination of racial or ethnic origins, caste status or gender;
- 'Cultural practices' – for example, discrimination against girls; marriage payments; prejudice against unmarried mothers (leading to the situation of babies being made available for commercial adoption); domestic violence at home;
- Fostering – in some societies a tradition of fostering allows a younger child to be sent to live and work in an urban centre with a member of the extended family, in exchange for a

promise of education or instruction in a trade. Taking advantage of this tradition, traffickers often position themselves as employment agents, inducing parents to part with a child, but then traffic the child into prostitution, domestic servitude or a commercial enterprise;

- Globalization and restrictions on migration – the rules of international trade have been modified to permit capital to move across frontiers and continents in an unrestricted way, whereas people (or 'labour') cannot move with the same freedom;
- Reduction in infant mortality in various developing countries has increased the number of poor families with large numbers of children. Unable to create new economic opportunities at home, sending one or more of the children away often seems a reasonable option;
- Ambition and hope for a better life elsewhere.

In addition, there is *demand* ('pull' factors) (US Department of State, 2007, pp. 18–28):

- Attraction of perceived higher standards of living elsewhere;
- Global demand for cheap, vulnerable and illegal labour;
- Demand for prostituted women, girls and boys;
- Sex tourism and child pornography have become worldwide industries, facilitated by technologies such as the internet, which vastly expand the choices available to paedophiles and permit instant and almost undetectable transactions;
- Temperament, such as obedience. In several parts of the world, notably West Africa and South East Asia, researchers reporting on child trafficking have observed that children from particular ethnic groups are regarded as more obedient or malleable than others. This apparently increases demand for them for specific uses (such as employment as a housemaid). In South East Asia, the readiness of girls to follow their parents' (or father's) wishes in leaving home to earn money through commercial sex is said to be caused by their strong sense of religious duty to obey their parents.

Predominant forms of trafficking

Incidents of human trafficking for sexual exploitation or forced labour may vary according to region and sub-region, with sexual exploitation reported by many sources in relation to Central and South Eastern Europe and by relatively few with regard to Africa. Where sources expressly report exploitation of boys, this tends to be in the labour market, while sexual exploitation is reported more frequently among female children.

The US Department of State *Trafficking in Persons Report* (2007) describes different forms of trafficking and slavery:

Labour trafficking

> Most instances of forced labor occur as unscrupulous employers take advantage of gaps in law enforcement to exploit vulnerable workers. Forced labor is a form of human trafficking that can be harder to identify and estimate than sex trafficking. It may not involve the same criminal networks profiting from transnational trafficking for sexual exploitation. (US Department of State, 2007, p. 18)

Bonded labour

> One form of force or coercion is the use of a bond, or debt, to keep a person under subjugation. This is referred to in law and policy as 'bonded labor' or 'debt bondage' ... Many workers around the world fall victim to debt bondage when traffickers or recruiters unlawfully exploit an initial debt the worker assumed as part of the terms of employment or when workers inherit debt in more traditional systems of bonded labor. Traditional bonded labor in South Asia enslaves huge numbers of people from generation to generation. (US Department of State, 2007, p. 18)

Involuntary servitude

People become trapped in involuntary servitude when they believe an attempted escape from their situation would result in serious physical harm to them or others, or when they are kept in a condition of servitude through the abuse or threatened abuse of the legal processes. Victims are often economic migrants and low-skilled laborers who are trafficked from less developed communities to more prosperous and developed places. Many victims are physically and verbally abused, experience breach of an employment contract, and/ or are held captive (or perceive themselves as held captive). (US Department of State, 2007, p. 19)

Debt bondage and involuntary servitude among guest workers

The vulnerability of migrant laborers to trafficking schemes is especially disturbing because this population is so sizeable in some regions. Three potential contributors can be discerned: 1) Abuse of contracts; 2) Inadequate local laws governing the recruitment and employment of migrant laborers; and 3) The intentional imposition of exploitative and often illegal costs and debts on these laborers in the source country or state, often with the complicity and/or support of labor agencies and employers in the destination country or state. (US Department of State, 2007, p. 21)

In reality, a range of combined factors come into play whenever conditions of migrant works are not well regulated, or local laws are not well enforced. This has often resulted in migrant workers becoming easy prey for various kinds of exploitation. Rather than focusing on rescuing individuals who are exploited, churches must recognize that more effective responses should focus on structural factors such as labour laws monitoring the employment of foreign workers, adequate protection of new guest workers, and stiff penalties whenever these strict regulations are infringed. The *Trafficking in Persons Report* notes:

Costs imposed on laborers for the 'privilege' of working abroad can place laborers in a situation highly vulnerable to debt bondage. However, these costs alone do not constitute debt bondage or involuntary servitude. When combined with exploitation by unscrupulous labor agents or employers in the destination country, these costs or debts, when excessive, can become a form of debt bondage. (US Department of State, 2007, p. 22)

Involuntary domestic servitude

Domestic workers may be trapped in servitude through the use of force or coercion, such as physical (including sexual) or emotional abuse. Children are particularly vulnerable. Domestic servitude is particularly difficult to detect because it occurs in private homes, which are often unregulated by public authorities. (US Department of State, 2007, p. 24)

Forced child labour

The sale and trafficking of children and their entrapment in bonded and forced labor are clearly the worst forms of child labor. Any child who is subject to involuntary servitude, debt bondage, peonage or slavery through the use of force, fraud or coercion is a victim of trafficking in persons regardless of the location of that exploitation. (US Department of State, 2007, p. 24)

Sex trafficking and forced prostitution

Sex trafficking is considered the largest specific subcategory of transnational modern-day slavery. Sex trafficking would not exist without the demand for commercial sex flourishing around the world ... Prostitution and related activities, including pimping and patronizing or maintaining brothels, encourage the growth of modern-day slavery by providing a façade behind which traffickers for sexual exploitation operate. Where prostitution is tolerated, there is a greater demand for human trafficking victims and nearly always an increase in the number of women and children trafficked into commercial sex slavery. (US Department of State, 2007, p. 27)

In summary, human trafficking is a complex evil that is transnational and with causes that are interconnected with problems in developing-world and low-income communities.

Although the root problems such as poverty, lack of economic power, education and social care made women easy prey for human traffickers, the continuing growth of sex trafficking is also caused by the demand for illegal sex in the Western world. Behind personal stories of women and men being trafficked from their home countries are the realities of income inequality in our global world. Therefore, co-ordinated global efforts are required if we are to combat the evils of human trafficking. Some focus should be directly on its victims (their rescue and rehabilitation); another focus should be on the arresting of the criminals who operate this enormously profitable criminal activity; while a more socio-political approach is also needed to focus on the struggle against regional poverty which makes millions of people vulnerable to exploitation.

Re-framing the mission of the Church if we are to address human trafficking effectively

Modern slavery and human trafficking is a systemic problem, meaning the Church will need a comprehensive understanding of its mission with regard to this problem. Mission is Christian witness, but it is also demonstration in word and deed. Whenever churches are more interested in the religious affairs of churches, we tend to demonstrate a lack of involvement or social concern with regard to the problems of modern slavery. Such a limited understanding of the mission of the Church could be the reason why human trafficking features poorly within the concerns of British Christians. Many non-Christian activists who are deeply engaged with problems of refugees, migrants and human trafficking question the credibility of Christians who are generally disengaged from the huge problem of human trafficking in the UK.

First, the source of mission is God himself. God created and sustained our world. Despite our rebellion and brokenness, God is the source of mission because he loves and cares for all his created ones. Humans are placed as communities to participate in the mission of God, as God's stewards, to care for all creation (Gen. 1.26–29; Ps. 8.1–8):

> When I look at your heavens, the work of your fingers, the moon and the stars that you have established; what are human beings that you are mindful of them, mortals that you care for them? Yet you have made them a little lower than God, and crowned them with glory and honour. You have given them dominion over the works of your hands; you have put all things under their feet. (Ps. 8.3–6)

Foundational to a creation-based understanding of mission is the unequivocal affirmation that all humanity, regardless of station in life, religion or race, is created in the image of God: to mirror God on earth, to represent him, and to be highly valued. Humanity's purpose is to discover, at the end of our life's journey, whether we have lived out the purposes of God, in valuing one another as God's 'crown of creation', made just a little lower than God (or 'the angels' in some translations). Modern slavery cannot be ignored or we become complicit in treating other people like animals or properties to be enslaved, bought or sold at will for selfish purposes. Humanity's worth is not based on something we have accomplished but something God had set for us, just a little lower than the angels/God himself.

Our brief biblical deliberations on the mass of humanity under slavery today challenges us to reflect on both the changing spheres of the mission of the Church and the unchanging mission of God. When things go wrong in our world, it is not due to the weakness of God but the fact that humans have chosen to betray God's purposes in creation by abusing fellow humans and have exploited fellow humans. We are no longer good stewards of all creation.

Missiologists such as David Bosch (1991), Lesslie Newbigin (1989, 1996) and others developed the idea that mission begins with God himself. Rather than focusing on the task and activities of mission, it should be understood as privileged participation in *missio Dei*. Not in the lost-ness of the world, nor the Great Commission, but in the saving sovereignty of God that overflows into his creation: 'God our Saviour, who desires everyone to be saved and to come to the knowledge of the truth. For there is one God; there is also one mediator between God and humankind, Christ Jesus, himself human' (1 Tim. 2.3–5). Mission is God's 'job description', describing what God does, and thus who God is.

Second, churches need to reframe their focus so that the locus of mission is not just 'the ends of the earth' but also 'mission at our doorsteps'. Traditionally, Christians in the West think about mission as sending mission workers overseas. The contributions of this book raise the new mission frontiers, and people groups who are now enslaved within our neighbourhoods and communities. In most smaller towns in the UK, we will find migrants who are working in bondage labour conditions, whether migrant workers in car washes, prostitution in most towns, those working in poor labour conditions (such as nail spas), and the stories of refugees who come to our churches. The mission of the gospel is to be witnesses in Jerusalem, Judea and Samaria, and to the ends of the earth.

Arising from such an understanding of the mission of God, the Church too is 'missionary by its very nature' because it shares in God's mission through its participation in the life of Christ through the Spirit. The Church's mission, therefore, is not additional to its being. The Church is as it is sent and active in its mission. It builds itself up for the sake of its mission and in relation to it.

Instead of seeing mission as primarily something British churches do (sending workers or funds overseas), churches need to recognize that mission opportunities are on our doorsteps. The mission of the Church is not only to reach out to people from diaspora communities who come to church, but to focus on those who are unjustly treated, the poor, and especially those whose human rights are trampled upon, such as exists in modern slavery.

Finally, the comprehensive understanding of the mission of the Church must move beyond mission being evangelism and the Church *preaching* Christ for the first time, but *demonstrating* it, which is also the act of Christians struggling against *injustice* and oppression; and it is the binding of wounds in *reconciliation*. Mission is challenging systemic and unjust structures that enslave humanity.

Responding to the challenges of modern slavery, could it be that the average church in the UK is still stuck with a traditional understanding of mission as preaching the gospel overseas and church planting – activities to extend the growth of local churches, rather than radical involvement as salt and light in our communities? Such a privatized understanding of the gospel has allowed Christians not to be outraged by the bondage labourers, forced prostitutions and prevalence of injustices committed in our neighbourhoods. God is King and he appointed all humanity to be his vice-regent, or crown prince.

The Church as ushering in the kingship of God among the poor

In summary, the Church must earn the right to be heard in postmodern Britain and that right has to do with authenticity of faith demonstrated in how God's kingship is expressed in the quality of the Church's responses to issues such as modern slavery. Based on the preceding section on how our theology flows into the mission of the Church, if we set such a high value for humanity then Christians must face the challenge that the kingship of God requires that we understand God's redemption as being over the whole of life and the well-being of whole communities (not only those who come to church but the poor and marginalized in our communities).

The Church is neither concerned with ghosts nor corpses, but with people. It is neither an underground railway to heaven nor another philanthropic organization, but instead is the Body of Christ. Christians must be salt and light in society, being God's eyes, hands and feet, and whereby we make a discernible difference in fighting against human trafficking, forced prostitution or bonded labour. It is an affront to the Christian gospel when a huge number of Christians seem to be so passionate about holding to their perceived truths of the gospel, but hardly about demonstrating the compassion and effective social actions in eradicating modern slavery in our communities.

This Body of Christ must include the whole of humanity. Such a radical understanding of the whole gospel for the whole world is not a recent popular slogan by modern mission movements such as the Lausanne Movement, but was the foundation for Protestant Christianity. Lesslie Newbigin outlined a comprehensive understanding of the Church as a missional community with the following expression:

> The primary reality of which we have to take account in seeking for a Christian impact on public life is the Christian congregation ... The only hermeneutic of the gospel is a congregation of men and women who believe it and live by it ... This community will have, I think, the following six characteristics:
>
> * It will be a community of praise.
> * It will be a community of truth.
> * It will be a community that does not live for itself.
> * It will be a community ... sustained in the exercise of the priesthood in the world.
> * It will be a community of mutual responsibility.
> * It will be a community of hope. (Newbigin, 1989, pp. 222–33)

Everything about the Church is an expression of a worship of a creator God who loves all people and desires that they live flourishing lives. The above six characteristics of vibrant and fruitful living should not be enjoyed merely within the confines of the four walls of Christians in local churches. Rather, such a vision of vibrant communities should belong to every refugee and every migrant who comes to the West in search of a better life, desiring a vision of shalom.

Through active engagement with the problem of modern slavery, the Church will rediscover its true identity as a missional community. The key to delivering the Church from its paralysis lies in the transformation of its identity and thus its expectations. In 1 Peter 2.9–10, it states that the Church is no longer to be just a religious order, but it needs to be:

- A Chosen Race – a new social order;
- A Royal Priesthood – a new religious order;
- A Holy Nation – a new political order;
- God's possession – a new economic order;
- People of mercy – a new vocational order.

How would such an understanding of the Church combat modern slavery and human trafficking today? Can we not envision the new chosen and religious order to include survivors of modern slavery? Can we envision the Church as a reconciling community whereby both perpetrators and human traffickers find repentance and reconciliation through the gospel of Jesus Christ, and fellowship as new humanity in Christ? Can we re-imagine the Church as a new economic order whereby its members only engage in buying ethically sources products? Can British Christians translate their religious worship into establishing businesses to help those exploited to find employment? Shouldn't the Church's vocational order be about protecting and safeguarding the most vulnerable in society by caring for survivors of modern slavery? When Christians in the UK begin to take seriously how society treats the most vulnerable communities under bondage in our streets and neighbourhood, we rediscover that these migrants are agents of transformation rather than mere beneficiaries requiring our help. Why? Because we then follow a Jesus who speaks to the consciences, moral vision and values of contemporary and global societies.

Awakening our slumber: some practical and collaborative mission responses

Historically, mission history is full of stories of God's people responding in mission against the injustices of slavery. In 1791, William Wilberforce presented the first Bill to ban the slave trade, but this was defeated by a landslide in Parliament. The following year, on 2 April 1792, Henry Dundas suggested an amendment be made to the Abolition Bill: the important introduction of the word 'gradual'. The Bill passed as amended and became law, the final date for slave trading to end, being later fixed at 1796. But this gave the slave traders' lobby the room to manoeuvre. Parliamentary delaying tactics came into play, further evidence was demanded, and it became clear that gradual abolition was to mean *no* abolition. Undeterred, Wilberforce persevered and brought his Bill back almost every year in the 1790s, but opposition against the abolition of slavery increased. Eventually, the 1807 Slave Trade Act became law on 25 March 1807.

During the height of oppositions against slavery in Britain, the Baptist Missionary Society (later known as BMS World Mission) was formed in 1792 by a group of Particular Baptists to send out William Carey and John Thomas as their first missionaries in 1793. While in Leicester, Carey 'belonged to a radical group that was outspoken against slavery and resolved to give up sugar because it was produced by slave labour in the West Indian estates' (Abraham, 1964, p. 12). Carey wrote *An Enquiry into the Obligations of Christians to use Means for the Conversion of the Heathens* (1792) and spoke of the 'accursed slave-trade in the coasts of Africa'. Therefore, since the early days of BMS, pioneers such as William Carey were involved in social reforms in India, in particular lobbying the British parliament to abolish *sati*, the practice of widow-burning in India. Later, BMS began to send missionaries to Africa and the Caribbean. Supporters of BMS in England became aware of slavery and discriminatory practices in places such as Jamaica. For example, there was a Bill in Jamaica that prevented 'Persons of Colour or Negroes' from attending meetings before sunrise or after sunset, and required preachers as well as meeting places to be legally registered. Joseph Gutteridge, a BMS supporter and General Council member of BMS in Britain, was involved in writing protest letters to Parliament about this Bill.

Although early BMS missionaries were instructed to avoid interference with local politics, others such as Lee Compere, who was sent to Jamaica, refused to remain silent in speaking against slavery (Stanley, 1992, p. 71). As early as July 1823, *The Baptist Magazine* of BMS claimed that it was 'high time for the British nation to awake from its slumber' and for Christians to petition parliament to abolish the slave trade (Stanley, 1992, p. 72). Sam Sharpe, a Jamaican Baptist leader, was recognized as instrumental in leading a campaign of resistance against the slave trade, and on 1 August 1834 slaves throughout the British West Indies received their freedom. However, various forms of bondage labour persisted in the guise of the apprenticeship system. After the initial slow and cautious responses: 'By 1837 the missionaries of BMS had earned a reputation on the island as the most vocal and consistent critics of the apprenticeship system' (Stanley, 1992, p. 81).

Our brief historical account raises significant parallels for today. Likewise, there is a need for concerted and collaborative actions by interest groups, both faith groups and civil and human rights groups, to respond to the complex problem of modern slavery. In the following section, we will highlight some practical examples of collaborative actions by Christians in combating modern slavery. In addition to prayers and individual church actions, there is a need for specialized mission groups to work together with other like-minded groups to dismantle some of the complex webs of human trafficking and modern slavery in Britain.

and Turkey to support the local and emerging Church in its holistic and contextually appropriate witness to predominantly Muslim members of the refugee community in a variety of contexts.

- *Discipleship and leadership development* programmes (training schools) to build the faith and leadership potential of new followers of Christ from Muslim backgrounds – who will then witness and lead discipleship activities within their own communities in a variety of contexts.
- A range of *humanitarian and missional responses* to refugee communities within the three contexts (source, route, destination) including core focuses, where relevant, on areas of ministry such as discipleship-making, educational provision, healthcare, development, relief, peace-building and leadership development.
- The *placement of personnel* (including volunteers, specialist short-, mid- and long-term personnel) from a variety of contexts into a variety of contexts where there is a missional engagement with vulnerable members of the refugee community through churches, networks and partner organizations.

In all the above activities, BMS World Mission will need to work with churches, networks and individuals who are passionate in wanting to combat modern slavery.

BMS World Mission ethical investment policy as combating human trafficking

BMS World Mission has an ethical investment policy that resulted in our organization working alongside the Church Investors Group, a membership organization for religious investors with over £25 billion of assets and that also encourages the companies that we invest in to take significant action to address the prevalence of slavery within their supply chains and to promote full compliance with the Modern Slavery Act.

Given the systemic nature of human trafficking and modern slavery, there are few (if any) businesses that can claim with any degree of certainty to operate slavery-free supply chains. Although the UK government, through the establishment of the Modern Slavery Act, overtly denounces any practices of modern slavery, in reality the enforcement of such clear rulings is rather weak.

Regulation outlawing forced labour, human trafficking and slavery is to be found in international human rights law and in the legislation of many sovereign states (including through the UK Modern Slavery Act, 2015). Further, eradicating modern slavery is one of the UN's Sustainable Development Goals.

As part of our shared commitment, BMS's ethical investment policy enabled us to join with the Church Investors Group in calling upon UK-listed companies to:

- Increase their efforts to identify human trafficking, forced labour and modern slavery in their supply chains;
- Review, assess and disclose the effectiveness of their attempts to address these issues;
- Support the provision of remedy to victims of modern slavery within their supply chain.

The Church Investors Group encourages companies to take a more robust approach to addressing slavery. Our investment managers are authorized to vote against the Annual Report and Accounts of companies deemed to be breaching the letter and spirit of section 54 of the Modern Slavery Act. Public listed companies have begun to respond to their corporate social responsibilities so that most businesses only stand to benefit from enhanced engagement with the risks of human rights abuses in their supply chains. We note that human trafficking and modern slavery has a significant economic impact globally, and that individual companies may suffer irreparable brand and reputational damage should their operations be found to be linked to human trafficking and modern slavery. BMS supports the inclusion of Transparency in Supply Chain (TISC)[5] in the Modern Slavery Act as a means to encourage all business in the UK to engage with the risks – for the good of their investors and customers, but also to protect potential victims.

In embracing a comprehensive understanding of the mission of God, local churches could likewise begin to reflect on how to respond to the challenges of modern slavery beyond traditional understandings. Although it is important to reach out to victims of trafficking in terms of evangelism, discipleship and church outreaches, there is a need to review churches' ethical investment policies, pension investments, and to educate members to evaluate whether our daily purchases inadvertently enable certain companies to neglect their corporate responsibilities relating to human bondage and trafficking. Christians working in marketplaces and businesses can also fulfil their social responsibilities through advocacy, raising questions and awareness so that their company policies have a robust and regular review into not being complicit in allowing modern slavery to continue unchecked.

Conclusion

So what difference will we make to modern slavery? In this chapter we have sought to approach the problem of modern slavery as phenomena whereby transnational actors have capitalized on vulnerable communities through the interconnected social pull and push factors, which has resulted in millions of people being trapped illegally and involuntarily without the possibility of freedom. We have argued here, first, that the Church's response should be grounded theologically within an understanding of who God is – as a creator God who created humanity as highly valued, and accorded the highest dignity to every person as a 'crown of creation'. Such an understanding of a loving Creator makes the presence of modern slavery a serious affront to God and demands compassionate responses from those who claim to follow God. Second, the Church's missiological response must embrace a comprehensive scope of mission that moves beyond a religious and personal dimension of mission, to become one that engages with structural and justice issues in the UK today. Like the coronavirus, modern slavery will continue to be a form of global pandemic that requires a global collaborative response by Christians, in participation with corporations and civil society. Just as historically the slave trades were funded by economic British interests, certain corporate trade practices and capitalist lifestyles of modern Britain likewise contribute to the perpetual supply of people as chattels for illegal trades today. Christian holistic mission responses to the presence of modern slavery and human trafficking demands a change of lifestyle as we become more sensitive to our contributions in feeding supply chains of corporate businesses in Western societies. We concluded with some practical and collaborative responses, ranging from ethical investment policies to intentional mission strategies, whereby mission groups such as BMS World Mission can work in partnership with local churches and Christians to combat the problem of modern slavery in the UK.

Bibliography

Abraham, C. E., 1964, *Carey and the Indian Church*, Calcutta: Baptist Mission Press.

Bosch, D., 1991, *Transforming Mission: Paradigm Shifts in Theology of Mission*, New York: Orbis Books.

Carey, W., 1792, *An Enquiry into the Obligations of Christians to Use Means for the Conversion of the Heathens*, Leicester (printed and sold by Anne Ireland). Refer to www.wmcarey.edu/carey/enquiry/an enquiry.pdf, accessed 8.04.21.

Lake, Q. et al., 2016, *Corporate Leadership on Modern Slavery*, Summary Report, November 2016, Hult International Business School and Ethical Trading Initiative, available from www.ethicaltrade.org/sites/default/files/shared_resources/corporate_leadership_on_modern_slavery_summary_o.pdf, accessed 12.12.20.

Minderoo Foundation, 2018, 'Global Slavery Index', available from www.walkfree.org/projects/the-global-slavery-index/, accessed 12.12.20.

Moyo, J., 2016, 'Corporate leadership on modern slavery: helping businesses do better, faster', Ethical Trading Initiative, available from www.ethicaltrade.org/blog/corporate-leadership-modern-slavery-helping-business-do-better-faster, accessed 12.12.20.

Newbigin, L., 1989, *The Gospel in a Pluralist Society*, Grand Rapids, MI: Eerdmans.

Newbigin, L., 1996, *The Open Secret: An Introduction to the Theology of Mission*, Grand Rapids, MI: Eerdmans.

Pierce, S., 2014, 'The vital difference between human trafficking and migrant smuggling', openDemocracy, available from www.opendem ocracy.net/en/beyond-trafficking-and-slavery/vital-difference-between-human-trafficking-and-migrant-smuggling/, accessed 12.12.20.

Stanley, B., 1992, *The Baptist Missionary Society*, Edinburgh: T & T Clark.

US Department of State, 2007, *US Trafficking in Persons Report*, available from https://2009-2017.state.gov/j/tip/rls/tiprpt/2007/index.htm, accessed 12.12.20.

Notes

1 Refer to www.legislation.gov.uk/ukpga/2015/30/contents/enacted, accessed 22.02.21.

2 Further information is available from www.opendemocracy.net/en/beyond-trafficking-and-slavery/vital-difference-between-human-traf ficking-and-migrant-smuggling/, accessed 22.02.21.

3 Research data in this section was compiled by Kat Wagner in 2014 for BMS World Mission.

4 BMS Strategy on 'People on the Move' is spearheaded by Arthur Brown, BMS Director of Mission. This section is taken from an unpublished BMS Internal Strategy document developed under Arthur's leadership.

5 Refer to https://assets.publishing.service.gov.uk/government/uploads/system/uploads/attachment_data/file/649906/Transparency_in_Supply_Chains_A_Practical_Guide_2017.pdf, accessed 22.01.21.

14

Exploitation of the Earth, Exploitation of People

JOHN WEAVER

Introduction

The growing expansion of economic activity throughout the world is placing great pressure on both the planet and the human population. Alongside the environmental crisis there is also a social crisis – immense poverty, social exclusion and attacks on human dignity in a world that is rich in consumer goods and opportunities for the economically secure. While those who profit from modern slavery and human trafficking are directly responsible for the harm and suffering that results for the most vulnerable, governments and business corporations must also take responsibility. The political ideologies, policies and actions of governments, and the economic, market and social decisions of global companies, have contributed to the exclusion and impoverishment of many poorer peoples, who remain largely voiceless.

In his encyclical *Laudato si'*, the Pope expresses his concern about our common home and the need for global, sustainable, integral development. He challenges us to avoid the short-term outlook that has dominated politics, and calls for a new political will. He maintains that we recognize that the destruction and wanton disregard for the environment is both a sin against ourselves and against God.

He outlines the scientific consensus and develops the thesis of the climate as a common good or a global common. In rehearsing the scientific observations of drought, flood, loss of rainforests, reduction in biodiversity, aquifers, coral reefs and glaciers, he challenges the developed world to see the impacts on the poor in the form of water poverty and crop failure. These demonstrate global inequality and injustice, and threaten the breakdown of society. He observes that world leaders fail to hear the cry of the earth and the cry of the poor. He concludes that, 'In the meantime, economic powers continue to justify the current global system where priority tends to be given to speculation and the pursuit of financial gain, which fail to take the context into account, let alone the effects on human dignity and the natural environment' (*Laudato si'*, para. 56).

Anthony Annett draws on *Laudato si', mi' signore* (Praise be to you, my Lord), observing that the desolation of the earth and the degradation of human dignity spring from the same flawed mind-set, a mind-set that seeks conquest over care, competition over cooperation and selfishness over solidarity. This mind-set turns people into masters, consumers and ruthless exploiters who ignore the needs of others and operate with a 'might is right', 'winner takes all' mentality (Annett, 2017, p. 162).

It is in such a context that exploitation through modern slavery and human trafficking is established and thrives. The anthropocentric ethical stance with its extrinsic values, which governs much of Western attitudes to the environment, extends into the commodification of people whereby relationships, the common good and the intrinsic value of persons, a function of theocentric ethics, is lost.

Pope Francis calls for integral and sustainable human development. Here there needs to be an integrated attitude that sees the development of the whole person and every person, giving all people the opportunity to flourish and to live fulfilling and dignified lives. We are called to combine combating poverty and restoring dignity with protecting nature and environmental stewardship. Economic growth must no longer be the sole goal of economic life (Annett, 2017, p. 164).

In his encyclical *Evangelii Gaudium*, Pope Francis identifies the abuse of people as a result of such an attitude focused on economic growth, and laments:

I have always been distressed at the lot of those who are victims of various kinds of human trafficking. How I wish that all of us would hear God's cry: 'Where is your brother?' (Gen. 4.9). Where is your brother or sister who is enslaved? Where is the brother and sister whom you are killing each day in clandestine warehouses, in rings of prostitution, in children used for begging, in exploiting undocumented labour? Let us not look the other way. There is greater complicity than we think. The issue involves everyone! This infamous network of crime is now well established in our cities, and many people have blood on their hands as a result of their comfortable and silent complicity.

Doubly poor are those women who endure situations of exclusion, mistreatment and violence, since they are frequently less able to defend their rights. Even so, we constantly witness among them impressive examples of daily heroism in defending and protecting their vulnerable families. (*Evangelii Gaudium*, paras 211, 212)

Michael Northcott reminds us that the Old Testament prophets criticized the people for breaking the covenant through their unjust treatment of the poor and the vulnerable, and through their failure to care for the land, as demonstrated in God's warning given by Isaiah (Isa. 24.5–6; Northcott, 2001, pp. 221–2). The exclusion of the poor and the degradation and exhaustion of the environment are seen as the results of ignoring God's care of creation and God's justice expressed in the Covenant. We can also note that Isaiah presents the alternative covenantal way of life (Isa. 24.4–12; cf. Isa. 5.1–7; 19.9; 32.14–20; 41.18–19; 55; 58.13–14), which brings peace and fruitfulness as opposed to the destruction that comes through foreign gods, and political, economic and military alliances. In Isaiah chapters 40—55, hope is presented when relationships are restored between God and humanity, and the earth is restored to fruitfulness and harmony (Isa. 55.10). Ultimately the earth will be full of God's knowledge and glory (Isa. 11.9; 6.3) and will be made new (Isa. 65.17).

Climate change

Climate change is the result of the build-up of greenhouse gases, especially CO_2 and methane in the lower atmosphere, producing an atmospheric 'duvet' that heats up the earth's surface. CO_2 is emitted through the burning of fossil fuels in industry and transport, and methane largely through the increase in pastoral agriculture. The science is unequivocal and the situation the world faces is urgent. The year 2019 was the warmest on record, and 18 of the top 19 warmest years have occurred since 2000.

The Intergovernmental Panel on Climate Change (IPCC) published in October 2018 a special report on the impacts of global warming of 1.5°C above pre-industrial levels.[1] In it they noted that extreme weather events are becoming more intense and more frequent. On a worldwide scale there will be more droughts, more flash floods and less reliable rain; there will be more frequent storm surges, coastal flooding and an increasing rise in sea level. It will be harder for many fisheries to make a living, especially tropical ones, as the seas get warmer and more acidic, and coastal ecosystems change. More people will be forced to move to make a living, and migration will continue to increase.

Loss of diversity of species is already a reality, and it is projected that over 10 per cent of insects, plants and vertebrates would be at risk with a 2°C rise in temperature. Impacts on the plant and animal world associated with other risks such as forest fires, and the spread of invasive species, increase as temperatures rise through 1.5°C of global warming. Tundra and boreal forests are particularly at risk of degradation and loss. Limiting global warming to 1.5°C is projected to reduce the risk of the thawing over centuries of a permafrost area of 1.5 to 2.5 million km², with the attendant release of large amounts of methane to add to global warming. Ice sheets at the poles, glaciers and coral reefs are projected to decline. Coral reefs are projected to decline by a further 70–90 per cent at 1.5°C.

There are human impacts for such climate changes. Regions at disproportionately higher risk, in addition to the polar ice caps, include dry-land regions, small-island developing states, and least developed countries, with up to several hundred million people susceptible to poverty by 2050.

Agriculture is particularly at risk with warming beyond 1.5°C, and reductions in yields of maize, rice, wheat, and other cereal crops are projected to result, particularly in sub-Saharan Africa, South East Asia, and Central and South America. The climate change impacts on sustainable development, the eradication of poverty and reducing inequalities would be greater if global warming increases beyond 1.5°C.

Limiting global warming requires limiting the emissions of CO_2 and methane. Global warming is likely to reach 1.5°C between 2030 and 2050. Therefore, to stay within a 1.5°C global surface temperature rise will require rapid and far-reaching transitions in the economy: in energy use, land management and farming, urban development and infrastructure (including transport and buildings), and in industry. These transitions imply drastic emissions reductions in all sectors, a wide portfolio of mitigation options and a significant upscaling of investment in the green economy.

We can draw three conclusions from the scientific assessment of climate change: the science of global climate change is unequivocal; the human causation is clearly demonstrated; and the effects are already obvious. The UN is agreed that it is important to aim for a maximum 1.5°C rise in global surface temperature and see global greenhouse gas emissions peak in the first half of the twenty-first century, and then begin to come down. Probably the biggest challenge for the IPCC is to make the bridge between the global science and an understanding of what people can do locally.

The impact of climate change on society involves issues of social justice and equality. We see the impacts on ecosystems with the mass extinction of species, and the availability of natural resources, with some places becoming uninhabitable, which is leading to migration. It can also be suggested that global climate change is resulting in civil unrest as the need to secure usable agricultural land and fresh water leads to violence.

Stuart Cohen and his colleagues note that the Brundtland Commission affirmed that:

Problems of human development (poverty, inequity, basic human needs) could not be separated from, indeed were *causally* connected with, environmental problems of resource depletion, biodiversity, pollution and life support systems ... [and that] the explicit linkage of the population and development 'problem' in developing countries with the 'consumption' problem in industrialized countries meant that SD [sustainable development] was inherently a global concept. (Cohen, 2018, p. 149)

Johan De Tavernier identifies a problem with the Brundtland Report in that it encourages a 'weak' sustainable development alongside a model of economic growth (De Tavernier, 2018, p. 150). He recognizes nine critical processes regulating the earth's ecosystem: land-system change; biosphere integrity; climate change; ocean acidification; novel entities; stratospheric ozone depletion; atmospheric aerosol loading; biochemical flows (nitrogen and phosphorus cycles); and freshwater processes.

While elements of ecological sustainability can be scientifically based, measuring social sustainability is often more uncertain. De Tavernier notes that farmers, for example, consider eight sustainability values: economic efficiency; community connectedness; stewardship; justice; ecological resilience; self-reliance; preservationism; and health. But he maintains that there is a human impact on the planet's life-support systems through increased food production, the introduction of new varieties, fertilizers, herbicides and pesticides, and through mechanization, including an increase in dairy and beef farming (De Tavernier, 2018, pp. 151–2).

Such production increases the burden placed on natural resources and makes a large contribution to greenhouse gas emissions, and causes a distortion in the nitrogen and phosphorus cycles. There are negative effects on land use, soil, nutrients, water and energy. Among the human effects is the displacement of people, with their resulting vulnerability. Climate change is predicted to lead to over 300 million refugees in the next 20 years.

Civil unrest, migration and vulnerability

In 2019 the United Nations High Commissioner for Refugees (UNHCR) reported that the number of forcibly displaced people had reached 70.8 million.[2] These included 41.3 million internally displaced; 25.9 million refugees; and 3.5 million asylum seekers. But statistics do not help us to fully understand; we need to recognize that each number is a person with a name, a family, a home and a history. Contrary to popular opinion, the Western nations, predominantly those of Europe and North America, are not flooded with refugees, as 82 per cent of all refugees are hosted in non-Western countries, which have few resources to meet the needs.

It is likely that there will be larger numbers of environmental migrants as sea levels rise and desertification and other factors take effect. It can be suggested, by viewing global maps comparing the worst effects of climate change and areas of civil unrest, that many of our current conflicts are partly a result of environmental factors. As large populations begin to search for fresh water, land that will sustain agriculture, and safety from violence and war, pressure builds in the places where migrants travel and political tensions arise between nations.

Degradation of the environment leads to marginalized communities migrating to avoid natural disasters and in response to lack of resources. Conflict and violence often erupt as a result. For example, the civil war in Syria, and the resulting rise of ISIS/Daesh, emerged in the aftermath of a year-long drought and water shortage in the Tigris–Euphrates River Basin, with climate change acting as a trigger in a complex political situation. Millions of people were driven from parched farmland to the cities. The massive population shifts led to tensions in the cities that contributed to the outbreak of civil war. This has been followed by hundreds of thousands of vulnerable people seeking to flee to Europe, with their resulting exploitation by criminal gangs, including those who trap these refugees in trafficking (Dávila, 2017, p. 149).

Manfred Steger observes that the Syrian crisis is an example of the problems, where impoverished land and poverty among the population led to the democracy movement in 2011. With the continuing escalation of civil unrest, over a quarter of the population, some six million people, have been internally displaced. Over five million have left the country, many finding themselves in refugee camps in Jordan, Lebanon and Turkey. Others have fled across the Mediterranean to Europe (Steger, 2017, p. 68). Such large movements of people pose a global challenge that is both political and humanitarian, and one that requires religious communities to address the concomitant issues of racism, discrimination and abuse, especially trafficking of vulnerable people.

In their book *Strangers in the Kingdom*, Rupen Das and Bret Hamoud ask what it means 'to be a follower of Christ and a people of God in a world where large numbers of people are forcibly displaced and where others migrate because they are seeking to live life with dignity' (Das and Hamoud, 2017, p. xix). Sadly, they note that racism, xenophobia and the closing of borders to unwanted foreigners have entered the political sphere.

Migration is a universal part of the history of the world population. Some have moved to find better land and climate conditions, some to escape overpopulation, and others have been forcibly displaced through wars and conflicts. Many have been trafficked as slaves.

The Bible is clear about the call on God's people to welcome the stranger and the migrant. Yet today they are seen as a threat and have become a growing social and political issue.

We can be pleased at the extensive work by Christian and secular NGOs in supporting and providing for migrants and refugees, but at nearly all levels of existence, displacement undercuts the security of belonging. There is a loss of community; homes and villages are destroyed, families separated, lives lost, and dreams of the future crushed.

Among people at risk of trafficking and slave labour are those defined as internally displaced persons. They have not crossed an international border and remain within their own country. While there is no international law that protects these people, the UN has drafted guiding principles that monitor such people, and holds national governments to account to protect those who are internally displaced. However, we can note that the national governments themselves may be responsible for persecuting and displacing people in the first place (Das and Hamoud, 2017, p. 18).

Stateless persons have no official country of belonging. There are estimated to be some ten million such people. They are among the most vulnerable to exploitation as they are unable to claim basic human rights. There are migrant workers, defined as anyone employed in a state of which they are not a national. There are both legal and illegal migrants. The latter have no protection and are often at the mercy of unscrupulous employers and criminal gangs, unable to find proper accommodation, without access to healthcare, and under the threat of deportation (Das and Hamoud, 2017, p. 21).

Throughout the world, and especially in Eastern Europe, Asia, South America and Africa, modern slavery and human trafficking is an everyday reality, where many women and girls are trafficked into the sex industry, and young men find themselves working in factories, mines or the construction industry for little or no pay, threatened with violence, and unable to leave. Modern slavery can be divided into four categories:

- Chattel slavery, where someone is sold into a family, often as a domestic slave;
- Bonded labour, also known as debt bondage, where a person is repayment for a loan – such labour is especially common in India, Pakistan and South America, where victims work in domestic jobs, mines, agriculture and brickmaking;
- Forced labour that occurs through trickery (the promise of a good job) or kidnap – migrant workers being particularly vulnerable;
- Sex slavery. (Carson, 2015, pp. 11–15)

Modern slavery and human trafficking is aided by corrupt political and economic systems. This is not something that is confined to the developing world but, as the UK's Modern Slavery Act[3] illustrates, is also present in so-called democratic societies under a well-developed and enforced judicial system.

In all countries where it is found, slavery is exploitation of the poor and the vulnerable, and human traffickers treat people as commodities to be bought and sold.

Climate change and social disruption

Michael Northcott notes that a climate-challenged planet without significant mitigation of fossil-fuel use will see a growth in civil conflict and mass migration of populations, together with increasing energy, food and water insecurity. As the century progresses, if there is no dramatic decrease in the burning of fossil fuels, billions of people will be forced to migrate from their ancestral lands. The majority of these people live in Asia (Northcott, 2014, p. 10). Northcott suggests that there will be conflicts between India and China as a result of the de-glaciation of the Himalayas, and in Africa, South America and Asia as a result of decreasing areas of habitable land as a direct result of a changing climate.

Climate change is not limited by political borders. Extremes of weather and ocean-level rise are leading to growing migration across national borders from the nations most severely affected, which is seen as a security threat to those nations whose productive capacities are less affected by climate change:

> The militarization of borders, the growing confinement of migrants to immigration camps or virtual prisons, and military interventions in climate-threatened regions against 'insurgents' – including presently Afghanistan, Mali, Pakistan, and Yemen – thus reveal the political response of nation-states to climate change more clearly than their claimed reductions in greenhouse gas emissions. (Northcott, 2014, p. 212)

It is these migrants who find themselves at the greatest risk from human traffickers.

Climate change increases the risk of natural disasters and places a strain on livelihoods; it exacerbates poverty and can potentially cause situations of conflict and instability. Yet climate change is rarely considered as a potential contributor to modern slavery and human trafficking in global discussions. Climate disasters, cumulative and sudden, can cause unexpected loss of land and lives, and destruction of means of livelihoods, instantly plunging those without safety nets into poverty. In the immediate aftermath of a disaster, displacement is likely to occur, giving space for traffickers to operate and exploit affected people in their desire for safety and search for means of income to help restore their lives.[4]

Many displaced persons who see migration as the only viable option to pursue better opportunities may seek assistance from human smugglers, placing themselves at risk of many of the forms of exploitation that are commonly associated with trafficking, such as sexual exploitation, forced labour, forced marriage, as well as organ removal. Trafficking takes place in camps/camp-like settings established to shelter those displaced by natural disasters.

Populations who depend on natural resources are affected by events such as coastal erosion, sea-level rise and glacial retreat, and may take proactive measures to diversify their income, which may lead them to collude with traffickers.[5]

Climate migrants who move to nearby cities often live in slums. Without savings, education or advanced skills, and with limited access to employment, these migrants have minimal bargaining power to assert their rights and can become easy targets for exploitation. Many find themselves engaged in unregulated domestic work or in the construction sector or clothing factories. Women are especially vulnerable as reports by the UN Migration Agency show that incidents of women originating from climate-vulnerable areas are being exploited. Criminal agents promise employment, but instead sell vulnerable women to brothels where they are sexually exploited.

Many industries that are open to human trafficking or labour exploitation also have a detrimental impact on the environment and contribute to climate change. In Asia, they often lie at the root of supply chains that connect the global economy. There are numerous, well-documented cases in which environmentally damaging extractive industries are underpinned by large numbers of migrant workers in forced labour situations. In South East Asia and Brazil, the lucrative palm oil industry is heavily dependent on less-than-ethical recruitment of foreign labour, as well as coercive labour practices. This industry exemplifies the link between forced labour associated with modern slavery, industrial-scale and often unregulated logging, and the widespread destruction of the Amazonian, Bornean and Sumatran rainforests.[6]

There is a hidden violence behind cheap clothing produced for a Western market. People involved in the production of cheap clothing are often exposed to harsh chemicals and unsafe conditions, such as crumbling buildings, overcrowded facilities and little ventilation – often receiving poor pay for long hours and no overtime pay (Dávila, 2017, pp. 150–3).

In many cases ethnic or religious conflict adds to the pressure on people to leave. For example, religious violence against the stateless, Muslim minority in Myanmar sent nearly a million Rohingya across the border to Bangladesh, where they sought shelter. From these camps women and children are being trafficked into exploitative domestic work and others into brothels.[7] Men can be subjected to forced labour, while others are fleeing to different countries in South East Asia.[8]

It is important that data collection and research on exploitation and trafficking trends should also include an assessment of environmental conditions and climate impacts on livelihoods, particularly if this appears as a primary driver towards trafficking or smuggling.[9]

We are now recognizing issues beyond the obvious for what climate change is going to mean. It has to be understood in the wider context of migration, human trafficking and the movement of people in a warming world.

Michael Gerrard, director of the Sabin Centre for Climate Law at Columbia University (in an article in *The Revelator*), worries that international agreements and domestic laws might not be able to combat the scale of human trafficking as a result of climate change. He writes: 'Unless there's a corresponding dramatic rise in the governmental resources devoted to enforcement, we simply won't have enough people carrying out the enforcement.' In order to mitigate the amount of trafficking projected to increase as a result of global climate change, the world's economies need to transition from using fossil fuels, which will decrease greenhouse gas emissions and can make the impacts of climate change less severe.[10]

It is also vital to improve the ability of vulnerable communities to stay in place so that they won't be tempted or lured away by human traffickers. To do this people will need to have access to clean water and adequate food supplies, and build homes that can withstand climate change – for example, building houses on stilts to protect against flood and rises in the sea level.

Human values, ecology and the environment

In addressing environmental degradation, there is a need to approach the context for human inhabitants, with their social, cultural, historical, economic, religious and environmental ties (Artinian-Kaiser, 2018, p. 167). For Christians, it is God who brings about redemption. Oliver O'Donovan (1994, p. 55) suggests that the resurrection (a) affirms the goodness of creation (as having its own meaning and purpose) *and* (b) holds forth the promise that 'all shall be made alive' one day (Artinian-Kaiser, 2018, p. 173). Through resurrection, creation is both restored and transformed and enlivened in new ways. We can add that in Romans 8.18–25 we are challenged to understand that the redemption of all creation is enabled by Christians acting in a Christlike way through the Spirit.

Divine wisdom bound up in love seeks to understand the complex relationships in the human and non-human environments. We seek to know how God's Spirit may be calling the world out of brokenness and into a new way of being, and be challenged as to how we might be involved. We ask how God may be calling us to participate in God's redeeming and transforming purposes for the world, a world in which human and non-human creatures flourish with abandon (Artinian-Kaiser, 2018, pp. 175–6).

The destruction of lives and the environment is not confined to the developing world. The twenty-first-century freshwater crises and conflicts result from complex intersections of hydrogeology, globalized political economies predicated on (established) resource extraction, and diverse cultural understandings or social norms regarding the distribution and use of water (Zenner, 2018, p. 179).

Christiana Zenner outlines the example of the Dakota Access Pipeline to transport oil from North Dakota to Illinois, and explores the dangers to water resources for the native American peoples of the region. She maintains that, like many extractive projects worldwide, the Dakota Access Pipeline is 'inextricably interwoven with legacies of racism, economic exploitation, and histories' that are similar for other marginalized communities (Zenner, 2018, p. 186).

She challenges political leaders to recognize that it is important that the historically marginalized and vulnerable populations, rather than the more powerful parties, are able to take the decisions in any projects. Scholarly authority is not the same as lived cultural praxis on matters of ecological and social values. She emphasizes that water is life – this truth must be upheld against the structures, legal regimes and physical oppressions that accompany our particular forms of neocolonialism, such as the Dakota Access Pipeline (Zenner, 2018, p. 194).

In *Laudato si'*, Pope Francis recognizes the seriousness of the global environmental crisis and draws out its implications for the world's poor and disadvantaged. He identifies the human causes, and lays the blame fairly and squarely on the activities of the developed world. The environmental crisis disproportionately impacts the poor in the form of water poverty and crop failure. These demonstrate global inequality and injustice, and threaten the breakdown of society. He rightly recognizes that ecology teaches us that everything is interconnected, as environmental degradation affects social structures and cultural identity, the very meaning of life and community. We must consider what kind of world we want to leave for those who come after us. This leads us to consider the meaning of our own lives – Who are we, and what are we here for? (*Laudato si'*, paras 48–52).

The consequences of climate change affect the most vulnerable people, and we recognize that it is one of the causes of poverty and forced migration, which are breeding grounds for modern slavery and human trafficking, forced labour, prostitution and organ trafficking.

The Pope commends to the Church new lifestyles that demonstrate a covenant between humanity and the environment. Furthermore, he challenges us to an ecological conversion whereby the effects of our encounter with Jesus Christ become evident in our relationship with the world around us. He calls us to find joy and peace in a life of simplicity, with love overflowing in our acts of care for creation. Environmental harm and ecological harm both directly impact the poor and are the result of destruction and exploitation through a web of production and consumption that is environmentally unsustainable and spiritually toxic (Dávila, 2017, pp. 145–59).

One of the deepest connections made in *Laudato si'* is how care for creation directly impacts real human beings, real communities and entire societies, especially the poor and racially marginalized. This is a case of environmental justice as it is the poorest who suffer the most. 'Conflict arises when the best intentions, in this case to "save the planet", run into our inability to overcome racism, xenophobia, and classism that mark human interactions in [some countries] and globally' (Dávila, 2017, p. 146).

The goods of God's creation are to be shared with all. There is a need to care for the material well-being of a person at the communal, social, national and international level. We need:

a solidarity with the poor and the marginalized as we work together in the struggle against injustice and oppression, the option[;] for the poor offers a comprehensive vision of what Christian discipleship ought to look like in historical circumstances marked by radical differences and human suffering as a result of the sin of the world. (Dávila, 2017, pp. 148–9)

It is the responsibility of all Christians to be attentive to the cry of the poor, developing an ability to listen to the vulnerable and oppressed.

Our moral and spiritual engagement with the effects of climate change among the poorest of the world must acknowledge that the environmental crisis creates conflict and material hardship. We must be attentive to the plight of migrants and refugees and their exploitation, often as trafficked people, and recognize how our lifestyle has contributed to it.

A central message of the Bible is of a redeeming God who sets the captives free. Christians are challenged to join in God's mission to bring liberation to the vulnerable and displaced. The Old Testament year of Jubilee (Lev. 25) was to include cancelling all debts and setting all slaves free, but it was never celebrated, and it is only with Jesus that Jubilee is declared (Luke 4.18–19), which caused his hearers to be amazed. Jesus declared that he had come to set the captives free.

God approaches broken humanity with a desire to comfort, heal and provide for needs. God does this through the call to the people of God to care for the widow, the orphan and the stranger as a key part of the Church's mission. In addressing human displacement, we understand God's care for all human beings, especially the poor, the vulnerable and those who do not belong.

Marion Carson states that Christians of all traditions are agreed that slavery is unacceptable. She challenges us to uphold the United Nations' Declaration that freedom is a human right: 'no one should be able to view another as his or her property. We believe that no one should be able to force another person to work without pay or by means of coercion and deceit' (Carson, 2015, p. 1). This is against everything we understand about God's justice in the world.

Love of God; love of neighbour; exploitation, vulnerability and justice

There is no prospect of actualization for the Pope's call to ecological conversion without reform of the purpose and governance of corporations. The corporation has become a machine generating shareholder value. Those employed are cogs in the machine. The modern corporation is a non-human embodiment of power and technology, yet its origin lies in a community of persons. There is a need to 'dethrone the cult of shareholder primacy' and recognize the corporation as a community of enterprise. The mind-set that has no sincere concern for the environment also has no concern for the most vulnerable members of society (Hayes, 2018, pp. 85–6).

Society can and must change if humanity is to survive climate change, but necessary change demands a conversion that recognizes the integral ecology we inhabit. It is possible that the pace of economic growth will slow if its true costs to the earth and the poor are internalized by business. The external costs of fossil-fuel energy are beginning to be accepted (Hayes, 2018, pp. 91–2).

Women are more affected by environmental degradation as they are the ones typically responsible for the daily sustenance of families and community. Oppression of the poor finds women and girls at the bottom of the pile. This is because the political will is lacking. The UN advocacy for sustainable development is ineffectual as states obstruct international agreements in the name of national interests.

In rural areas women constitute the majority of agricultural labour. In developing countries women farmers account for 43 per cent of all food production and 67 per cent of livestock keepers. But less than 20 per cent are landowners and less than 5 per cent in north and west Africa. Indigenous women especially, with their knowledge of biodiversity and of edible and medicinal plants, should play a leading role in the response to climate change.

Lisa Sowle Cahill is right to observe that:

We must realize that at a very basic level, when women are excluded from essential means of sustenance, subjugated in family and community, and regularly exposed to physical violence, advocacy for women's dignity in general is a precondition of environmental empowerment. (Cahill, 2018, pp. 135–46)

Pope Francis, in *Laudato si'*, rightly observes that progress has become the dominant argument, but such progress must be in the service of all humanity. He challenges us to recover Christian values and goals in our relationship with the environment, others and God. The Pope believes we need a Christlike attitude, one that recognizes that all people are made in the image of God and none is superfluous; and that all species give glory to God, who cares for each one (Luke 12.6; Matt. 6.26). He outlines a sacramental creation where God is manifest and present in the whole created world, and where all things are created, redeemed and reconciled through Christ (Col. 1.15–20). He goes further and states that 'every act of cruelty towards any creature is contrary to human dignity.' He sees the earth as a collective good, a shared inheritance, which offers fundamental rights to the poor (Hodson and Hodson, 2017).

Liberation theologians side with the marginalized of society and of the world itself. The association of the devastation of the land with poverty has meant that the cry of the poor is joined by the cry of the earth (Deane-Drummond, 2017, p. 37).

The glory of God, expressed in the gift of life, is concerned with the well-being of all creatures in a way that challenges and seeks to transform current economic practice. Sin is a move away from such flourishing at individual or institutional levels.

Economic thinking based purely on the market tends to assume that there are unlimited natural resources, which clearly there are not. We cannot put a monetary value on environmental good – ecological concern reflects human values as citizens, whereas the market economy presupposes preferences as consumers. We need to judge according to common good and intrinsic value.

Extreme poverty, social exclusion and environmental injustice appear together in communities all over the world. This is one reason for the environmental justice movement. Ecological issues need to find a place on the political agenda in our concern for future generations. One of the difficulties of a global market economy is that it serves to undermine the economic authority and political power of individual nation states, and the protection of the most vulnerable (Deane-Drummond, 2017, p. 119).

The UN Secretary-General António Guterres, speaking on the need to step up protection for the most vulnerable, observed that most countries have the necessary laws in place, but 'more needs to be done to bring transnational trafficking networks to justice and, most of all, to ensure that victims are identified and can access the protection and services they need.'[11]

The UN Office on Drugs and Crime (UNODC) representative urged member states to step up efforts towards, and investment in, long-term solutions to ensure compensation for people who are trafficked. Maria Grazia Giammarinaro, Special Rapporteur on trafficking of persons, has stressed that 'restrictive and xenophobic migration policies and the criminalization of migrants, as well as of NGOs and individuals providing humanitarian aid, are incompatible with effective action against human trafficking.' Presenting social inclusion as the 'only and right answer' to exploitation and trafficking, she argued that 'politicians fuelling hatred, building walls, condoning the detention of children and preventing vulnerable migrants from entering their territories are working against the interests of their own countries.'

She further asserted that making provision for the social integration of migrants is 'crucial also for victims of trafficking, including women suffering discrimination, gender-based violence and exploitation, and children subjected to abuse during their journey, especially when travelling alone'. Therefore she proposed that all member states should 'remove obstacles hampering access to justice for victims by giving residency status to people who have been trafficked, and by ensuring they are not detained or prosecuted for illegal activities they may have been involved in as a result of being trafficked'.[12]

The political response can be summed up by the principles presented under the Earth Charter (Foltz, 2003, pp. 591–6), which included among its principles: to respect the earth and life in all its diversity; to care for the community of life with understanding, compassion and love; to protect and restore the integrity of the earth's ecological systems – biodiversity and natural processes; to adopt patterns of production, consumption and reproduction that safeguard the earth's regenerative capacities, human rights, and community well-being; and to ensure that economic activities and institutions at all levels promote human development in an equitable and sustainable manner.

Conclusion

As Christians we have a moral responsibility. Christ is not only Lord of the lives and bodies of Christians, but Lord of the whole created order. The implications of the resurrection extend beyond the lives of Christians to reveal God's intention to restore the righteous peace, or *shalom*, of the whole of creation.

Righteousness and justice, which are intrinsic to the being of God, are also writ large in the material and moral framework of the creation that God has made, and with which God remains in continuing relationship. We have in this tradition, then, a powerful insight into the ecological nature of divine justice, and so of created justice (Northcott, 2001).

In Jesus, God is a participant in creation, totally committed and personally present (Heb. 4.14–16; John 1.14; 3.16). It is God's grace that is our ultimate hope, and it is God who seeks the redemption of the whole of creation. Christians who regularly pray 'Thy kingdom come, Thy will be done, on earth as in heaven' are part of God's mission (Rom. 8.18–25). Unlike the nations surrounding it, Israel was to be an alternative society but its people became like their neighbours and found that they were under God's judgement in exile. The Church (or, more specifically, Christians) is now called to be that alternative society – God's kingdom people on earth, which creation waits for with eager longing.

God promises to be present with us in the realities of life (Ps. 23; Isa. 43.1–5; Matt. 28.20), and encourages us to hold on to hope in the face of uncertainty. We learn from both Amos and Jeremiah that the false prophets promised hope without catastrophe, while God's prophets offer hope beyond catastrophe.

We can speak of the hope of judgement; that there is accountability for our lack of care of the poor and of the environment. Our hope is based on God and God's justice and grace, which is not thwarted by human sinfulness.

Ultimate hope is in God and is eternal, while human hope is temporal and uncertain. As Christians we are called to a hopeful discipleship in the light of our ultimate hope in God's promises and purposes (Weaver, 2012, pp. 134–55). We live as those who are created in the image of God and cooperate with God's transformative action in and for the world. We cannot separate the religious parts of our life from the rest; God is active and inhabits every part of our world and our lives. We are called to work with God in renewing and transforming this world. Every person is made in God's image and every person is offered God's grace and, in turn, the opportunity to work together with God in the creation and re-creation of the world.

Our response is to act with particular concern and compassion for the vulnerable, the oppressed, the trafficked, the voiceless and the powerless. As Christians we are called to love God and love our neighbour, which will include the example that we present in our lifestyle: our attitude to those who the world often ignores or despises; our consumption, and especially our use of fossil fuels. This will also include our political will through our engagement in the political process, seeking to influence politicians to make social and environmental considerations a priority in legislation.

In a world where modern slavery and human trafficking is a hidden and overlooked blight on humanity, Christian disciples are called to embody an alternative narrative, sovereignty and hope – to express a different model of society.

In Christ we live as hopeful disciples, restored to our full humanity as God's stewards of creation, embodying the image of God, who has declared creation good and calls on human beings to exercise a godly care of the whole of creation.

Bibliography

Annett, A., 2017, 'The economic vision of Pope Francis', in Vincent J. Miller (ed.), *The Theological and Ecological Vision of Laudato si': Everything is Connected*, London: T & T Clark.

Artinian-Kaiser, R., 2018, 'Restoration and transformation: a theological engagement with ecological restoration', in C. Deane-Drummond and R. Artinian-Kaiser (eds), *Theology and Ecology across the Disciplines: On Care for our Common Home*, London: T & T Clark.

Cahill, L. S., 2018, 'The environment, the common good and women's participation', in C. Deane-Drummond and R. Artinian-Kaiser (eds), *Theology and Ecology across the Disciplines: On Care for our Common Home*, London: T & T Clark.

Carson, M. L. S., 2015, *Setting the Captives Free: The Bible and Human Trafficking*, Eugene, OR: Cascade Books.

Cohen, S. et al., 2018, 'Climate change and sustainable development: towards dialogue', *Global Environmental Change* 8(4) (1998), quoted in J. De Tavernier 'The planetary boundaries framework and food production: a radical redefinition of sustainable development', in C. Deane-Drummond and R. Artinian-Kaiser (eds), *Theology and Ecology across the Disciplines: On Care for our Common Home*, London: T & T Clark.

Das, R. and Hamoud, B., 2017, *Strangers in the Kingdom: Ministering to Refugees, Migrants, and the Stateless*, Carlisle: Langham Global Library.

Dávila, M. T., 2017, 'The option for the poor in *Laudato si'*: connecting care for creation with care for the poor', in V. J. Miller (ed.), *The Theological and Ecological Vision of Laudato si'. Everything is Connected*, London: T & T Clark.

Deane-Drummond, C., 2017, *A Primer in Ecotheology: Theology for a Fragile Earth*, Eugene, OR: Cascade Books.

De Tavernier, J., 2018, 'The planetary boundaries framework and food production: a radical redefinition of sustainable development', in C. Deane-Drummond and R. Artinian-Kaiser (eds), *Theology and Ecology across the Disciplines: On Care for our Common Home*, London: T & T Clark.

Foltz, R. (ed.), 2003, *Worldviews, Religion, and Environment: A Global Anthology*, Toronto: Wadsworth/Thomson Learning.

Hayes, M. G., 2018, 'Creation and creativity', in C. Deane-Drummond and R. Artinian-Kaiser (eds), *Theology and Ecology across the Disciplines: On Care for our Common Home*, London: T & T Clark.

Hodson, M. J. and Hodson, M. R., 2017, *An Introduction to Environmental Ethics*, Cambridge: Grove Books E184.

Northcott, M., 2001, 'Ecology and Christian ethics', in R. Gill (ed.), *The Cambridge Companion to Christian Ethics*, Cambridge: Cambridge University Press.

Northcott, M., 2014, *A Political Theology of Climate Change*, London: SPCK.

O'Donovan, O., 1994, *Resurrection and Moral Order: An Outline of Evangelical Ethics*, Leicester: Apollos.

Pope Francis, 2013, *Evangelii Gaudium*, London: Catholic Truth Society.

Pope Francis, 2015, *Laudato si', mi' Signore*, Rome: Vatican.

Steger, M. B., 2017, *Globalisation: A Very Short Introduction*, Oxford: Oxford University Press.

Weaver, J., 2012, 'Hopeful disciples in a time of climate change', in S. Finamore and J. Weaver (eds), *Wisdom, Science and the Scriptures: Essays in Honour of Ernest Lucas*, Oxford: Regent's Park College and Bristol Baptist College, Eugene, OR: Wipf & Stock.

Zenner, C., 2018, '*Laudato si'* and standing rock: water justice and indigenous ecological knowledge', in C. Deane-Drummond and R. Artinian-Kaiser (eds), *Theology and Ecology across the Disciplines: On Care for our Common Home*, London: T & T Clark.

Notes

1 https://report.ipcc.ch/sr15/pdf/sr15_spm_final.pdf, accessed 9.12.19.

2 UNHCR, 'Figures at a Glance', www.unhcr.org/figures-at-a-glance.html, accessed 9.12.19.

3 www.legislation.gov.uk/ukpga/2015/30/contents, accessed 9.12.19.

4 The Climate Change-Human Trafficking Nexus, https://publications.iom.int/system/files/pdf/mecc_infosheet_climate_change_nexus.pdf, accessed 4.12.19.

5 The Climate Change-Human Trafficking Nexus.

6 The Climate Change-Human Trafficking Nexus.

7 Rashid, T., 2018, 'Inside the Bangladesh brothels where Rohingya girls are suffering', available from www.pbs.org/newshour/world/inside-the-bangladesh-brothels-where-rohingya-girls-are-suffering, accessed 4.12.19.

8 Reuters, 2018, *Fishermen rescue Rohingya Muslims at sea off Indonesia, with more arrivals expected*, available from www.reuters.com/article/us-myanmar-rohingya-indonesia/fishermen-rescue-rohingya-muslims-at-sea-off-indonesia-with-more-arrivals-expected-idUSKCN1HD0RG, accessed 4.12.19.

9 www.pbs.org/newshour/world/inside-the-bangladesh-brothels-where-rohingya-girls-are-suffering, accessed 5.12.19.

10 *The Revelator*, an initiative of the Centre for Biological Diversity, https://therevelator.org/climate-change-human-trafficking/, accessed 4.12.19.

11 See also https://thediplomat.com/2015/02/climate-change-and-human-trafficking-a-deadly-combination/, accessed 4.12.19.

12 https://news.un.org/en/story/2019/07/1043391, accessed 4.12.19.

PART 5

Prayers in Response

I

Prayers for Victims Being Exploited

1 Dear God, we pray for those who are vulnerable to being exploited; those stepping out into the unknown, perhaps moving away from home, sometimes to a different country or culture, those who have been tricked by the sale of false hope and a better life ahead of them. We pray too for the protection of people at risk in our own neighbourhoods; the defenceless and unprotected.

The Salvation Army

2 Liberating God, we pray for those who are exploited, trapped and suffering. In their pain and despair, may they know that your Spirit is with them. When they feel forgotten and invisible, help them to know they are remembered. When they feel worthless and devalued, send reminders that they are loved and cherished by you. We pray that you would provide opportunities for them to find safety and protection. Bring people across their paths who see them and can help. We pray that you would bring freedom to the captives and release to the prisoner; that your kingdom would come on earth as it is in heaven. Amen.

Dan Pratt, Together Free

3 Dear God, I thank you that all of us are precious to you. We pray for victims of modern slavery, for those who have been treated as commodities and held captive by the greed and violence of a broken world. For children, women and men who are bought and sold and abused by those who have forgotten the worth of a human being. May they rediscover their value in you.

The Salvation Army

2

Prayers for Survivors
Finding Freedom

1 Father God, we pray for all those who are, or who have been, victims of human trafficking and modern slavery. May they know your presence and your peace, and may they find safety and shelter given by those who are working to provide relief from all kinds of oppression.

God of justice, we pray for justice for those who have been wronged. We also pray that survivors will have the courage to speak out against their oppressors.

God of freedom, we pray for freedom for all those enslaved in any kind of oppressive situation.

God of healing, we pray for healing for the physical and mental scars experienced by those affected.

Father, your Word shows that you bring new joy and hope where previously there were only shame and fear. We pray for restoration for our brothers and sisters, who desperately need to accept that they can be made new.

We pray this through the powerful name of Jesus. Amen.

Garry Smith, The Medaille Trust

2 Dear God, we pray for the families and friends of victims and survivors. We long for a world where there is no need for an impoverished family to send a child into a trafficking situation; no need for a young person to leave home and fall victim to perpetrators. And we pray that when survivors return home, they will be reunited with their families with love, mercy and compassion.

The Salvation Army

3 God of love, we pray for those who have survived exploitation and trafficking. We know they have been through terrible experiences and we ask for their lives to be filled with your love.

God of freedom, we give thanks for those who have found physical freedom. We also acknowledge that true freedom is not a one-off event but an ongoing journey for all of us. We pray that those seeking to rebuild their lives will know true and lasting freedom.

God of strength, we pray for all those working with people who have survived trafficking and exploitation. We pray that they will have wisdom, patience and strength to journey with survivors as they heal from the past.

God of action, we pray for fair systems here in the UK. Where processes make recovery more difficult for survivors, we pray for change. Where inequality makes it hard for people to rise out of oppression, we pray for justice. Help each one of us to do our part to build a fairer society.

God of joy, we pray that survivors will enjoy many beautiful experiences to help them overcome painful memories from the past. We ask that they will be surrounded by people who genuinely care for them. May they discover all that is good and worth celebrating in life.

In Jesus' name we pray, Amen.

Emily Chalke, Ellas

3

Prayers for Church and Faith Communities

1 Almighty God, Creator of all, help us to share our trust in your love with those in whom your precious image is damaged through brutal exploitation and unthinking indifference.

May our eyes be opened to see the signs of suffering, so often subtly hidden in our midst.

May our hearts be opened to reach out with care and comfort.

May our voices be raised to champion the needs of those who are hurting, and to challenge the complacencies and criminality that keeps crushing your children.

Inspire and empower us in the grace of Jesus Christ, your Son, our Saviour. Amen.

Bishop Alastair Redfern, The Clewer Initiative

2 Father, we know from your Word that you care for all people but especially for the outcast, the dispossessed and the exploited. We recognize in our own lives the times we have not listened to you and have acted in such a way as to add to their exploitation. We are sorry for this. Please forgive us.

Help us to see those within our communities who are exploited; help us to understand how you care for them and how we and our church community can show your care. Help us to act and to work in such a way that we can challenge injustice and break the chains of exploitation. Help us to be with the oppressed. Remind us to care for them.

Father, please help us to help as well those who seek you.

We pray that we might be a light to your Church and to our communities as we respond to your Word and seek your righteousness in our lives.

Please hear us as we seek to rebuild our communities according to your will. Amen.

Caroline Virgo, The Clewer Initiative

3 Lord, who sees and hears all things, forgive us.
Our eyes have not seen and our ears have not heard the cries of your children caught in the grip of exploitation.
We acknowledge our blindfolds and our ear plugs.
We confess we have turned away from seeing and hearing the pain of human trafficking where we live, work and worship.

Silence

Response – Lord, help us to see, to hear and together walk the rocky path
Lord, who stirs the waters, who walks with us and before us into freedom, strengthen us.
Open our eyes to the possibilities, reassure us that all is possible with you and that change can come.
Let us hear the whisper that in our weakness there is your strength.
Stir our hearts to see and hear and love even in the chaos of this broken world.

Silence

Response – Lord, help us to see, to hear and together walk the difficult path
Lord, who is light and love, inspire us.
Inspire us to kneel and wash the feet of the broken. To turn aside on the road and bind the wounds of the beaten-up stranger.
Inspire us to join hands together across our communities and across all nations. Help us together, your Church as one, to hear, to see, to act and to speak.

Silence

Response – Lord, help us to see, to hear and together walk the freedom path
Lord, we look to you. Help us to see, to hear and to walk in your footsteps so that no child, no woman, no man may ever again be thrown into the despair of slavery and exploitation. In the name of the Father, the Son and the Holy Spirit. Amen.

Diane Watts, Baptists Together

4 Dear God, we pray for all of us who are intentionally or unintentionally creating demand, because of our desire for cheap food, goods and services. Help us to understand the way our choices may play a part in keeping others captive by creating demand for more slaves, and give us courage to make different choices.

The Salvation Army

4

Prayers for Exploiters and Traffickers

1 Dear Lord, we pray today for those people who have been a part of trafficking and enslaving men, women and children all around the world. We ask that your love would break through to their lives and that love would transform their thinking and their actions. Lord, break the cycle of hurt and open their eyes to the evil that they are committing, and help them to turn from their sins and repent. We know that no one is too far from the reach of your love, and we pray for salvation to come to them today.

Help us, Lord, to not judge those who are traffickers but to love them as you have called us to love our enemies.

God of Justice, we ask you to give help and strength to all police, law-enforcement agencies and charities who work to find, arrest and prosecute traffickers and see victims set free. Give courage to those survivors who are called to stand up in court to testify against their former captors. Let us see justice for victims and an end to all enslavement.

In your mighty name, Amen.

Tim Nelson, Hope for Justice

2 Dear God, we pray for a change of heart in the perpetrators of human trafficking. We ask for a miracle, that you would touch the hearts of those who enslave others. We pray that your light will break through their darkness and they will turn from their ways, finding freedom from greed and violence.

The Salvation Army

PART 6

Resources

Organizations and resources

Below are some of the many organizations responding to modern slavery and human trafficking. Their resources include information, research, videos, apps, awareness literature and opportunities to get involved.

- Anti-Slavery International: www.antislavery.org.
- The Clewer Initiative: www.theclewerinitiative.org.
- Ellas: www.ellas.org.uk.
- Ethical Consumer: www.ethicalconsumer.org.
- Freedom Sunday: www.freedomsundayglobal.org.
- Freedom United: www.freedomunited.org.
- Global Slavery Index: www.globalslaveryindex.org.
- GOV.UK: www.gov.uk/government/collections/modern-slavery.
- Hestia: www.hestia.org.
- Hope for Justice: https://hopeforjustice.org.
- The Human Trafficking Foundation: www.humantrafficking foundation.org.
- Independent Anti-Slavery Commissioner: www.antislavery commissioner.co.uk.
- International Justice Mission: www.ijmuk.org.
- Justice and Care: www.justiceandcare.org.
- Migrant Help: www.migranthelpuk.org.
- Modern Slavery Helpline: www.modernslaveryhelpline.org.
- René Cassin: www.renecassin.org.
- Slavery Footprint: http://slaveryfootprint.org/survey/#where_do_you_live.

- Southend Against Modern Slavery Partnership: www.sams partnership.org.uk.
- Stop the Traffik: www.stopthetraffik.org.
- The Medaille Trust: www.Medaille-Trust.org.uk.
- The Ministry of Justice: www.gov.uk/government/ publications/modern-slavery-closer-than-you-think. *Includes foreign-language leaflets to provide advice and support to those affected by modern slavery. Leaflets are available in Albanian, Chinese, Czech, English, French, Lithuanian, Polish, Romanian, Slovak, Thai, Vietnamese and Welsh.*
- The Salvation Army: www.salvationarmy.org.uk/modern-slavery.
- Together Free: www.togetherfree.org.uk.
- Unseen: www.unseenuk.org.
- University of Nottingham Rights Lab: www.nottingham. ac.uk/research/beacons-of-excellence/rights-lab/index.aspx.

For help, safeguarding and to report concerns

Crimestoppers

An independent charity that enables anonymous reporting of crime.
Telephone: 0800 555 111
website: https://crimestoppers-uk.org

Gangmasters and Labour Abuse Authority (GLA)

The GLA investigates labour offences *in England and Wales only* including: gang-master offences, non-payment of the National Minimum Wage, forced and compulsory labour and any associated trafficking and other modern slavery offences.
Telephone: 0800 432 0804
website: www.gla.gov.uk

Modern Slavery Helpline

For advice and reporting. Available 24/7 with translators.
Telephone: 0800 0121 700
website: www.modernslaveryhelpline.org

National Crime Agency

Leads the UK's fight to cut serious and organized crime.
Telephone: 0370 496 7622
website: https://nationalcrimeagency.gov.uk

NSPCC (National Society for the Prevention of Cruelty to Children)

A charity providing safeguarding advice and referrals relating
to the abuse of children.
Telephone: 0808 800 5000
email: help@nspcc.org.uk
website: www.nspcc.org.uk

Police

Telephone: 999 (Emergency) or 101 (non-Emergency).

The Salvation Army

The Salvation Army provides safe houses for victims of
modern slavery.
Telephone: 0800 808 3733
website: www.salvationarmy.org.uk/modern-slavery

Resources

Survivors UK

Support for survivors of male rape or sexual abuse.
Email: info@survivorsuk.org
website: www.survivorsuk.org

Trading Standards

If someone has experienced a situation where they feel they
have been charged excessive amounts of money for services
provided, or pressurized into buying something they did not
want by unscrupulous traders, Trading Standards may be able
to help.
Telephone: 0808 223 1133
website: www.tradingstandards.uk

Victim Support

Victim Support is the independent charity for victims and
witnesses of crime in England and Wales.
Support line: 0808 16 89 111
website: www.victimsupport.org.uk

Women's Aid

A national charity working to end domestic violence against
women and children. Supports a network of over 500
domestic and sexual-violence services across the UK.
National Domestic Violence Helpline: 0808 2000 247
website: www.womensaid.org.uk

Index of Bible References

Index of Names and Subjects